SPIDER-MAN

AND THE

FANTASTIC FOUR

SPIDER-MAN/FANTASTIC FOUR. Contains material originally published in magazine form as SPIDER-MAN/FANTASTIC FOUR #1-4; PETER PARKER, THE SPECTACULAR SPIDER-MAN #42; and FANTASTIC FOUR #218. st printing 2011. ISBN# 978-0-7851-4423-6. Published by MARVEL WORLDWIDE, INC., a subsidiary of MARVEL ENTERTAINMENT, LLC. OFFICE OF PUBLICATION: 135 West 50th Street, New York, NY 10020. Copyright 1980, 2010 and 2011 Marvel Characters, Inc. All rights reserved. $14.99 per copy in the U.S. and $16.50 in Canada (GST #R127032852); Canadian Agreement #40668537. All characters featured in this issue and the tinctive names and likenesses thereof, and all related indicia are trademarks of Marvel Characters, Inc. No similarity between any of the names, characters, persons, and/or institutions in this magazine with those of y living or dead person or institution is intended, and any such similarity which may exist is purely coincidental. **Printed in the U.S.A.** ALAN FINE, EVP - Office of the President, Marvel Worldwide, Inc. and EVP & CMO rvel Characters B.V.; DAN BUCKLEY, Publisher & President - Print, Animation & Digital Divisions; JOE QUESADA, Chief Creative Officer; JIM SOKOLOWSKI, Chief Operating Officer; DAVID BOGART, SVP of Business Affairs alent Management; TOM BREVOORT, SVP of Publishing; C.B. CEBULSKI, SVP of Creator & Content Development; DAVID GABRIEL, SVP of Publishing Sales & Circulation; MICHAEL PASCIULLO, SVP of Brand Planning & nmunications; JIM O'KEEFE, VP of Operations & Logistics; DAN CARR, Executive Director of Publishing Technology; JUSTIN F. GABRIE, Director of Publishing & Editorial Operations; SUSAN CRESPI, Editorial Operations nager; ALEX MORALES, Publishing Operations Manager; STAN LEE, Chairman Emeritus. For information regarding advertising in Marvel Comics or on Marvel.com, please contact John Dokes, SVP Integrated Sales and rketing, at jdokes@marvel.com. For Marvel subscription inquiries, please call 800-217-9158. **Manufactured between 6/23/2011 and 7/12/2011 by QUAD/GRAPHICS, DUBUQUE, IA, USA.**

9 8 7 6 5 4 3 2 1

SPIDER-MAN
AND THE
FANTASTIC FOUR

Writer .... Christos Gage
Artist .... Mario Alberti
Letterer .... Jared K. Fletcher
Editor .... Tom Brennan
Supervising Editor .... Stephen Wacker

PETER PARKER,
THE SPECTACULAR SPIDER-MAN #42

Writer .... Bill Mantlo
Penciler .... Mike Zeck
Inker .... Jim Mooney
Colorist .... Janice Cohen
Letterer .... Irvine Watanabe
Color Reconstruction .... Jerron Quality Color

FANTASTIC FOUR #218

Writer .... Bill Mantlo
Penciler .... John Byrne
Inker .... Joe Sinnott
Colorist .... Ben Sean
Letterer .... Jim Novak
Editor .... Jim Salicrup
Color Reconstruction .... Jerron Quality Color

Collection Editor .... Jennifer Grünwald
Editorial Assistants .... James Emmett & Joe Hochstein
Assistant Editors .... Alex Starbuck & Nelson Ribeiro
Editor, Special Projects .... Mark D. Beazley
Senior Editor, Special Projects .... Jeff Youngquist
Senior Vice President of Sales .... David Gabriel
SVP of Brand Planning & Communications .... Michael Pasciullo
Book Design .... Jeff Powell

Editor in Chief .... Axel Alonso
Chief Creative Officer .... Joe Quesada
Publisher .... Dan Buckley
Executive Producer .... Alan Fine

While attending a demonstration in radiology, high school student Peter Parker was bitten by a spider which had accidentally been exposed to radioactive rays. Through a miracle of science, Peter soon found that he had gained the spider's powers... and had, in effect, become a human arachnid! From that day on he was...

the Amazing Spider-Man

Reed Richards, Mr. Fantastic! Ben Grimm, the Thing! Sue Storm, the Invisible Woman! Johnny Storm, the Human Torch! A team — and a family — of adventurers, explorers and imaginauts, the Fantastic Four lead lives both ordinary and extraordinary!

Fantastic Four

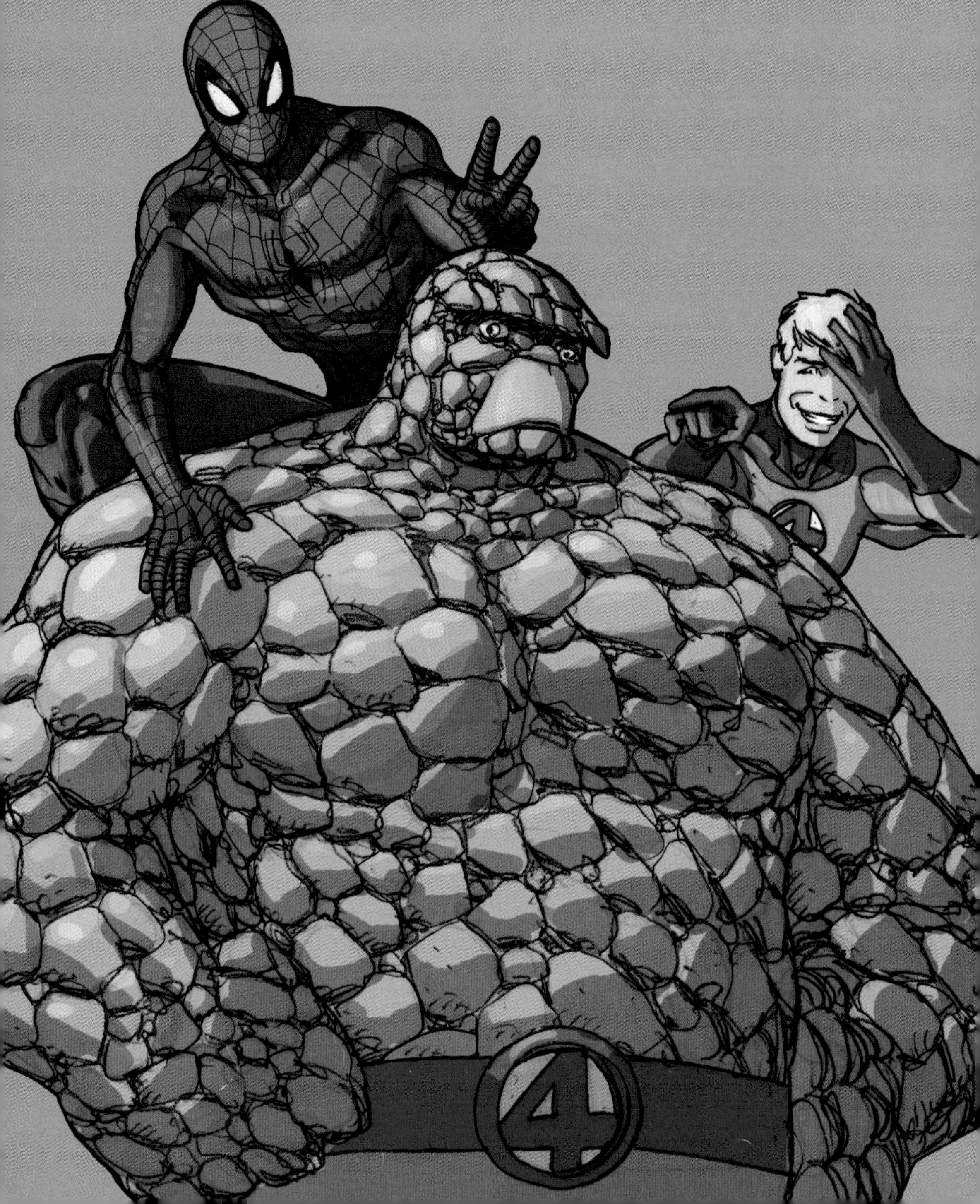

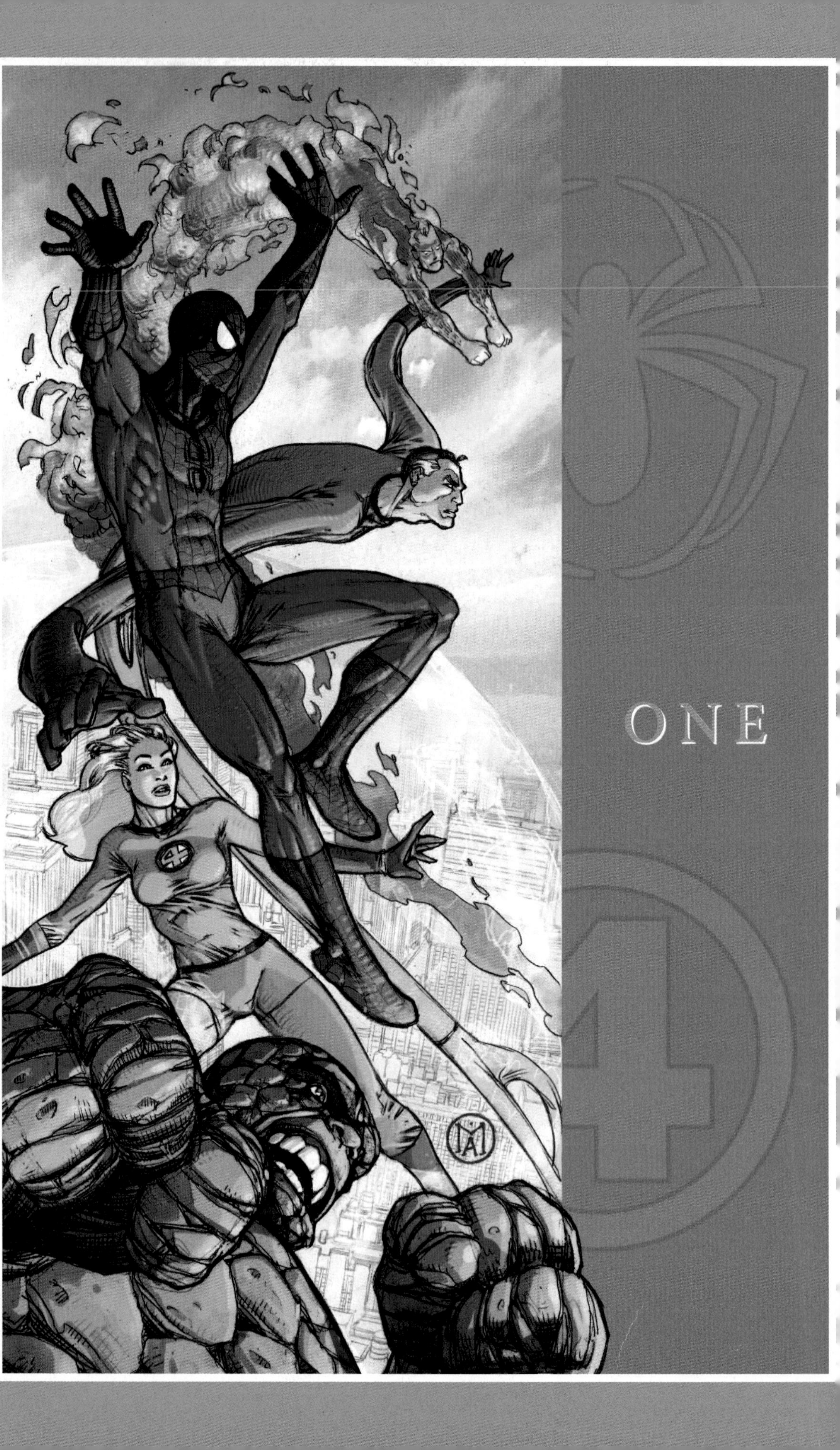

ONE

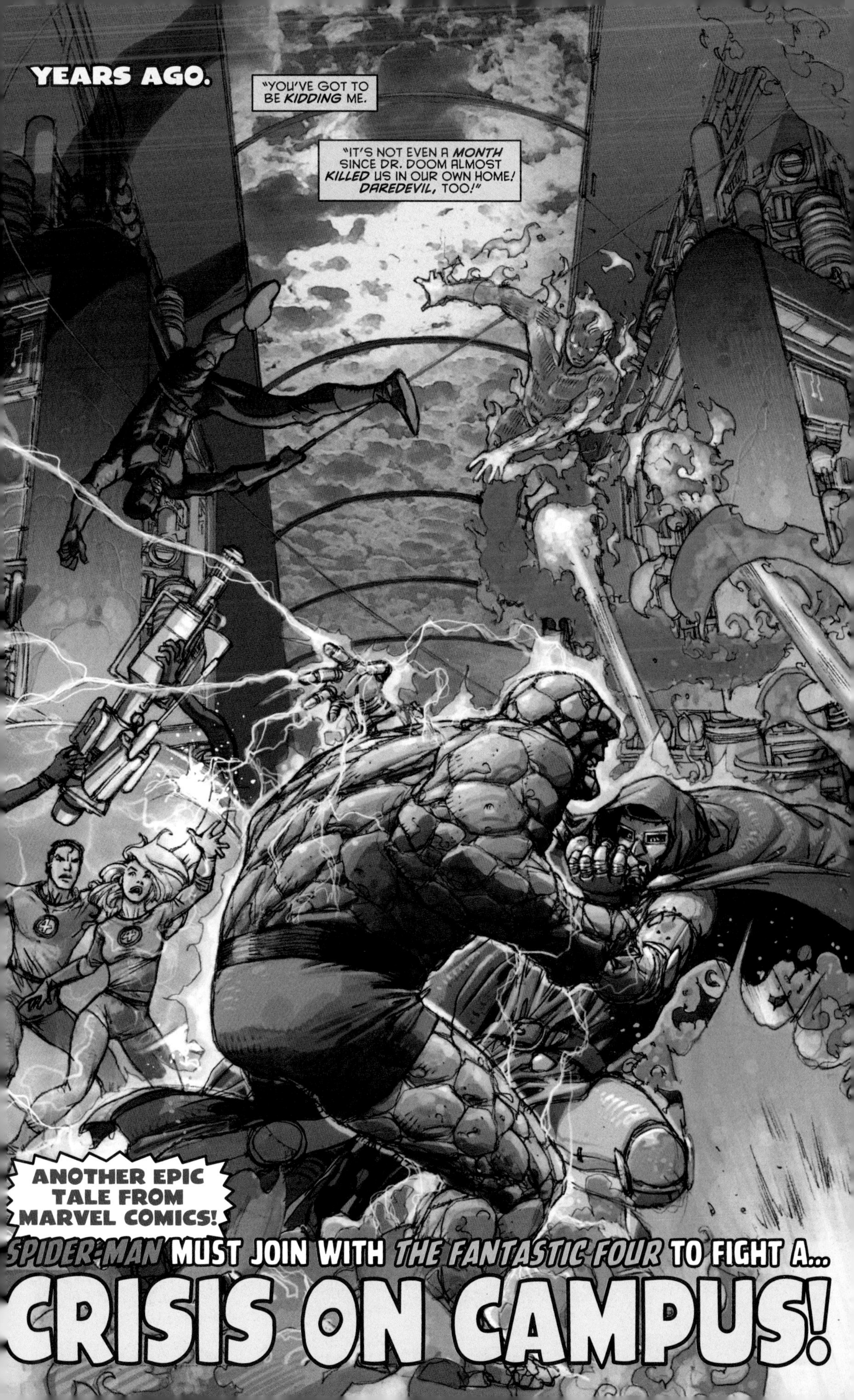
YEARS AGO.
"YOU'VE GOT TO BE KIDDING ME.
"IT'S NOT EVEN A MONTH SINCE DR. DOOM ALMOST KILLED US IN OUR OWN HOME! DAREDEVIL, TOO!"
ANOTHER EPIC TALE FROM MARVEL COMICS!
SPIDER-MAN MUST JOIN WITH THE FANTASTIC FOUR TO FIGHT A...
CRISIS ON CAMPUS!

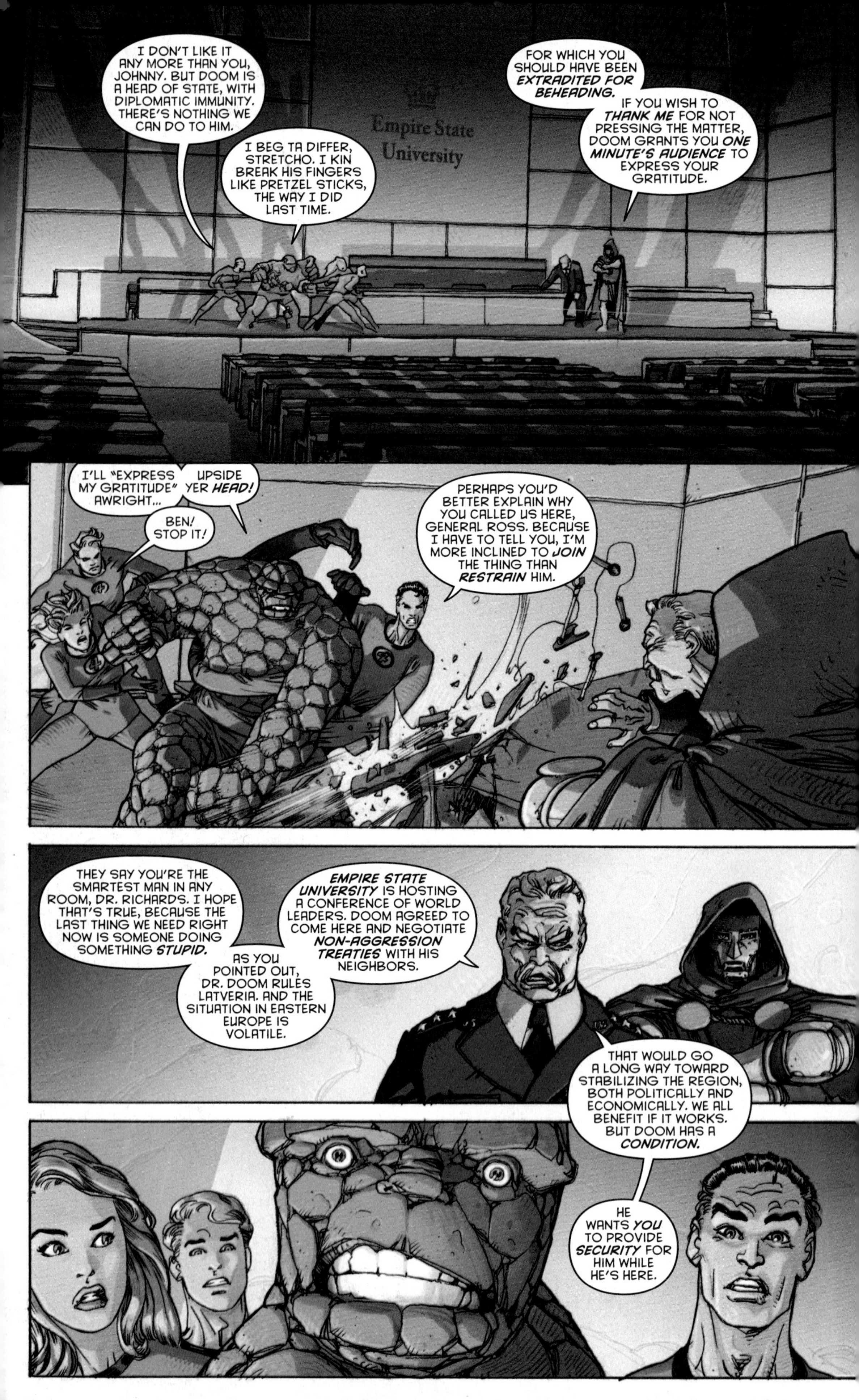
I DON'T LIKE IT ANY MORE THAN YOU, JOHNNY. BUT DOOM IS A HEAD OF STATE, WITH DIPLOMATIC IMMUNITY. THERE'S NOTHING WE CAN DO TO HIM.
Empire State University
I BEG TA DIFFER, STRETCHO. I KIN BREAK HIS FINGERS LIKE PRETZEL STICKS, THE WAY I DID LAST TIME.
FOR WHICH YOU SHOULD HAVE BEEN EXTRADITED FOR BEHEADING.
IF YOU WISH TO THANK ME FOR NOT PRESSING THE MATTER, DOOM GRANTS YOU ONE MINUTE'S AUDIENCE TO EXPRESS YOUR GRATITUDE.
I'LL "EXPRESS MY GRATITUDE" AWRIGHT...
UPSIDE YER HEAD!
BEN! STOP IT!
PERHAPS YOU'D BETTER EXPLAIN WHY YOU CALLED US HERE, GENERAL ROSS. BECAUSE I HAVE TO TELL YOU, I'M MORE INCLINED TO JOIN THE THING THAN RESTRAIN HIM.
THEY SAY YOU'RE THE SMARTEST MAN IN ANY ROOM, DR. RICHARDS. I HOPE THAT'S TRUE, BECAUSE THE LAST THING WE NEED RIGHT NOW IS SOMEONE DOING SOMETHING STUPID.
AS YOU POINTED OUT, DR. DOOM RULES LATVERIA. AND THE SITUATION IN EASTERN EUROPE IS VOLATILE.
EMPIRE STATE UNIVERSITY IS HOSTING A CONFERENCE OF WORLD LEADERS. DOOM AGREED TO COME HERE AND NEGOTIATE NON-AGGRESSION TREATIES WITH HIS NEIGHBORS.
THAT WOULD GO A LONG WAY TOWARD STABILIZING THE REGION, BOTH POLITICALLY AND ECONOMICALLY. WE ALL BENEFIT IF IT WORKS. BUT DOOM HAS A CONDITION.
HE WANTS YOU TO PROVIDE SECURITY FOR HIM WHILE HE'S HERE.

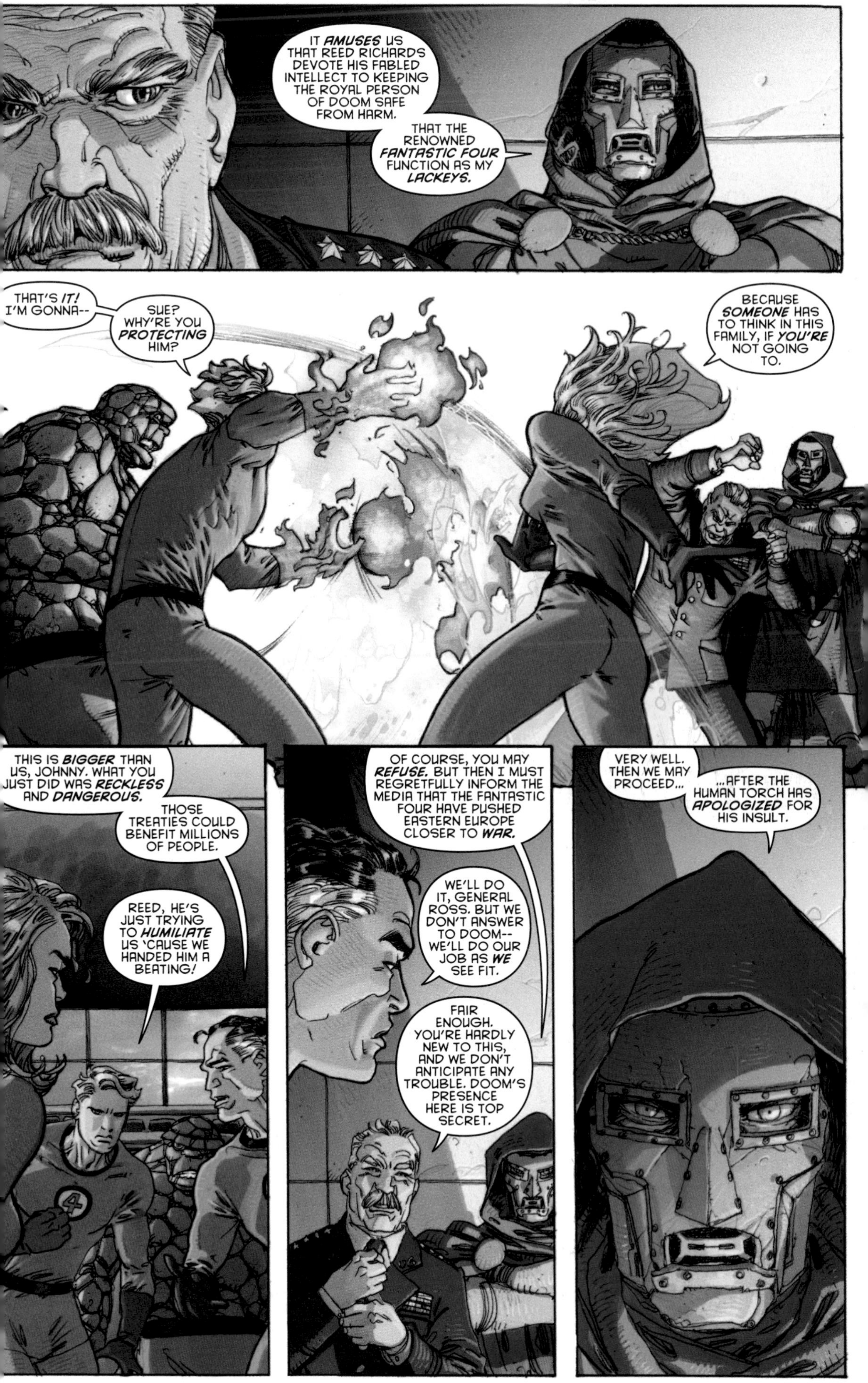
IT AMUSES US THAT REED RICHARDS DEVOTE HIS FABLED INTELLECT TO KEEPING THE ROYAL PERSON OF DOOM SAFE FROM HARM.
THAT THE RENOWNED FANTASTIC FOUR FUNCTION AS MY LACKEYS.
THAT'S IT! I'M GONNA--
SUE? WHY'RE YOU PROTECTING HIM?
BECAUSE SOMEONE HAS TO THINK IN THIS FAMILY, IF YOU'RE NOT GOING TO.
THIS IS BIGGER THAN US, JOHNNY. WHAT YOU JUST DID WAS RECKLESS AND DANGEROUS.
THOSE TREATIES COULD BENEFIT MILLIONS OF PEOPLE.
REED, HE'S JUST TRYING TO HUMILIATE US 'CAUSE WE HANDED HIM A BEATING!
OF COURSE, YOU MAY REFUSE. BUT THEN I MUST REGRETFULLY INFORM THE MEDIA THAT THE FANTASTIC FOUR HAVE PUSHED EASTERN EUROPE CLOSER TO WAR.
WE'LL DO IT, GENERAL ROSS. BUT WE DON'T ANSWER TO DOOM-- WE'LL DO OUR JOB AS WE SEE FIT.
FAIR ENOUGH. YOU'RE HARDLY NEW TO THIS, AND WE DON'T ANTICIPATE ANY TROUBLE. DOOM'S PRESENCE HERE IS TOP SECRET.
VERY WELL. THEN WE MAY PROCEED...
...AFTER THE HUMAN TORCH HAS APOLOGIZED FOR HIS INSULT.

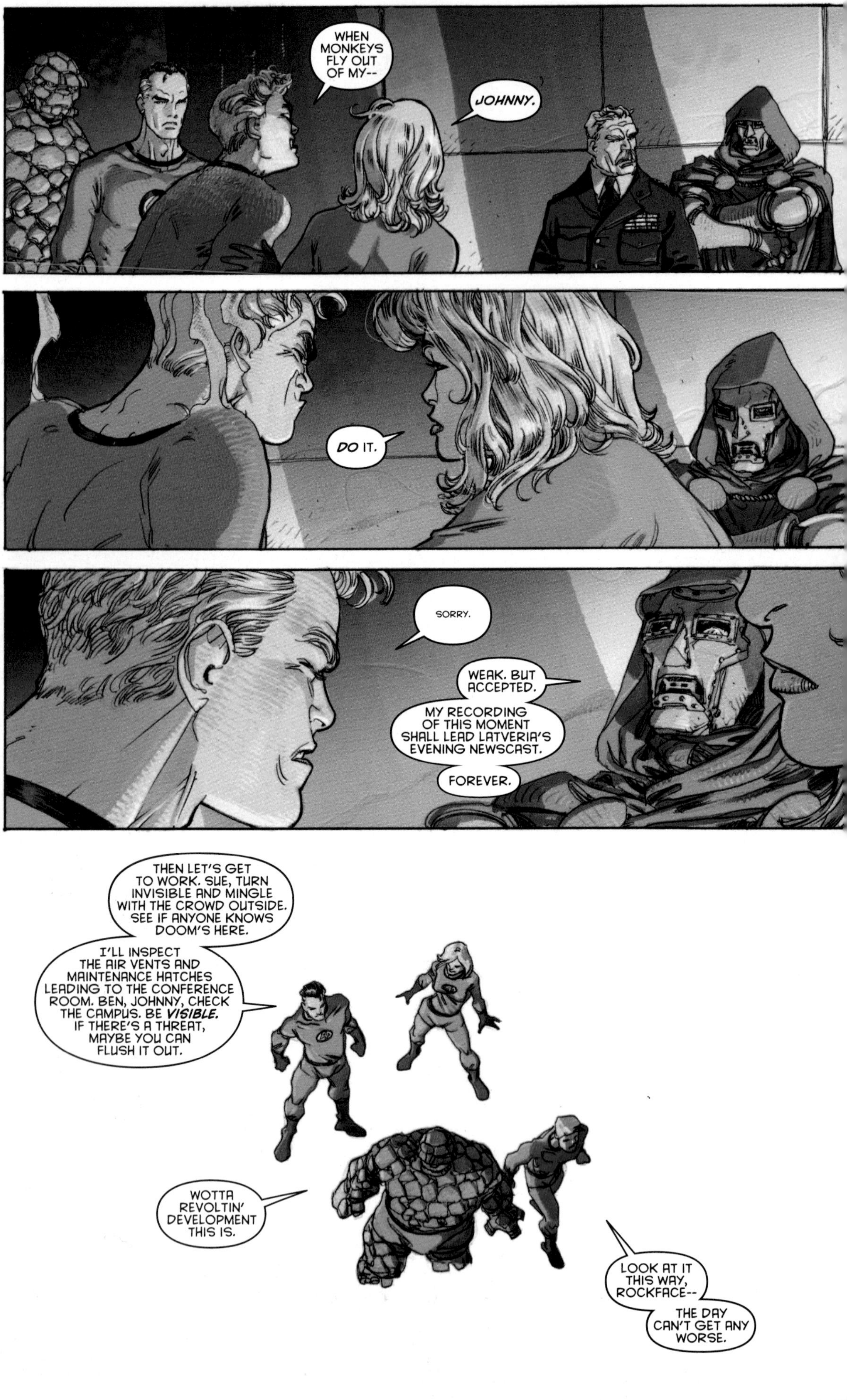
WHEN MONKEYS FLY OUT OF MY--
JOHNNY.
DO IT.
SORRY.
WEAK. BUT ACCEPTED.
MY RECORDING OF THIS MOMENT SHALL LEAD LATVERIA'S EVENING NEWSCAST.
FOREVER.
THEN LET'S GET TO WORK. SUE, TURN INVISIBLE AND MINGLE WITH THE CROWD OUTSIDE. SEE IF ANYONE KNOWS DOOM'S HERE.
I'LL INSPECT THE AIR VENTS AND MAINTENANCE HATCHES LEADING TO THE CONFERENCE ROOM. BEN, JOHNNY, CHECK THE CAMPUS. BE VISIBLE. IF THERE'S A THREAT, MAYBE YOU CAN FLUSH IT OUT.
WOTTA REVOLTIN' DEVELOPMENT THIS IS.
LOOK AT IT THIS WAY, ROCKFACE--
THE DAY CAN'T GET ANY WORSE.

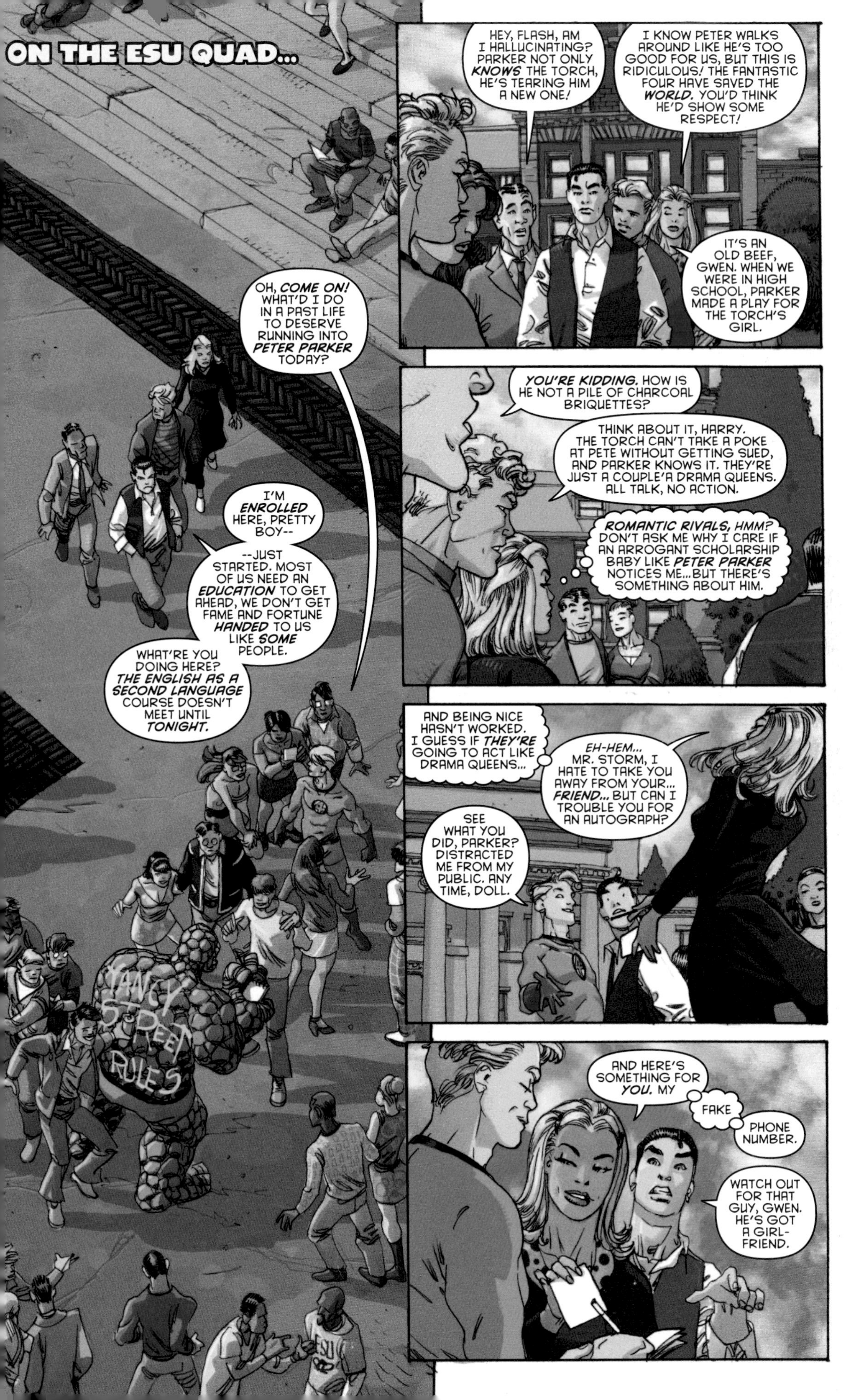
ON THE ESU QUAD...
HEY, FLASH, AM I HALLUCINATING? PARKER NOT ONLY KNOWS THE TORCH, HE'S TEARING HIM A NEW ONE!
I KNOW PETER WALKS AROUND LIKE HE'S TOO GOOD FOR US, BUT THIS IS RIDICULOUS! THE FANTASTIC FOUR HAVE SAVED THE WORLD. YOU'D THINK HE'D SHOW SOME RESPECT!
IT'S AN OLD BEEF, GWEN. WHEN WE WERE IN HIGH SCHOOL, PARKER MADE A PLAY FOR THE TORCH'S GIRL.
OH, COME ON! WHAT'D I DO IN A PAST LIFE TO DESERVE RUNNING INTO PETER PARKER TODAY?
I'M ENROLLED HERE, PRETTY BOY--
--JUST STARTED. MOST OF US NEED AN EDUCATION TO GET AHEAD, WE DON'T GET FAME AND FORTUNE HANDED TO US LIKE SOME PEOPLE.
WHAT'RE YOU DOING HERE? THE ENGLISH AS A SECOND LANGUAGE COURSE DOESN'T MEET UNTIL TONIGHT.
YANCY STREET RULES
YOU'RE KIDDING. HOW IS HE NOT A PILE OF CHARCOAL BRIQUETTES?
THINK ABOUT IT, HARRY. THE TORCH CAN'T TAKE A POKE AT PETE WITHOUT GETTING SUED, AND PARKER KNOWS IT. THEY'RE JUST A COUPLE'A DRAMA QUEENS. ALL TALK, NO ACTION.
ROMANTIC RIVALS, HMM? DON'T ASK ME WHY I CARE IF AN ARROGANT SCHOLARSHIP BABY LIKE PETER PARKER NOTICES ME...BUT THERE'S SOMETHING ABOUT HIM.
AND BEING NICE HASN'T WORKED. I GUESS IF THEY'RE GOING TO ACT LIKE DRAMA QUEENS...
EH-HEM... MR. STORM, I HATE TO TAKE YOU AWAY FROM YOUR... FRIEND... BUT CAN I TROUBLE YOU FOR AN AUTOGRAPH?
SEE WHAT YOU DID, PARKER? DISTRACTED ME FROM MY PUBLIC. ANY TIME, DOLL.
AND HERE'S SOMETHING FOR YOU. MY
FAKE
PHONE NUMBER.
WATCH OUT FOR THAT GUY, GWEN. HE'S GOT A GIRL-FRIEND.

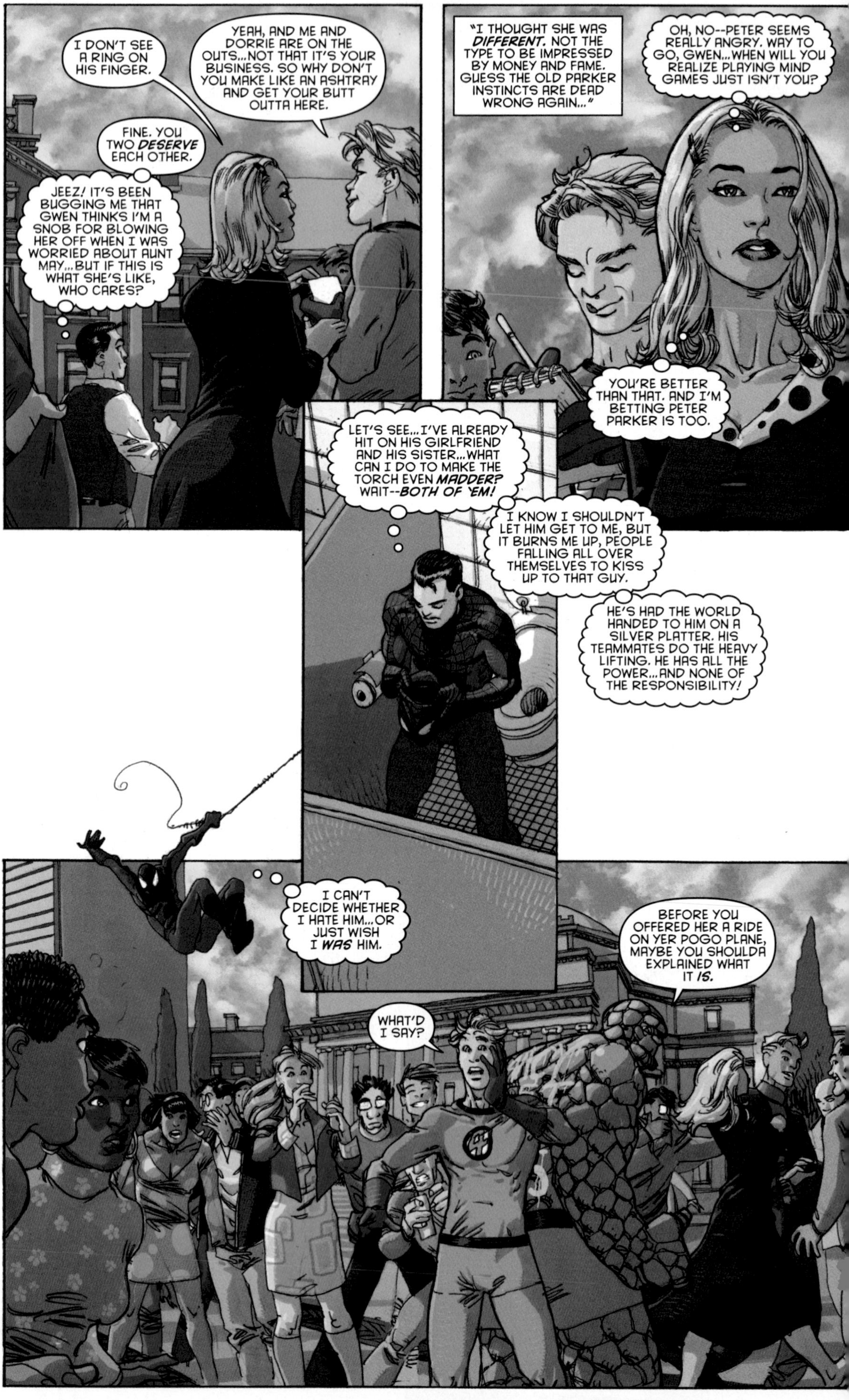

I DON'T SEE A RING ON HIS FINGER.
YEAH, AND ME AND DORRIE ARE ON THE OUTS...NOT THAT IT'S YOUR BUSINESS. SO WHY DON'T YOU MAKE LIKE AN ASHTRAY AND GET YOUR BUTT OUTTA HERE.
FINE. YOU TWO DESERVE EACH OTHER.
JEEZ! IT'S BEEN BUGGING ME THAT GWEN THINKS I'M A SNOB FOR BLOWING HER OFF WHEN I WAS WORRIED ABOUT AUNT MAY...BUT IF THIS IS WHAT SHE'S LIKE, WHO CARES?
"I THOUGHT SHE WAS DIFFERENT. NOT THE TYPE TO BE IMPRESSED BY MONEY AND FAME. GUESS THE OLD PARKER INSTINCTS ARE DEAD WRONG AGAIN..."
OH, NO--PETER SEEMS REALLY ANGRY. WAY TO GO, GWEN...WHEN WILL YOU REALIZE PLAYING MIND GAMES JUST ISN'T YOU?
YOU'RE BETTER THAN THAT. AND I'M BETTING PETER PARKER IS TOO.
LET'S SEE...I'VE ALREADY HIT ON HIS GIRLFRIEND AND HIS SISTER...WHAT CAN I DO TO MAKE THE TORCH EVEN MADDER? WAIT--BOTH OF 'EM!
I KNOW I SHOULDN'T LET HIM GET TO ME, BUT IT BURNS ME UP, PEOPLE FALLING ALL OVER THEMSELVES TO KISS UP TO THAT GUY.
HE'S HAD THE WORLD HANDED TO HIM ON A SILVER PLATTER. HIS TEAMMATES DO THE HEAVY LIFTING. HE HAS ALL THE POWER...AND NONE OF THE RESPONSIBILITY!
I CAN'T DECIDE WHETHER I HATE HIM...OR JUST WISH I WAS HIM.
BEFORE YOU OFFERED HER A RIDE ON YER POGO PLANE, MAYBE YOU SHOULDA EXPLAINED WHAT IT IS.
WHAT'D I SAY?

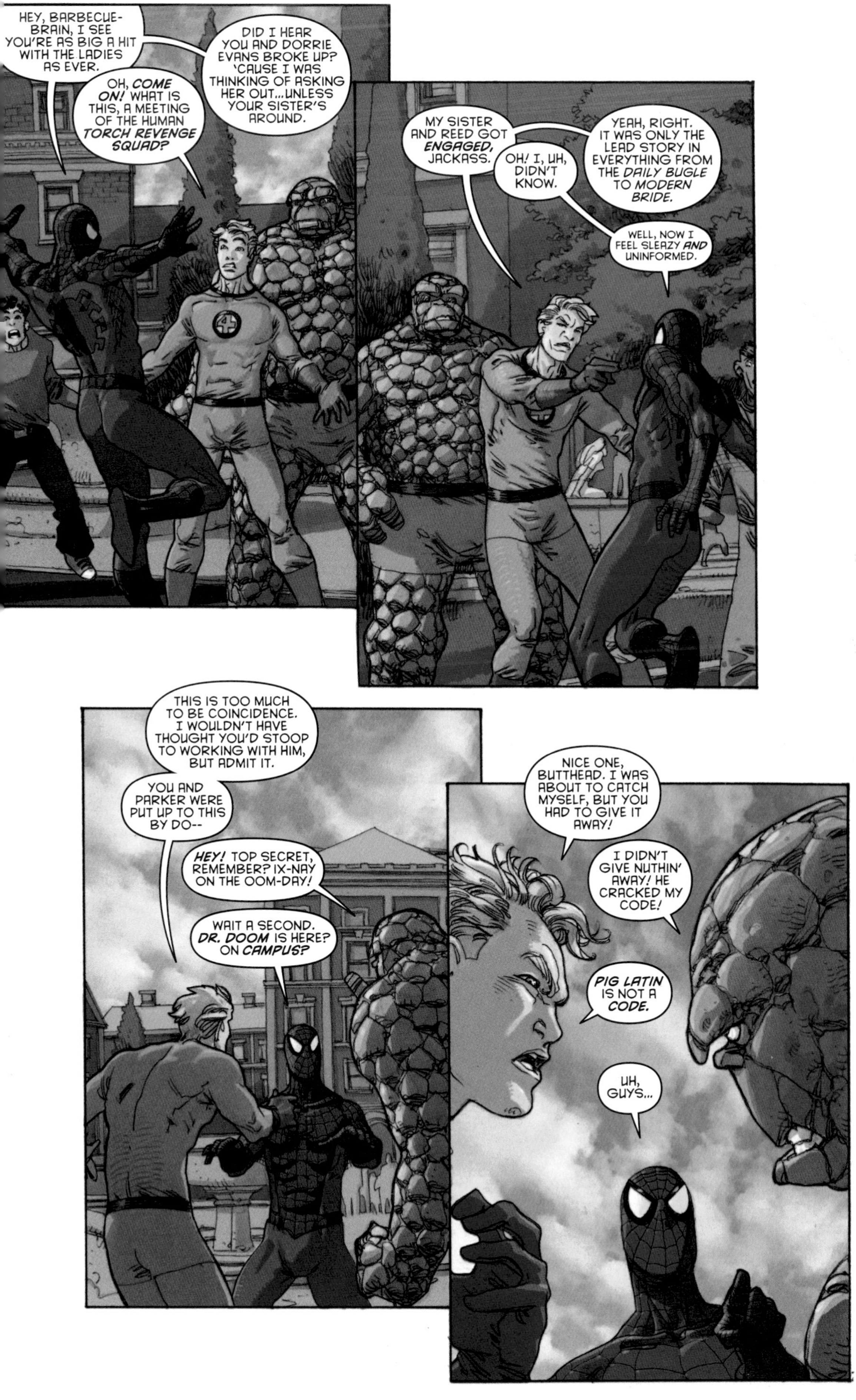

HEY, BARBECUE-BRAIN, I SEE YOU'RE AS BIG A HIT WITH THE LADIES AS EVER.
OH, *COME ON!* WHAT IS THIS, A MEETING OF THE HUMAN *TORCH REVENGE SQUAD?*
DID I HEAR YOU AND DORRIE EVANS BROKE UP? 'CAUSE I WAS THINKING OF ASKING HER OUT...UNLESS YOUR SISTER'S AROUND.
MY SISTER AND REED GOT *ENGAGED,* JACKASS.
YEAH, RIGHT. IT WAS ONLY THE LEAD STORY IN EVERYTHING FROM THE *DAILY BUGLE* TO *MODERN BRIDE.*
OH! I, UH, DIDN'T KNOW.
WELL, NOW I FEEL SLEAZY *AND* UNINFORMED.
THIS IS TOO MUCH TO BE COINCIDENCE. I WOULDN'T HAVE THOUGHT YOU'D STOOP TO WORKING WITH HIM, BUT ADMIT IT.
YOU AND PARKER WERE PUT UP TO THIS BY DO--
HEY! TOP SECRET, REMEMBER? IX-NAY ON THE OOM-DAY!
WAIT A SECOND. *DR. DOOM* IS HERE? ON *CAMPUS?*
NICE ONE, BUTTHEAD. I WAS ABOUT TO CATCH MYSELF, BUT YOU HAD TO GIVE IT AWAY!
I DIDN'T GIVE NUTHIN' AWAY! HE CRACKED MY CODE!
PIG LATIN IS NOT A *CODE.*
UH, GUYS...

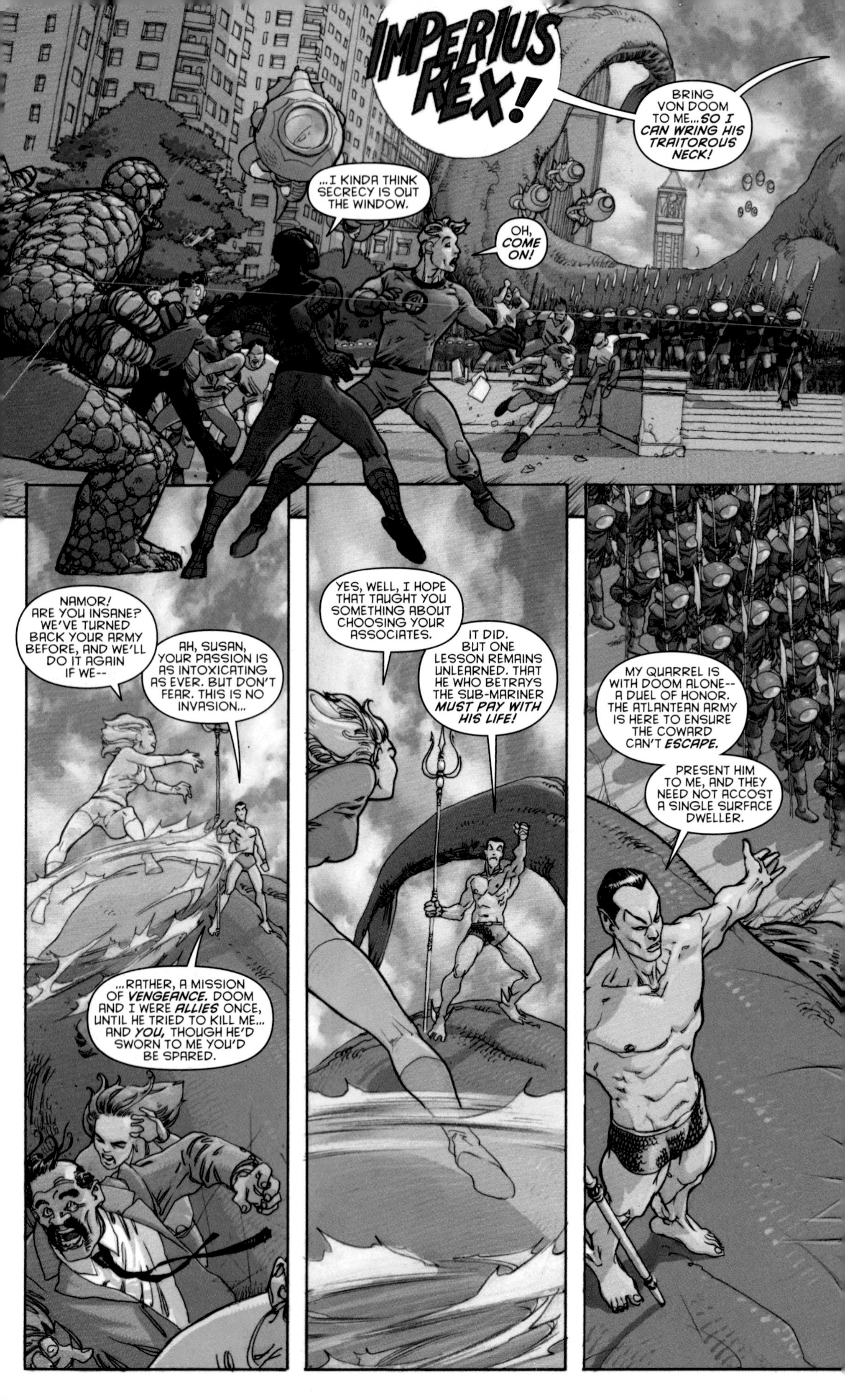
IMPERIUS REX!
BRING VON DOOM TO ME...SO I CAN WRING HIS TRAITOROUS NECK!
...I KINDA THINK SECRECY IS OUT THE WINDOW.
OH, COME ON!
NAMOR! ARE YOU INSANE? WE'VE TURNED BACK YOUR ARMY BEFORE, AND WE'LL DO IT AGAIN IF WE--
AH, SUSAN, YOUR PASSION IS AS INTOXICATING AS EVER. BUT DON'T FEAR. THIS IS NO INVASION...
...RATHER, A MISSION OF VENGEANCE. DOOM AND I WERE ALLIES ONCE, UNTIL HE TRIED TO KILL ME... AND YOU, THOUGH HE'D SWORN TO ME YOU'D BE SPARED.
YES, WELL, I HOPE THAT TAUGHT YOU SOMETHING ABOUT CHOOSING YOUR ASSOCIATES.
IT DID. BUT ONE LESSON REMAINS UNLEARNED. THAT HE WHO BETRAYS THE SUB-MARINER MUST PAY WITH HIS LIFE!
MY QUARREL IS WITH DOOM ALONE-- A DUEL OF HONOR. THE ATLANTEAN ARMY IS HERE TO ENSURE THE COWARD CAN'T ESCAPE.
PRESENT HIM TO ME, AND THEY NEED NOT ACCOST A SINGLE SURFACE DWELLER.

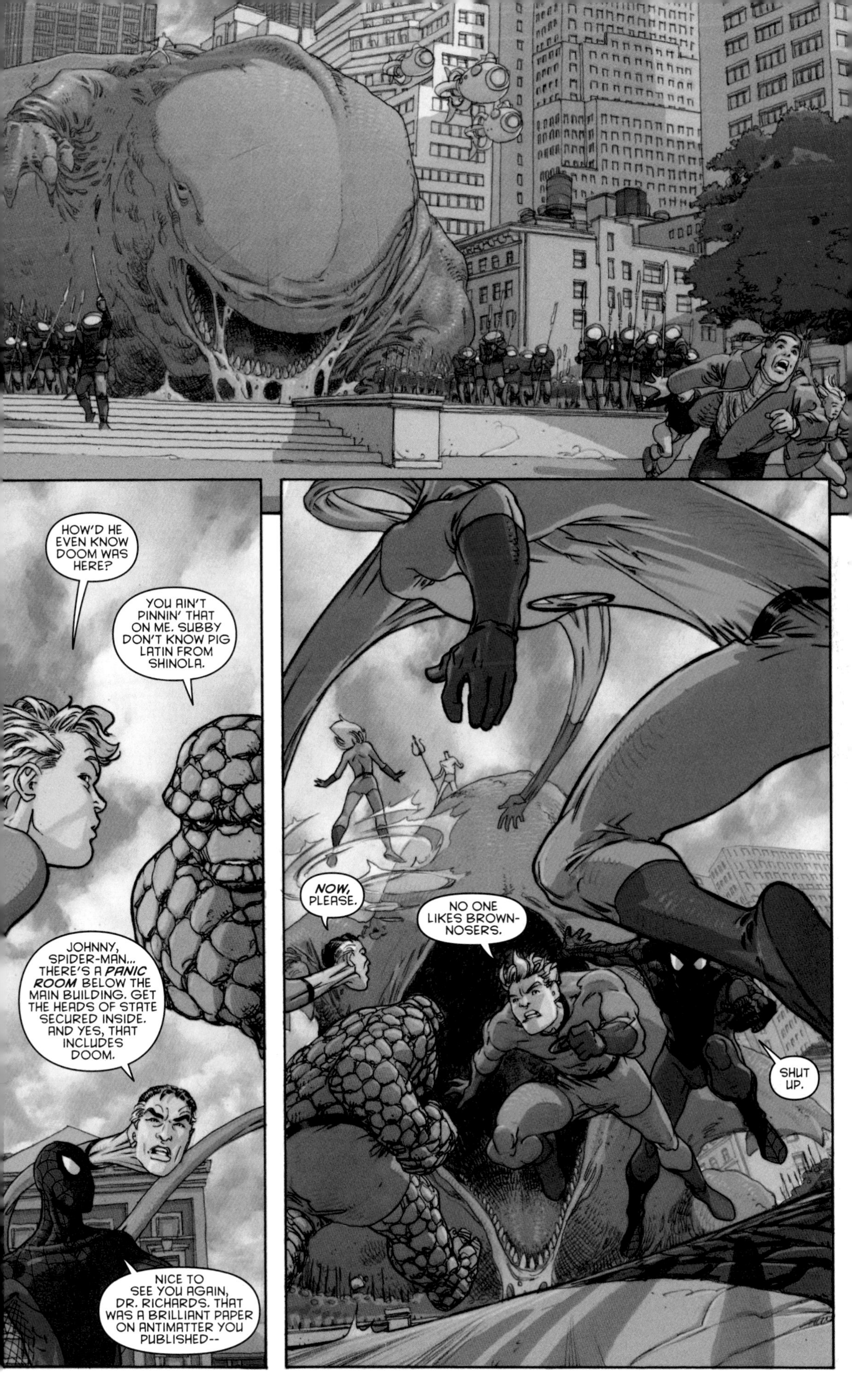
HOW'D HE EVEN KNOW DOOM WAS HERE?
YOU AIN'T PINNIN' THAT ON ME. SUBBY DON'T KNOW PIG LATIN FROM SHINOLA.
JOHNNY, SPIDER-MAN... THERE'S A ***PANIC ROOM*** BELOW THE MAIN BUILDING. GET THE HEADS OF STATE SECURED INSIDE. AND YES, THAT INCLUDES DOOM.
NICE TO SEE YOU AGAIN, DR. RICHARDS. THAT WAS A BRILLIANT PAPER ON ANTIMATTER YOU PUBLISHED--
NOW, PLEASE.
NO ONE LIKES BROWN-NOSERS.
SHUT UP.

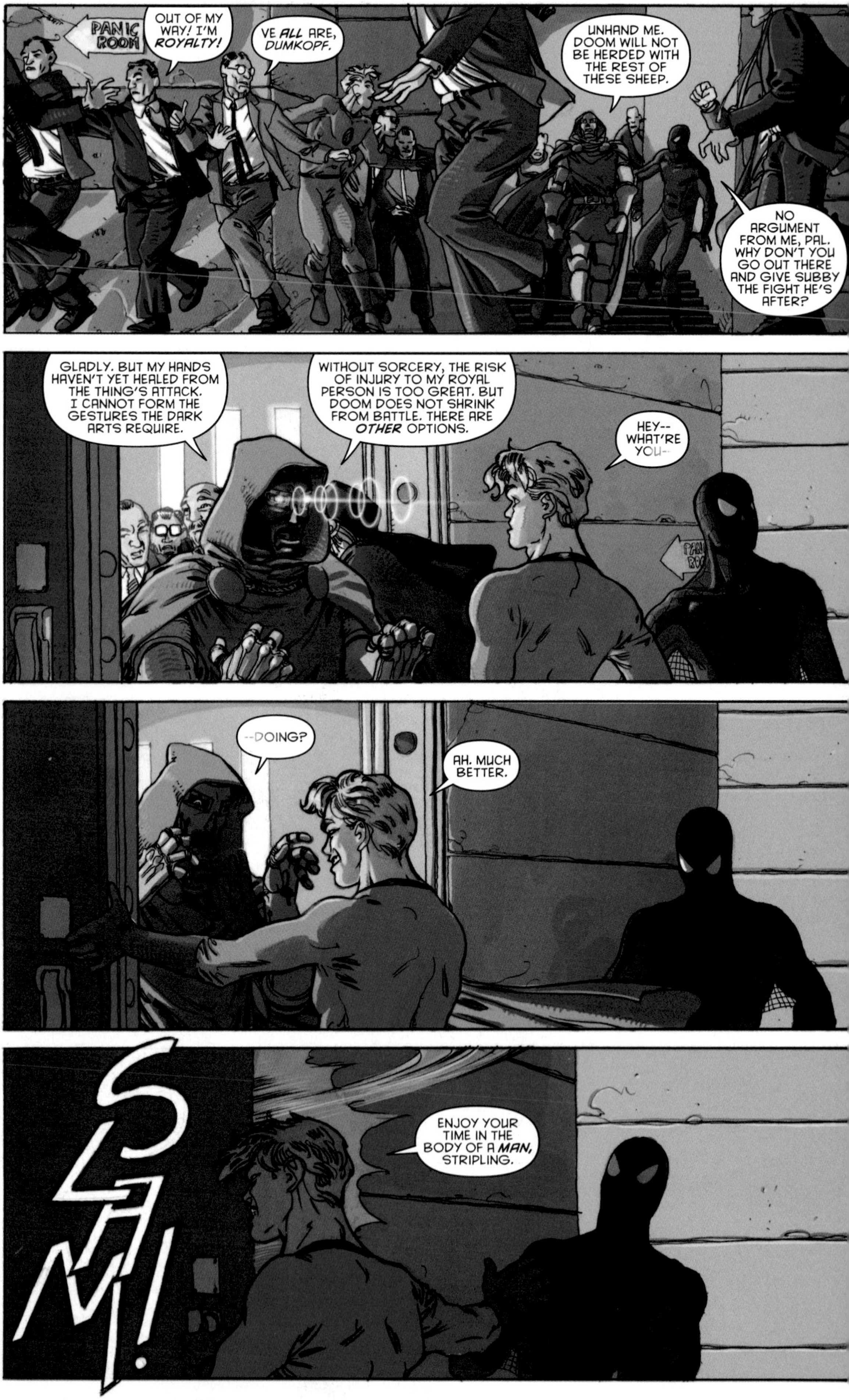
PANIC ROOM
OUT OF MY WAY! I'M ROYALTY!
VE ALL ARE, DUMKOPFF.
UNHAND ME. DOOM WILL NOT BE HERDED WITH THE REST OF THESE SHEEP.
NO ARGUMENT FROM ME, PAL. WHY DON'T YOU GO OUT THERE AND GIVE SUBBY THE FIGHT HE'S AFTER?
GLADLY. BUT MY HANDS HAVEN'T YET HEALED FROM THE THING'S ATTACK. I CANNOT FORM THE GESTURES THE DARK ARTS REQUIRE.
WITHOUT SORCERY, THE RISK OF INJURY TO MY ROYAL PERSON IS TOO GREAT. BUT DOOM DOES NOT SHRINK FROM BATTLE. THERE ARE OTHER OPTIONS.
HEY--WHAT'RE YOU--
--DOING?
AH. MUCH BETTER.
SLAM!
ENJOY YOUR TIME IN THE BODY OF A MAN, STRIPLING.

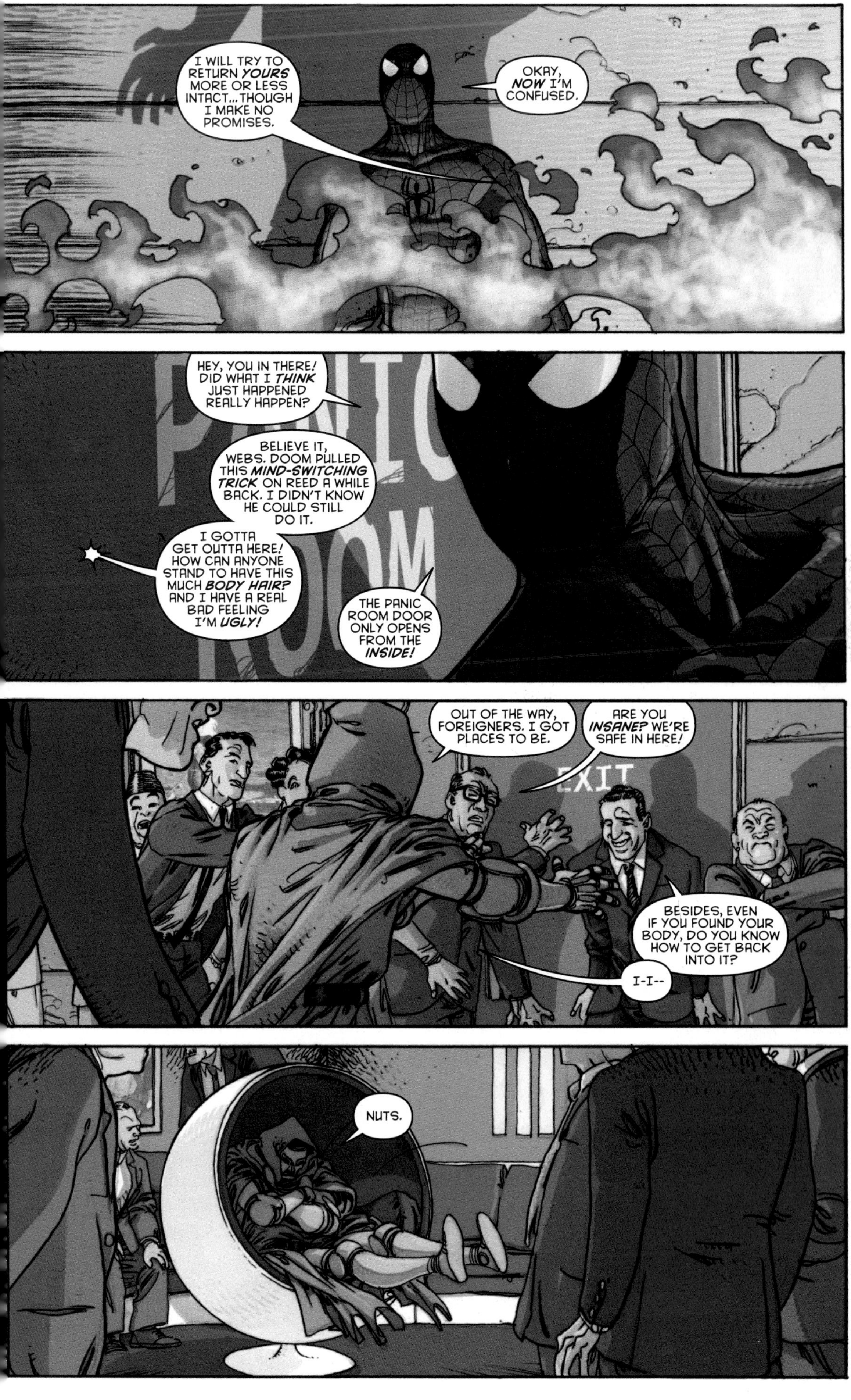
I WILL TRY TO RETURN YOURS MORE OR LESS INTACT...THOUGH I MAKE NO PROMISES.
OKAY, NOW I'M CONFUSED.
HEY, YOU IN THERE! DID WHAT I THINK JUST HAPPENED REALLY HAPPEN?
PANIC ROOM
BELIEVE IT, WEBS. DOOM PULLED THIS MIND-SWITCHING TRICK ON REED A WHILE BACK. I DIDN'T KNOW HE COULD STILL DO IT.
I GOTTA GET OUTTA HERE! HOW CAN ANYONE STAND TO HAVE THIS MUCH BODY HAIR? AND I HAVE A REAL BAD FEELING I'M UGLY!
THE PANIC ROOM DOOR ONLY OPENS FROM THE INSIDE!
OUT OF THE WAY, FOREIGNERS. I GOT PLACES TO BE.
ARE YOU INSANE? WE'RE SAFE IN HERE!
EXIT
BESIDES, EVEN IF YOU FOUND YOUR BODY, DO YOU KNOW HOW TO GET BACK INTO IT?
I-I--
NUTS.

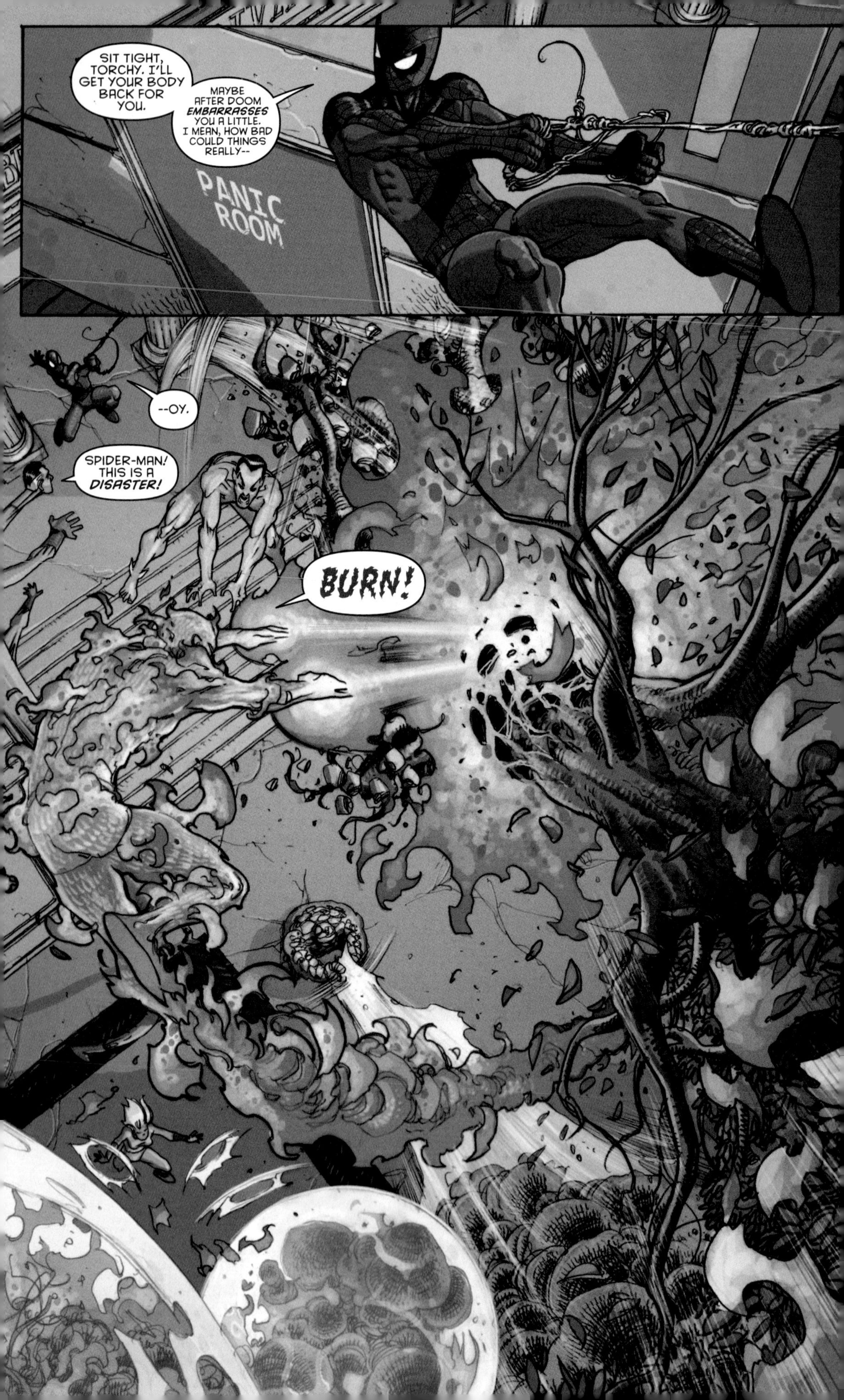
SIT TIGHT, TORCHY. I'LL GET YOUR BODY BACK FOR YOU.
MAYBE AFTER DOOM EMBARRASSES YOU A LITTLE. I MEAN, HOW BAD COULD THINGS REALLY--
PANIC ROOM
--OY.
SPIDER-MAN! THIS IS A DISASTER!
BURN!

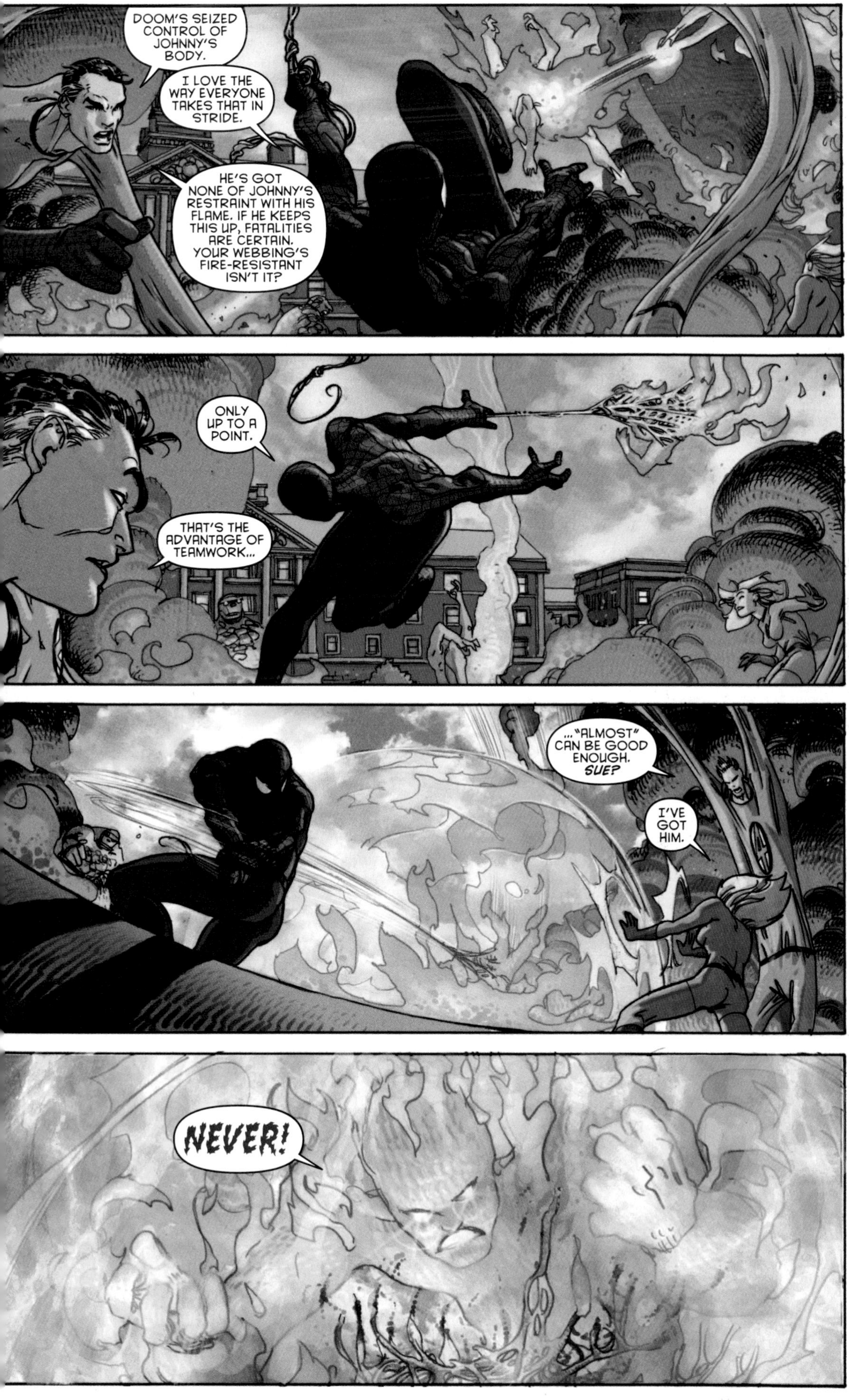
DOOM'S SEIZED CONTROL OF JOHNNY'S BODY.
I LOVE THE WAY EVERYONE TAKES THAT IN STRIDE.
HE'S GOT NONE OF JOHNNY'S RESTRAINT WITH HIS FLAME. IF HE KEEPS THIS UP, FATALITIES ARE CERTAIN. YOUR WEBBING'S FIRE-RESISTANT ISN'T IT?
ONLY UP TO A POINT.
THAT'S THE ADVANTAGE OF TEAMWORK...
..."ALMOST" CAN BE GOOD ENOUGH. *SUE?*
I'VE GOT HIM.
NEVER!

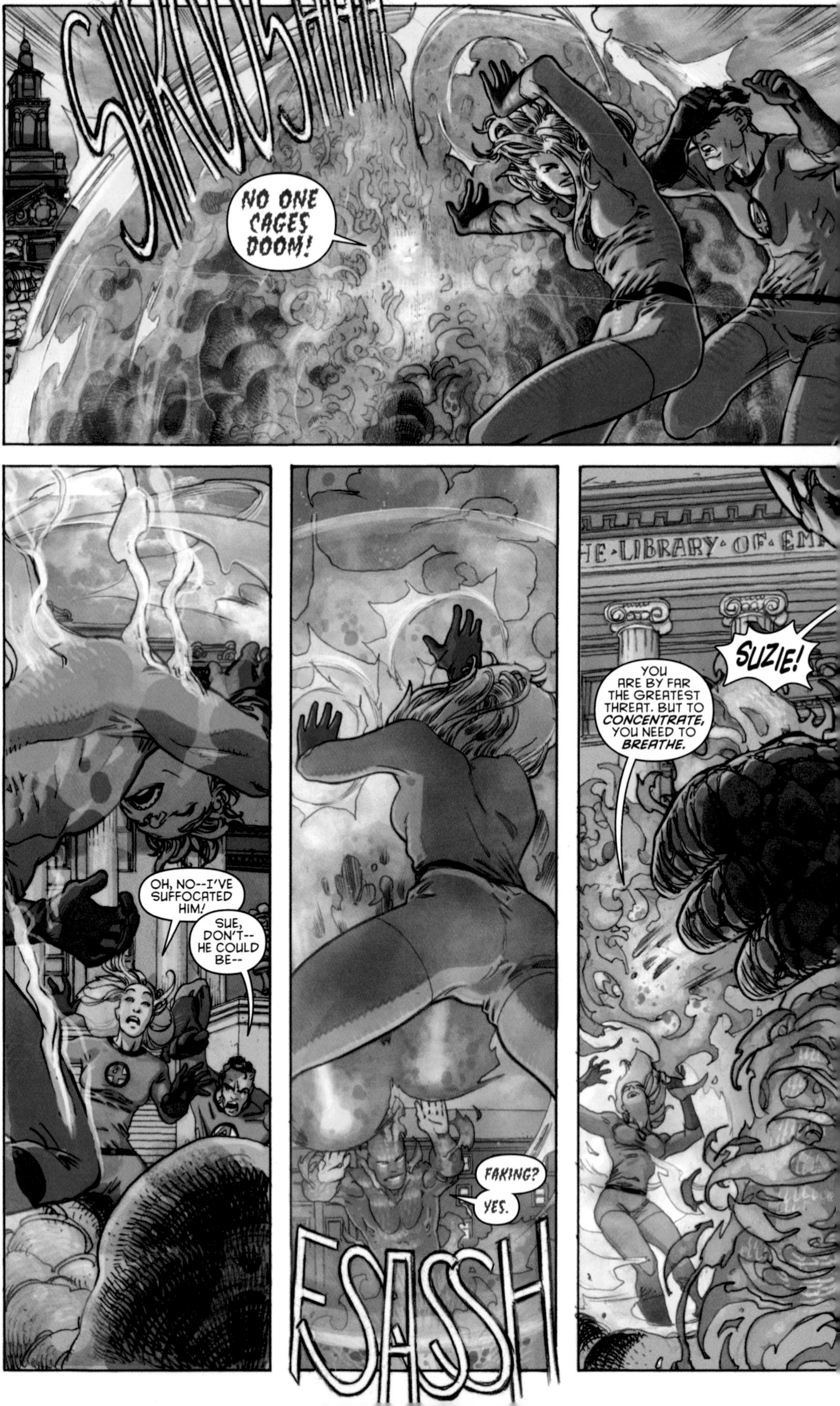
SHROOSHHHH
NO ONE CAGES DOOM!
OH, NO--I'VE SUFFOCATED HIM!
SUE, DON'T-- HE COULD BE--
FAKING?
YES.
ESASSH
HE LIBRARY OF EM
SUZIE!
YOU ARE BY FAR THE GREATEST THREAT. BUT TO CONCENTRATE, YOU NEED TO BREATHE.

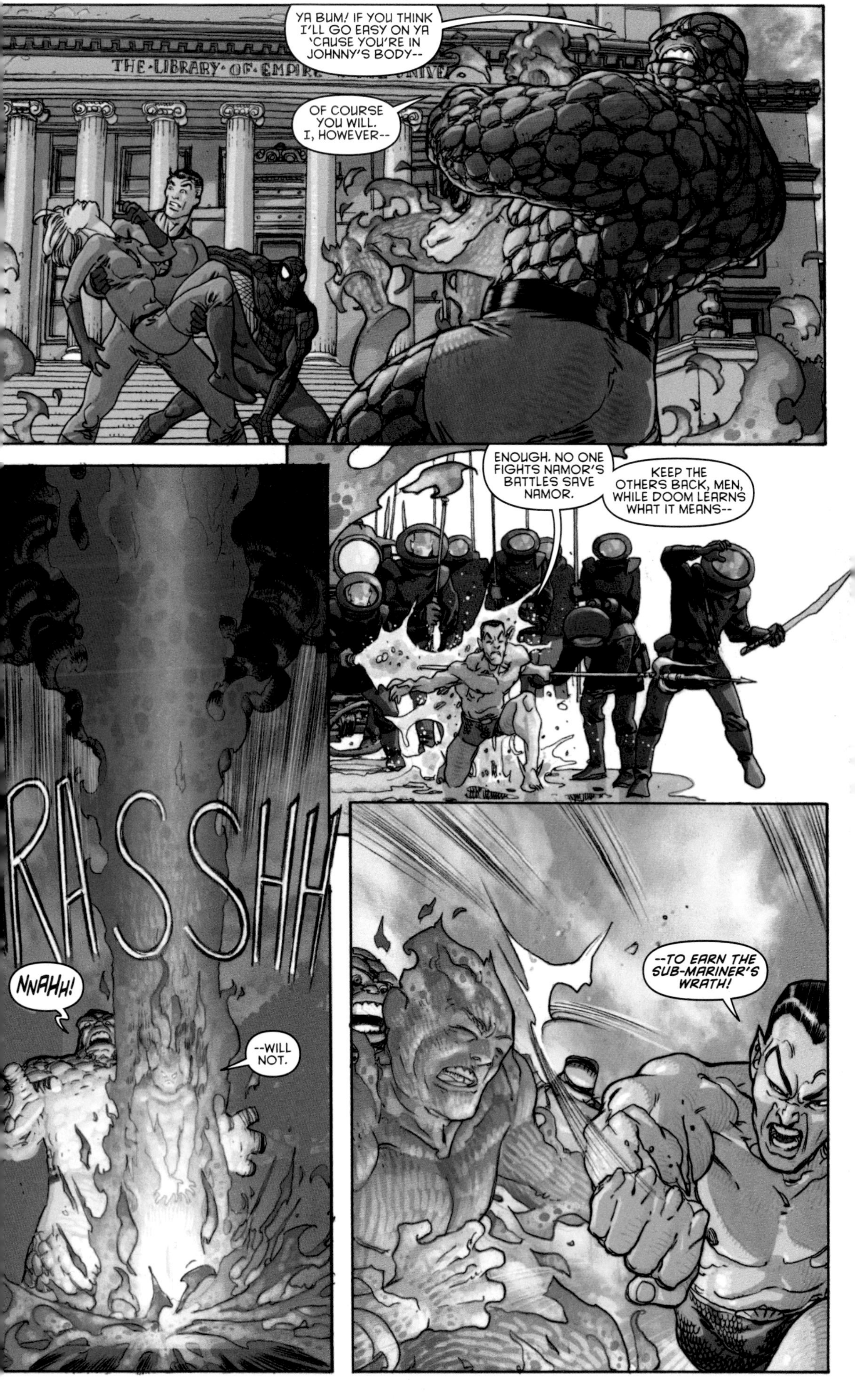
YA BUM! IF YOU THINK I'LL GO EASY ON YA 'CAUSE YOU'RE IN JOHNNY'S BODY--
THE LIBRARY OF EMPIRE
OF COURSE YOU WILL. I, HOWEVER--
ENOUGH. NO ONE FIGHTS NAMOR'S BATTLES SAVE NAMOR.
KEEP THE OTHERS BACK, MEN, WHILE DOOM LEARNS WHAT IT MEANS--
RASSHH
NNAHH!
--WILL NOT.
--TO EARN THE SUB-MARINER'S WRATH!

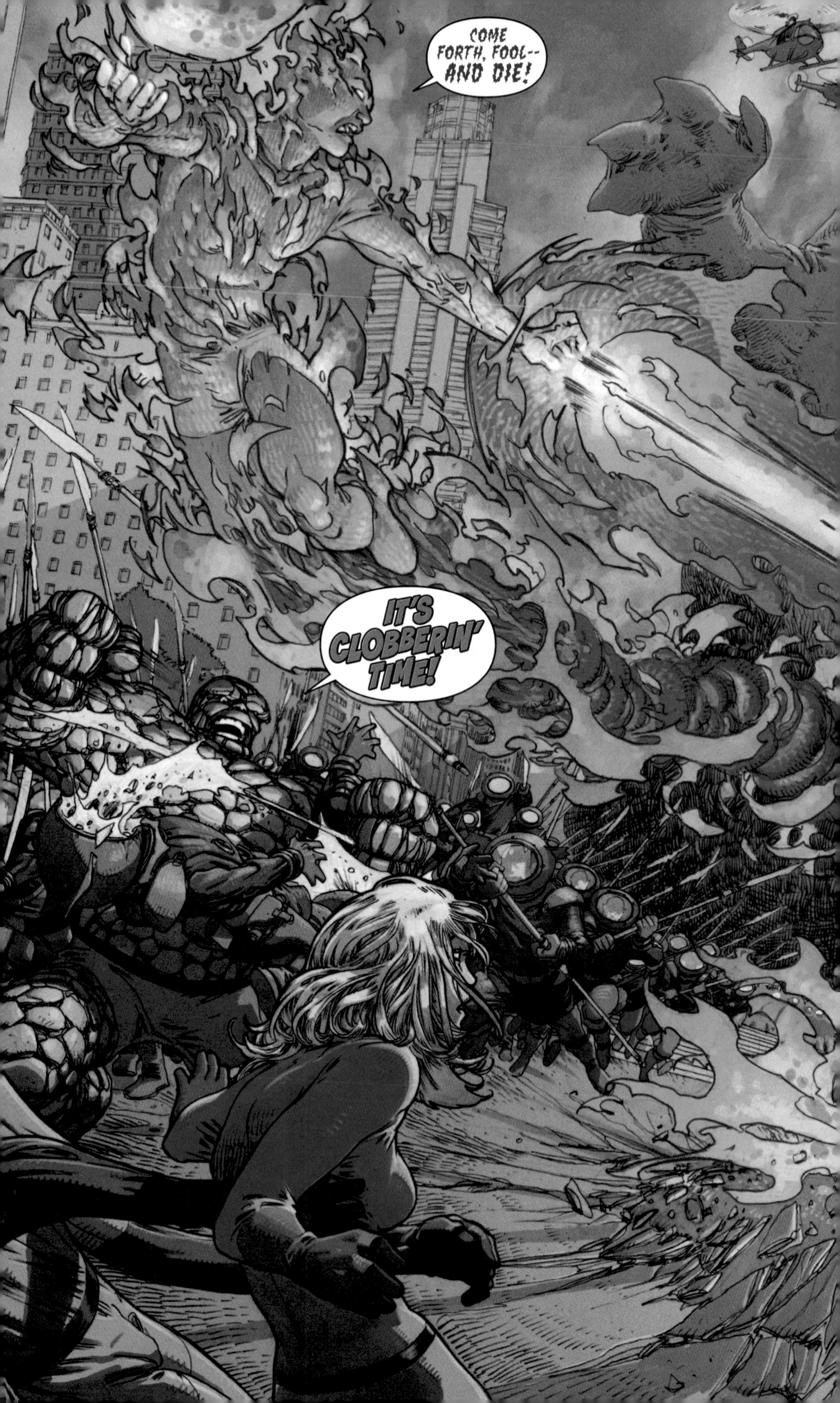
COME FORTH, FOOL-- AND DIE!
IT'S CLOBBERIN' TIME!

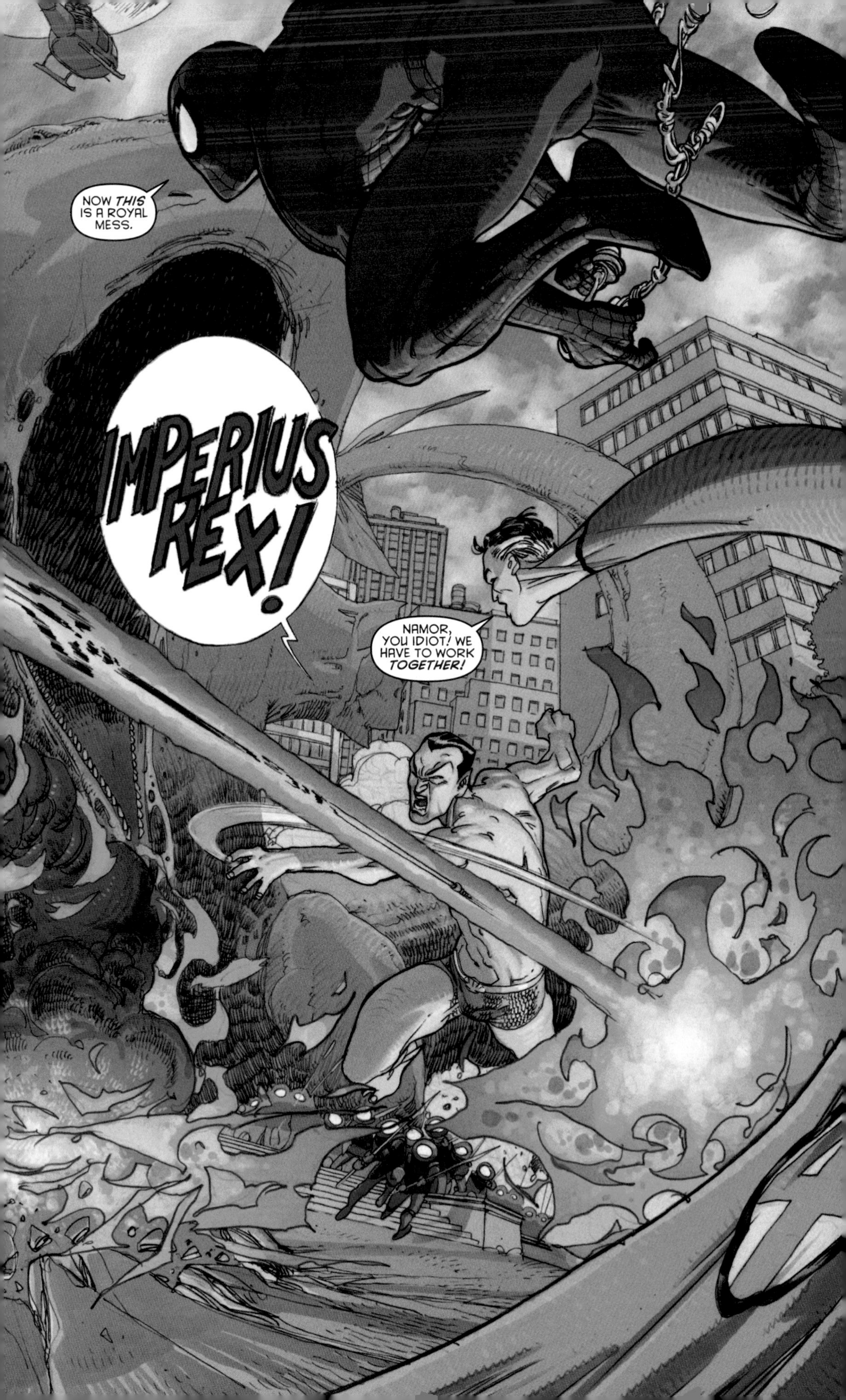
NOW THIS IS A ROYAL MESS.
IMPERIUS REX!
NAMOR, YOU IDIOT! WE HAVE TO WORK TOGETHER!

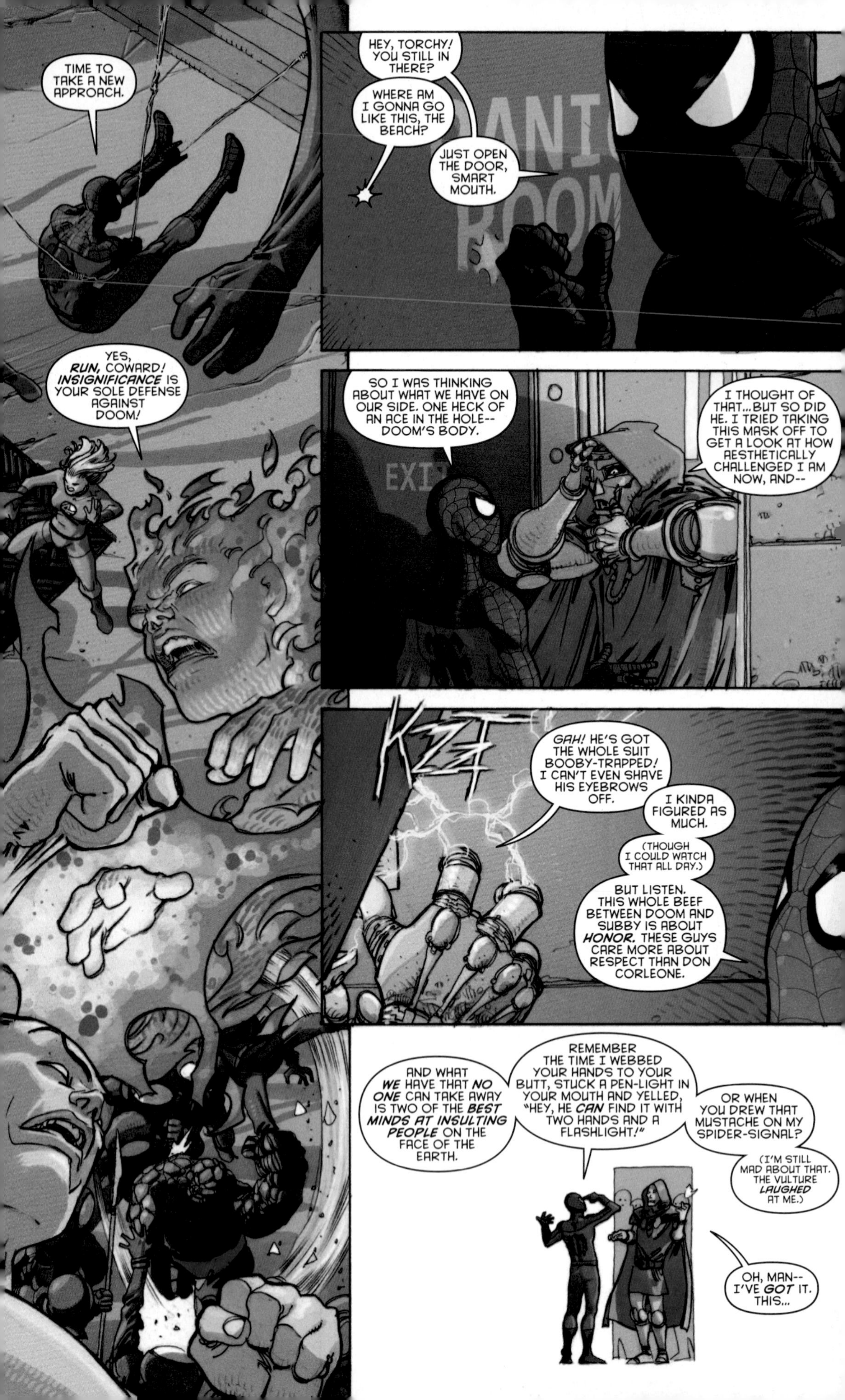
TIME TO TAKE A NEW APPROACH.
HEY, TORCHY! YOU STILL IN THERE?
WHERE AM I GONNA GO LIKE THIS, THE BEACH?
JUST OPEN THE DOOR, SMART MOUTH.
PANIC ROOM
YES, RUN, COWARD! INSIGNIFICANCE IS YOUR SOLE DEFENSE AGAINST DOOM!
SO I WAS THINKING ABOUT WHAT WE HAVE ON OUR SIDE. ONE HECK OF AN ACE IN THE HOLE-- DOOM'S BODY.
EXIT
I THOUGHT OF THAT...BUT SO DID HE. I TRIED TAKING THIS MASK OFF TO GET A LOOK AT HOW AESTHETICALLY CHALLENGED I AM NOW, AND--
KZZT
GAH! HE'S GOT THE WHOLE SUIT BOOBY-TRAPPED! I CAN'T EVEN SHAVE HIS EYEBROWS OFF.
I KINDA FIGURED AS MUCH.
(THOUGH I COULD WATCH THAT ALL DAY.)
BUT LISTEN. THIS WHOLE BEEF BETWEEN DOOM AND SUBBY IS ABOUT HONOR. THESE GUYS CARE MORE ABOUT RESPECT THAN DON CORLEONE.
AND WHAT WE HAVE THAT NO ONE CAN TAKE AWAY IS TWO OF THE BEST MINDS AT INSULTING PEOPLE ON THE FACE OF THE EARTH.
REMEMBER THE TIME I WEBBED YOUR HANDS TO YOUR BUTT, STUCK A PEN-LIGHT IN YOUR MOUTH AND YELLED, "HEY, HE CAN FIND IT WITH TWO HANDS AND A FLASHLIGHT!"
OR WHEN YOU DREW THAT MUSTACHE ON MY SPIDER-SIGNAL?
(I'M STILL MAD ABOUT THAT. THE VULTURE LAUGHED AT ME.)
OH, MAN-- I'VE GOT IT. THIS...

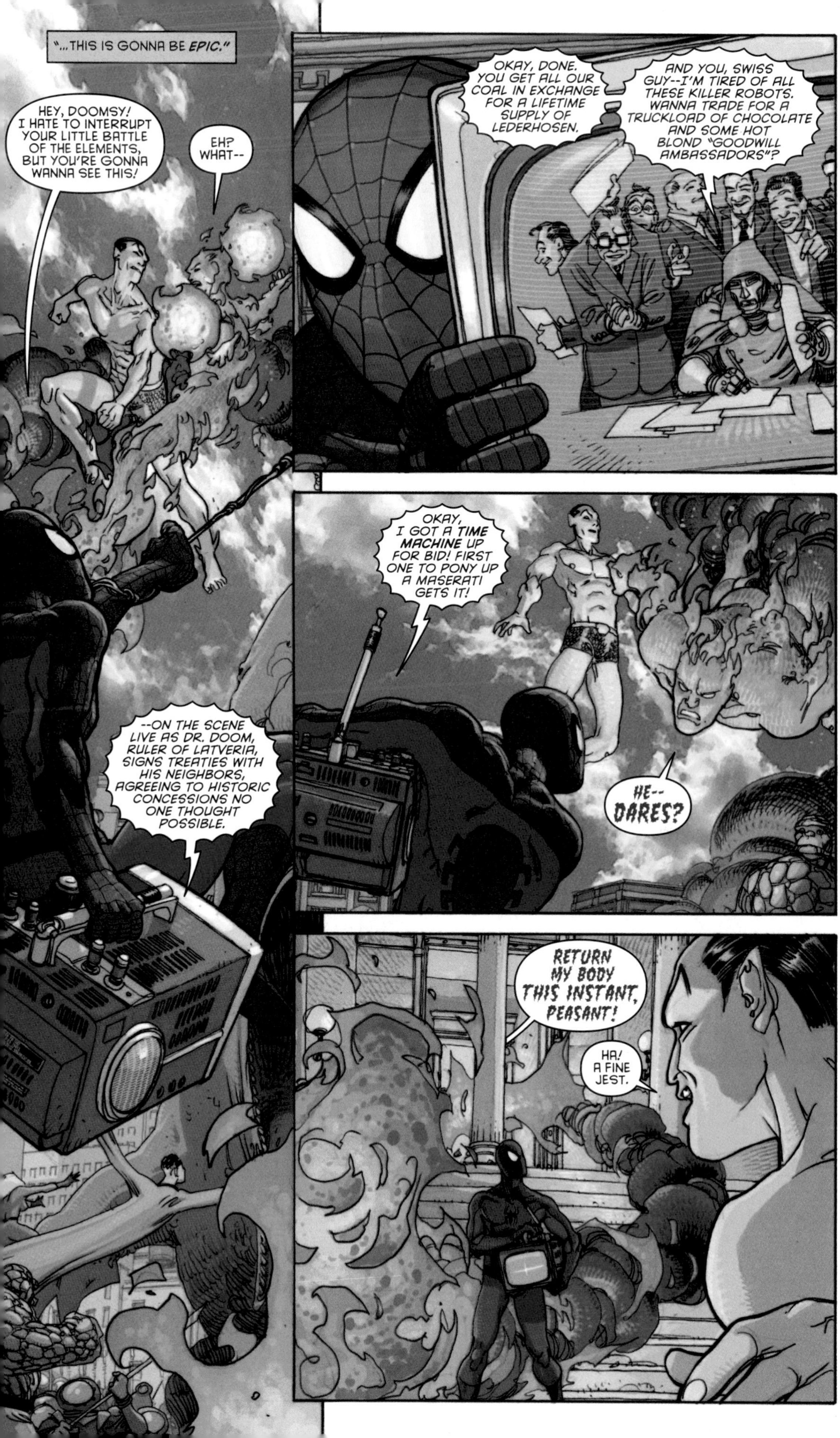
"...THIS IS GONNA BE EPIC."
HEY, DOOMSY! I HATE TO INTERRUPT YOUR LITTLE BATTLE OF THE ELEMENTS, BUT YOU'RE GONNA WANNA SEE THIS!
EH? WHAT--
OKAY, DONE. YOU GET ALL OUR COAL IN EXCHANGE FOR A LIFETIME SUPPLY OF LEDERHOSEN.
AND YOU, SWISS GUY--I'M TIRED OF ALL THESE KILLER ROBOTS. WANNA TRADE FOR A TRUCKLOAD OF CHOCOLATE AND SOME HOT BLOND "GOODWILL AMBASSADORS"?
--ON THE SCENE LIVE AS DR. DOOM, RULER OF LATVERIA, SIGNS TREATIES WITH HIS NEIGHBORS, AGREEING TO HISTORIC CONCESSIONS NO ONE THOUGHT POSSIBLE.
OKAY, I GOT A TIME MACHINE UP FOR BID! FIRST ONE TO PONY UP A MASERATI GETS IT!
HE-- DARES?
RETURN MY BODY THIS INSTANT, PEASANT!
HA! A FINE JEST.

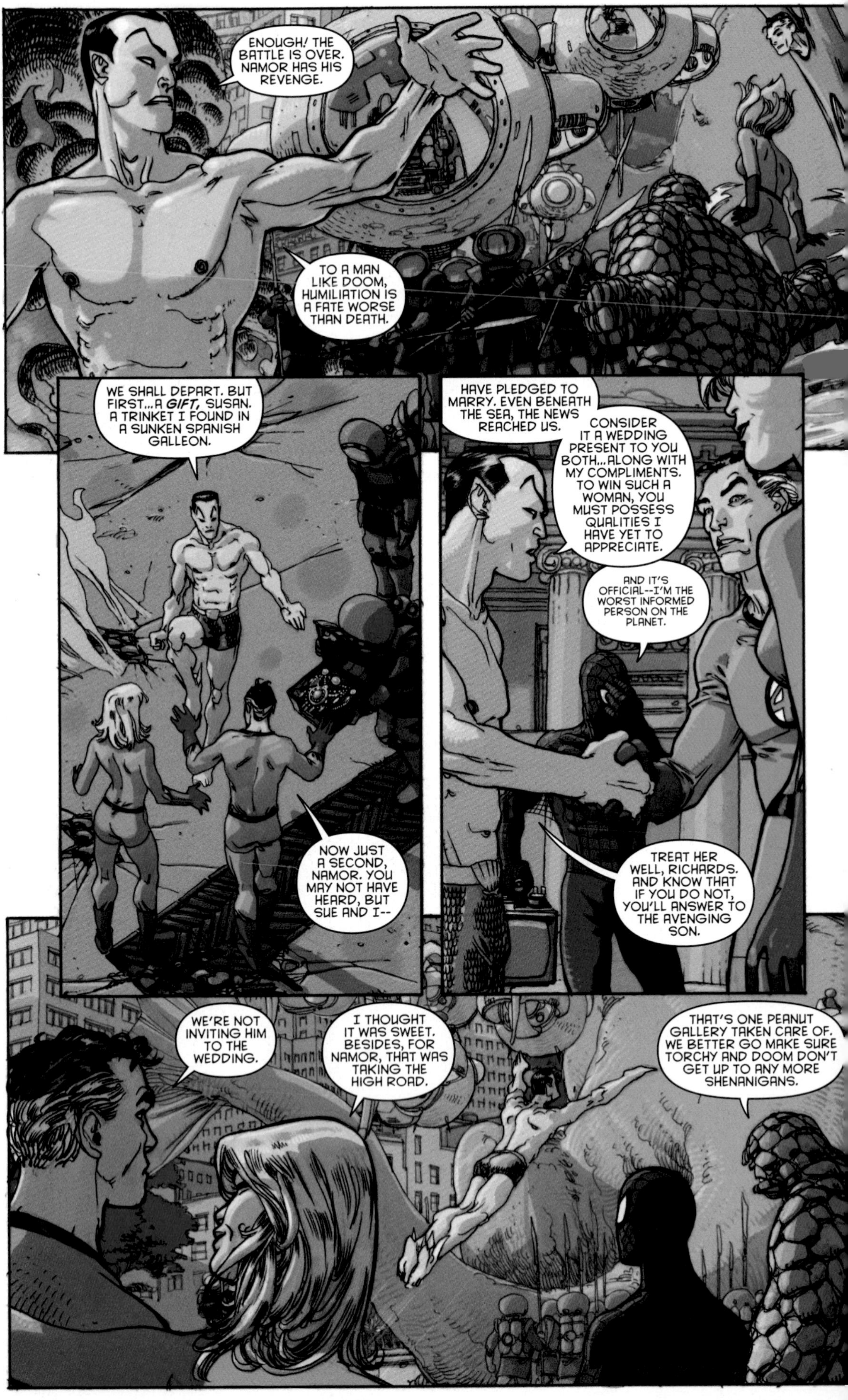
ENOUGH! THE BATTLE IS OVER. NAMOR HAS HIS REVENGE.
TO A MAN LIKE DOOM, HUMILIATION IS A FATE WORSE THAN DEATH.
WE SHALL DEPART. BUT FIRST... A *GIFT,* SUSAN. A TRINKET I FOUND IN A SUNKEN SPANISH GALLEON.
NOW JUST A SECOND, NAMOR. YOU MAY NOT HAVE HEARD, BUT SUE AND I--
HAVE PLEDGED TO MARRY. EVEN BENEATH THE SEA, THE NEWS REACHED US.
CONSIDER IT A WEDDING PRESENT TO YOU BOTH... ALONG WITH MY COMPLIMENTS. TO WIN SUCH A WOMAN, YOU MUST POSSESS QUALITIES I HAVE YET TO APPRECIATE.
AND IT'S OFFICIAL--I'M THE WORST INFORMED PERSON ON THE PLANET.
TREAT HER WELL, RICHARDS. AND KNOW THAT IF YOU DO NOT, YOU'LL ANSWER TO THE AVENGING SON.
WE'RE NOT INVITING HIM TO THE WEDDING.
I THOUGHT IT WAS SWEET. BESIDES, FOR NAMOR, THAT WAS TAKING THE HIGH ROAD.
THAT'S ONE PEANUT GALLERY TAKEN CARE OF. WE BETTER GO MAKE SURE TORCHY AND DOOM DON'T GET UP TO ANY MORE SHENANIGANS.

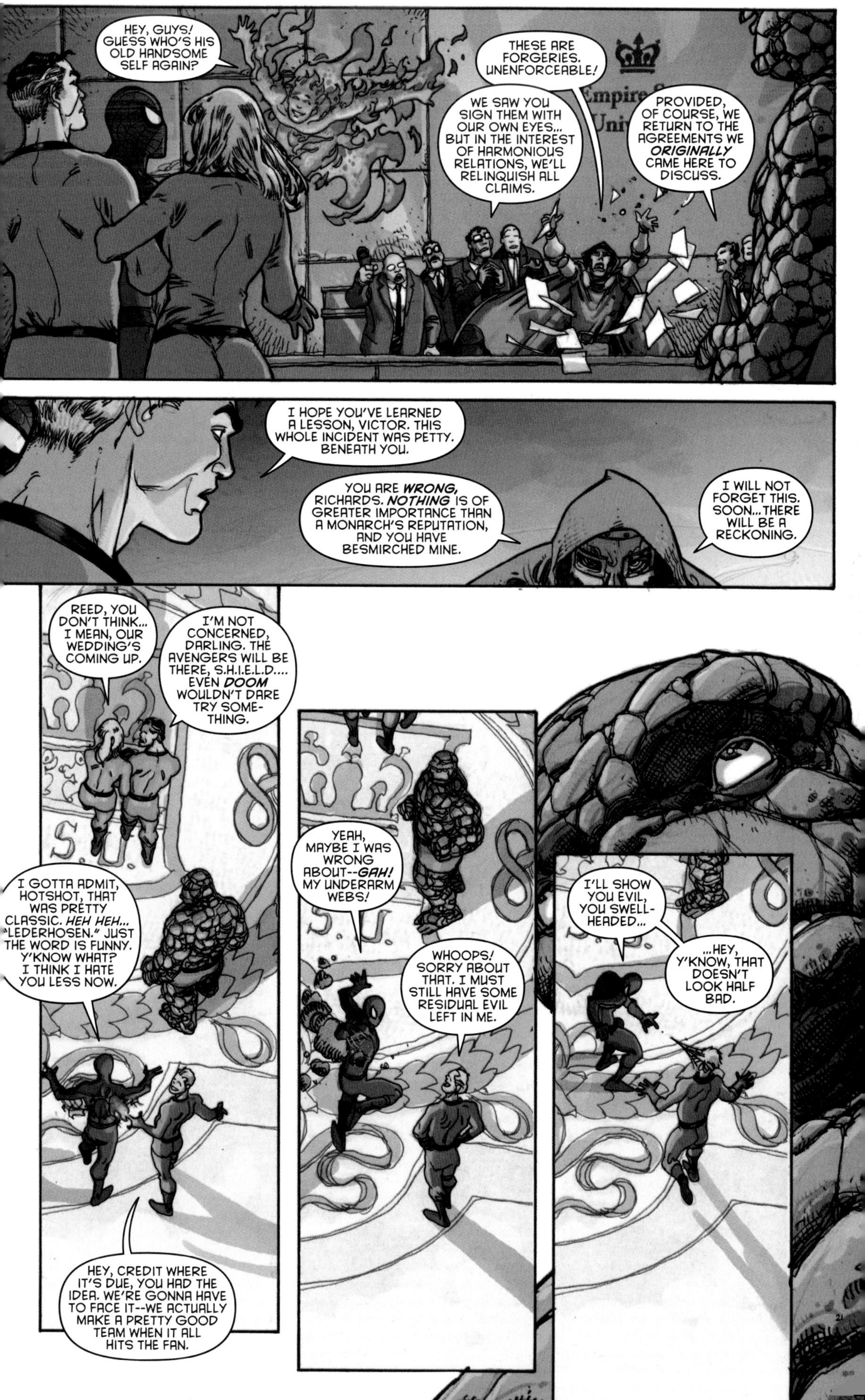

HEY, GUYS! GUESS WHO'S HIS OLD HANDSOME SELF AGAIN?
THESE ARE FORGERIES. UNENFORCEABLE!
WE SAW YOU SIGN THEM WITH OUR OWN EYES... BUT IN THE INTEREST OF HARMONIOUS RELATIONS, WE'LL RELINQUISH ALL CLAIMS.
PROVIDED, OF COURSE, WE RETURN TO THE AGREEMENTS WE *ORIGINALLY* CAME HERE TO DISCUSS.
I HOPE YOU'VE LEARNED A LESSON, VICTOR. THIS WHOLE INCIDENT WAS PETTY. BENEATH YOU.
YOU ARE *WRONG,* RICHARDS. *NOTHING* IS OF GREATER IMPORTANCE THAN A MONARCH'S REPUTATION, AND YOU HAVE BESMIRCHED MINE.
I WILL NOT FORGET THIS. SOON... THERE WILL BE A RECKONING.
REED, YOU DON'T THINK... I MEAN, OUR WEDDING'S COMING UP.
I'M NOT CONCERNED, DARLING. THE AVENGERS WILL BE THERE, S.H.I.E.L.D.... EVEN *DOOM* WOULDN'T DARE TRY SOME-THING.
I GOTTA ADMIT, HOTSHOT, THAT WAS PRETTY CLASSIC. *HEH HEH...* "LEDERHOSEN." JUST THE WORD IS FUNNY. Y'KNOW WHAT? I THINK I HATE YOU LESS NOW.
HEY, CREDIT WHERE IT'S DUE, YOU HAD THE IDEA. WE'RE GONNA HAVE TO FACE IT--WE ACTUALLY MAKE A PRETTY GOOD TEAM WHEN IT ALL HITS THE FAN.
YEAH, MAYBE I WAS WRONG ABOUT--*GAH!* MY UNDERARM WEBS!
WHOOPS! SORRY ABOUT THAT. I MUST STILL HAVE SOME RESIDUAL EVIL LEFT IN ME.
I'LL SHOW YOU EVIL, YOU SWELL-HEADED...
...HEY, Y'KNOW, THAT DOESN'T LOOK HALF BAD.

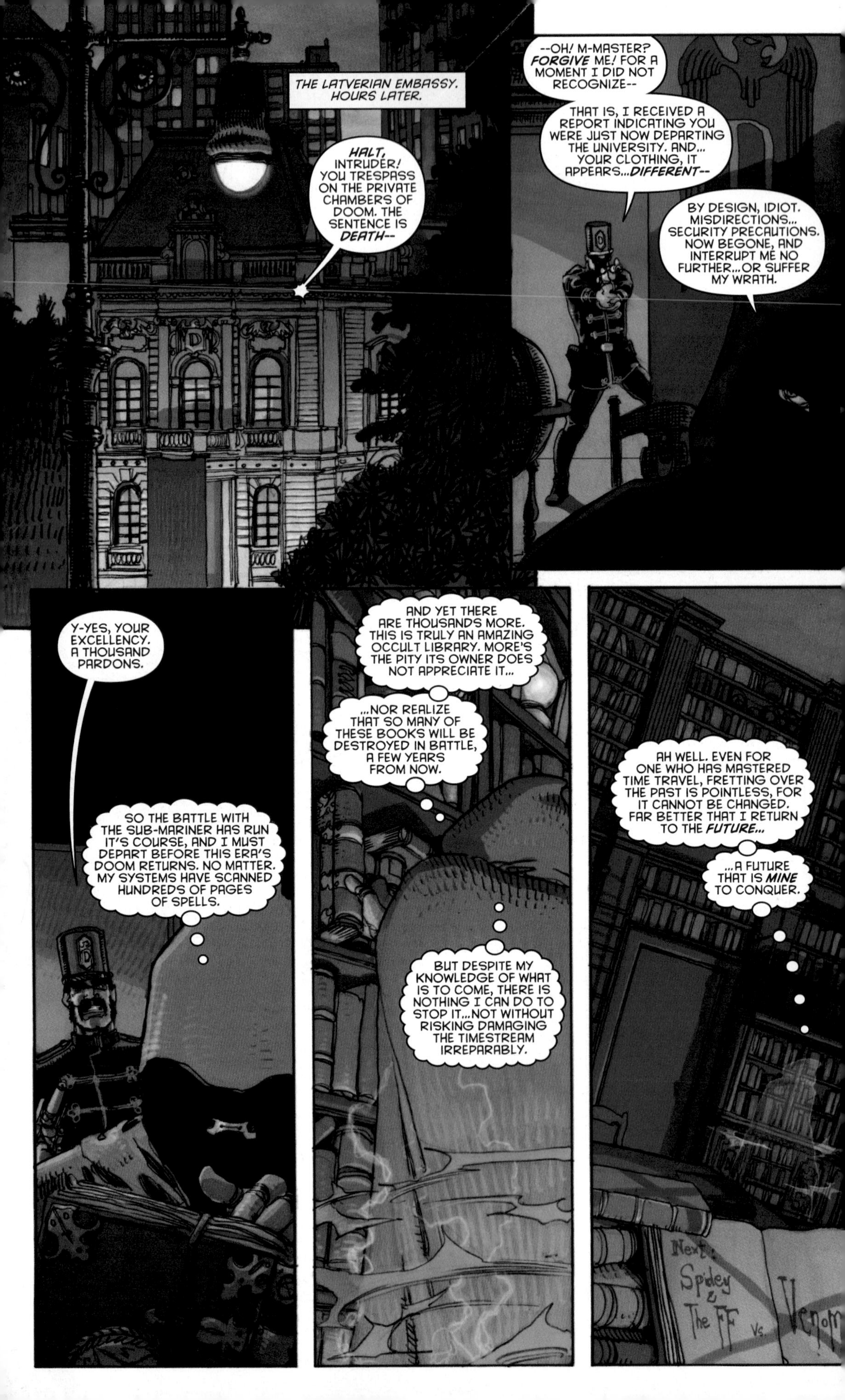
THE LATVERIAN EMBASSY. HOURS LATER.
HALT, INTRUDER! YOU TRESPASS ON THE PRIVATE CHAMBERS OF DOOM. THE SENTENCE IS DEATH--
--OH! M-MASTER? FORGIVE ME! FOR A MOMENT I DID NOT RECOGNIZE--
THAT IS, I RECEIVED A REPORT INDICATING YOU WERE JUST NOW DEPARTING THE UNIVERSITY. AND... YOUR CLOTHING, IT APPEARS...DIFFERENT--
BY DESIGN, IDIOT. MISDIRECTIONS... SECURITY PRECAUTIONS. NOW BEGONE, AND INTERRUPT ME NO FURTHER...OR SUFFER MY WRATH.
Y-YES, YOUR EXCELLENCY. A THOUSAND PARDONS.
SO THE BATTLE WITH THE SUB-MARINER HAS RUN IT'S COURSE, AND I MUST DEPART BEFORE THIS ERA'S DOOM RETURNS. NO MATTER. MY SYSTEMS HAVE SCANNED HUNDREDS OF PAGES OF SPELLS.
AND YET THERE ARE THOUSANDS MORE. THIS IS TRULY AN AMAZING OCCULT LIBRARY. MORE'S THE PITY ITS OWNER DOES NOT APPRECIATE IT...
...NOR REALIZE THAT SO MANY OF THESE BOOKS WILL BE DESTROYED IN BATTLE, A FEW YEARS FROM NOW.
BUT DESPITE MY KNOWLEDGE OF WHAT IS TO COME, THERE IS NOTHING I CAN DO TO STOP IT...NOT WITHOUT RISKING DAMAGING THE TIMESTREAM IRREPARABLY.
AH WELL. EVEN FOR ONE WHO HAS MASTERED TIME TRAVEL, FRETTING OVER THE PAST IS POINTLESS, FOR IT CANNOT BE CHANGED. FAR BETTER THAT I RETURN TO THE FUTURE...
...A FUTURE THAT IS MINE TO CONQUER.
Next: Spidey & The FF vs. Venom

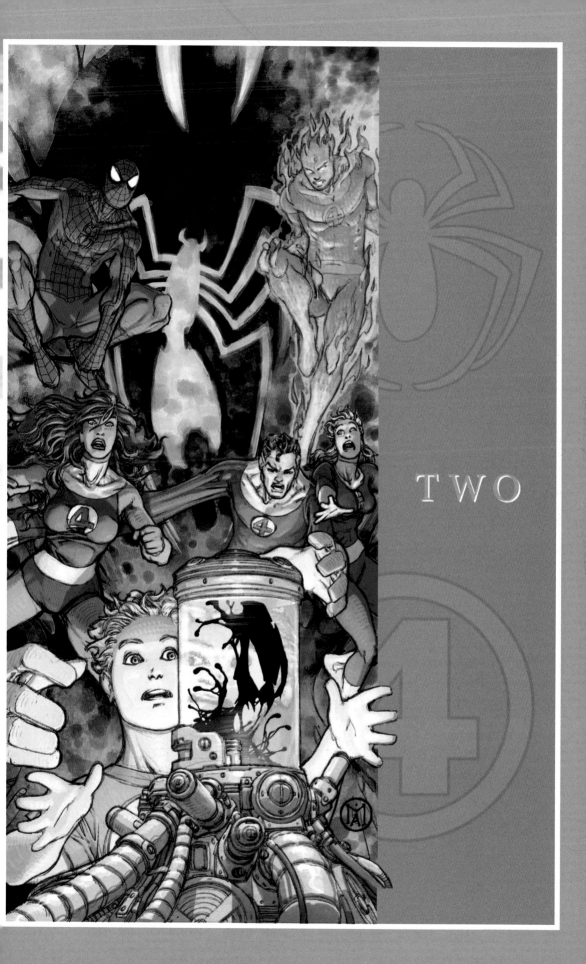

TWO

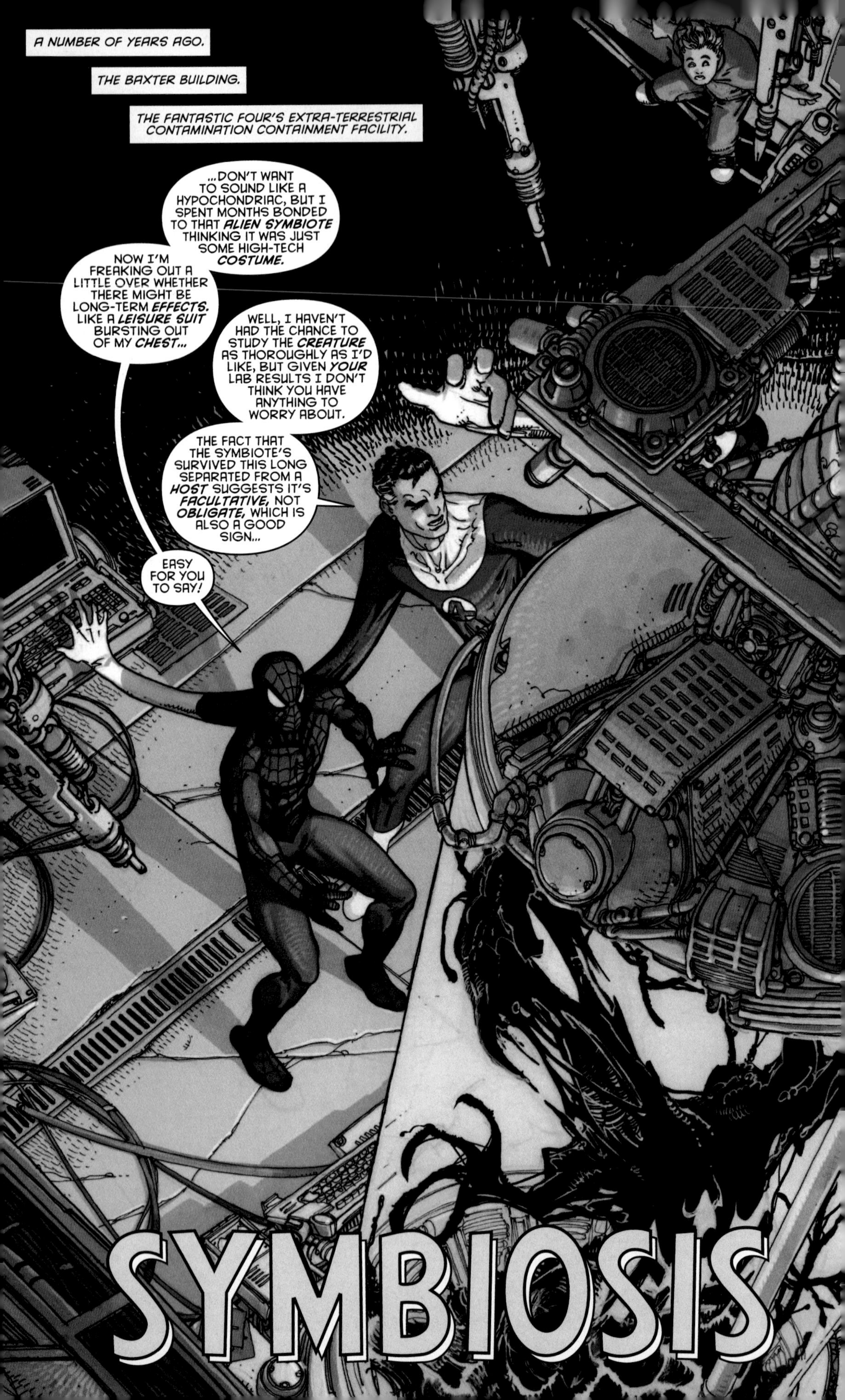
A NUMBER OF YEARS AGO.
THE BAXTER BUILDING.
THE FANTASTIC FOUR'S EXTRA-TERRESTRIAL CONTAMINATION CONTAINMENT FACILITY.
...DON'T WANT TO SOUND LIKE A HYPOCHONDRIAC, BUT I SPENT MONTHS BONDED TO THAT ALIEN SYMBIOTE THINKING IT WAS JUST SOME HIGH-TECH COSTUME.
NOW I'M FREAKING OUT A LITTLE OVER WHETHER THERE MIGHT BE LONG-TERM EFFECTS. LIKE A LEISURE SUIT BURSTING OUT OF MY CHEST...
WELL, I HAVEN'T HAD THE CHANCE TO STUDY THE CREATURE AS THOROUGHLY AS I'D LIKE, BUT GIVEN YOUR LAB RESULTS I DON'T THINK YOU HAVE ANYTHING TO WORRY ABOUT.
THE FACT THAT THE SYMBIOTE'S SURVIVED THIS LONG SEPARATED FROM A HOST SUGGESTS IT'S FACULTATIVE, NOT OBLIGATE, WHICH IS ALSO A GOOD SIGN...
EASY FOR YOU TO SAY!
SYMBIOSIS

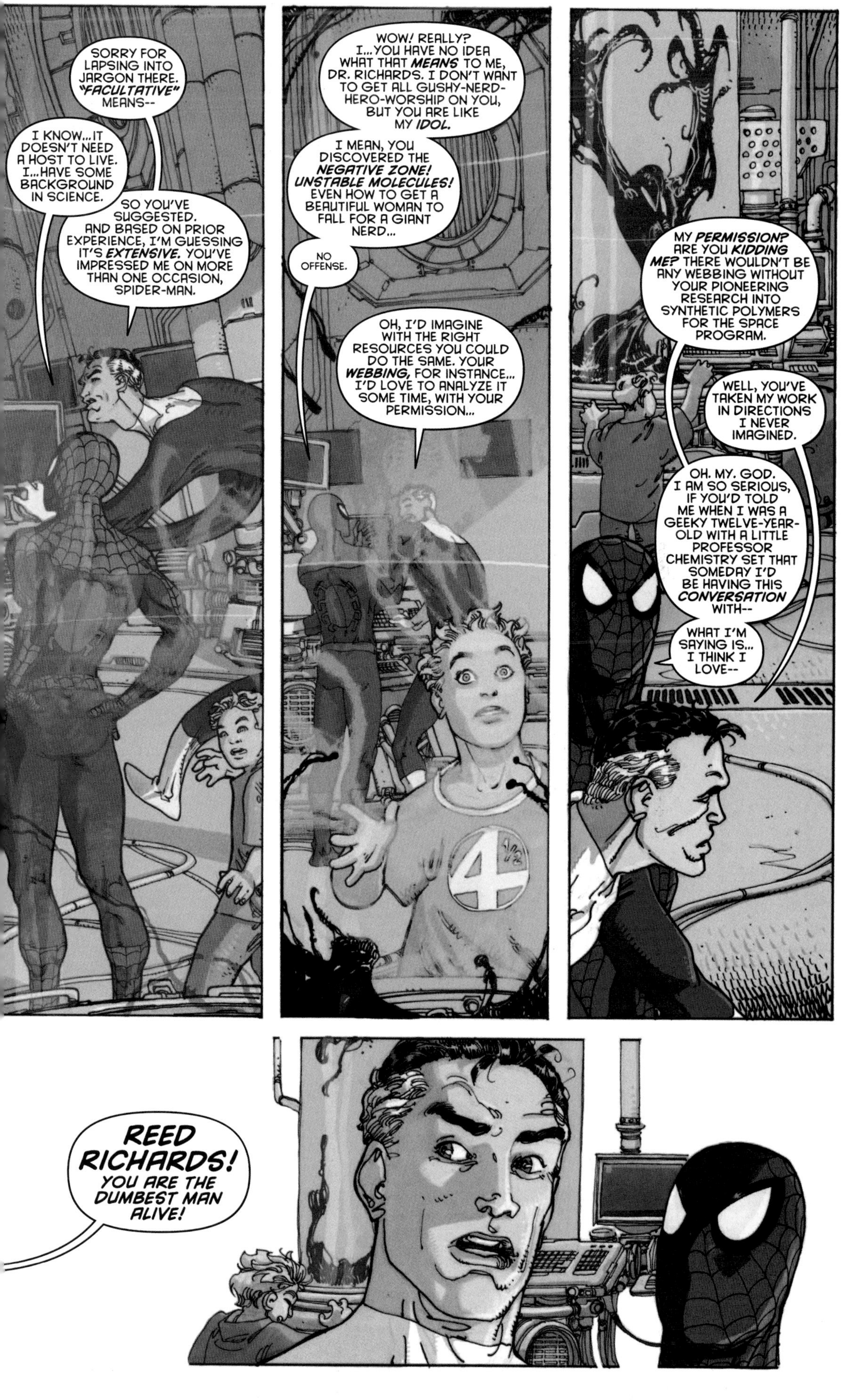
SORRY FOR LAPSING INTO JARGON THERE. "FACULTATIVE" MEANS--
I KNOW...IT DOESN'T NEED A HOST TO LIVE. I...HAVE SOME BACKGROUND IN SCIENCE.
SO YOU'VE SUGGESTED. AND BASED ON PRIOR EXPERIENCE, I'M GUESSING IT'S EXTENSIVE. YOU'VE IMPRESSED ME ON MORE THAN ONE OCCASION, SPIDER-MAN.
WOW! REALLY? I...YOU HAVE NO IDEA WHAT THAT MEANS TO ME, DR. RICHARDS. I DON'T WANT TO GET ALL GUSHY-NERD-HERO-WORSHIP ON YOU, BUT YOU ARE LIKE MY IDOL.
I MEAN, YOU DISCOVERED THE NEGATIVE ZONE! UNSTABLE MOLECULES! EVEN HOW TO GET A BEAUTIFUL WOMAN TO FALL FOR A GIANT NERD...
NO OFFENSE.
OH, I'D IMAGINE WITH THE RIGHT RESOURCES YOU COULD DO THE SAME. YOUR WEBBING, FOR INSTANCE... I'D LOVE TO ANALYZE IT SOME TIME, WITH YOUR PERMISSION...
MY PERMISSION? ARE YOU KIDDING ME? THERE WOULDN'T BE ANY WEBBING WITHOUT YOUR PIONEERING RESEARCH INTO SYNTHETIC POLYMERS FOR THE SPACE PROGRAM.
WELL, YOU'VE TAKEN MY WORK IN DIRECTIONS I NEVER IMAGINED.
OH. MY. GOD. I AM SO SERIOUS, IF YOU'D TOLD ME WHEN I WAS A GEEKY TWELVE-YEAR-OLD WITH A LITTLE PROFESSOR CHEMISTRY SET THAT SOMEDAY I'D BE HAVING THIS CONVERSATION WITH--
WHAT I'M SAYING IS... I THINK I LOVE--
REED RICHARDS! YOU ARE THE DUMBEST MAN ALIVE!

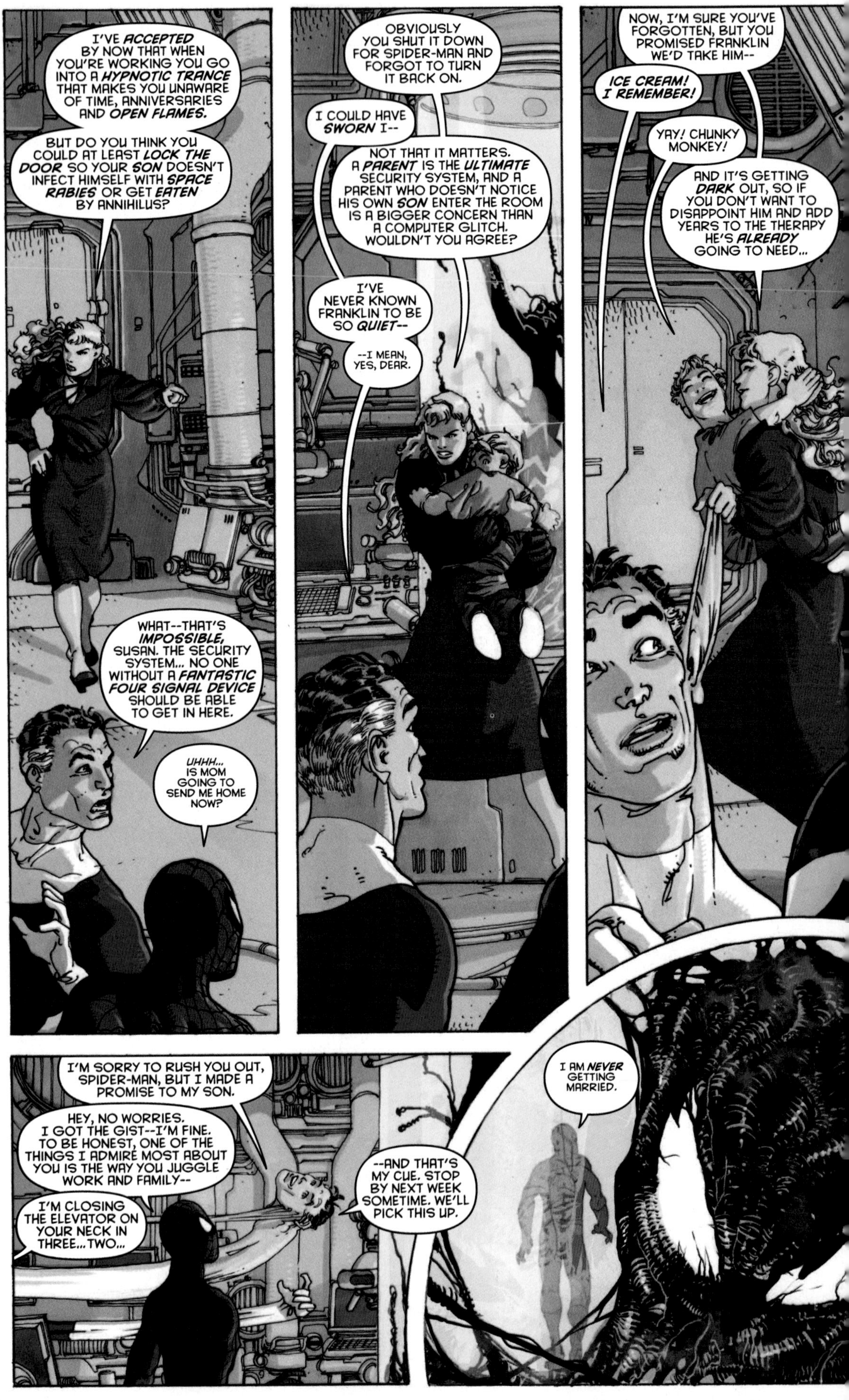
I'VE ACCEPTED BY NOW THAT WHEN YOU'RE WORKING YOU GO INTO A HYPNOTIC TRANCE THAT MAKES YOU UNAWARE OF TIME, ANNIVERSARIES AND OPEN FLAMES.
BUT DO YOU THINK YOU COULD AT LEAST LOCK THE DOOR SO YOUR SON DOESN'T INFECT HIMSELF WITH SPACE RABIES OR GET EATEN BY ANNIHILUS?
WHAT--THAT'S IMPOSSIBLE, SUSAN. THE SECURITY SYSTEM... NO ONE WITHOUT A FANTASTIC FOUR SIGNAL DEVICE SHOULD BE ABLE TO GET IN HERE.
UHHH... IS MOM GOING TO SEND ME HOME NOW?
OBVIOUSLY YOU SHUT IT DOWN FOR SPIDER-MAN AND FORGOT TO TURN IT BACK ON.
I COULD HAVE SWORN I--
NOT THAT IT MATTERS. A PARENT IS THE ULTIMATE SECURITY SYSTEM, AND A PARENT WHO DOESN'T NOTICE HIS OWN SON ENTER THE ROOM IS A BIGGER CONCERN THAN A COMPUTER GLITCH. WOULDN'T YOU AGREE?
I'VE NEVER KNOWN FRANKLIN TO BE SO QUIET--
--I MEAN, YES, DEAR.
NOW, I'M SURE YOU'VE FORGOTTEN, BUT YOU PROMISED FRANKLIN WE'D TAKE HIM--
ICE CREAM! I REMEMBER!
YAY! CHUNKY MONKEY!
AND IT'S GETTING DARK OUT, SO IF YOU DON'T WANT TO DISAPPOINT HIM AND ADD YEARS TO THE THERAPY HE'S ALREADY GOING TO NEED...
I'M SORRY TO RUSH YOU OUT, SPIDER-MAN, BUT I MADE A PROMISE TO MY SON.
HEY, NO WORRIES. I GOT THE GIST--I'M FINE. TO BE HONEST, ONE OF THE THINGS I ADMIRE MOST ABOUT YOU IS THE WAY YOU JUGGLE WORK AND FAMILY--
I'M CLOSING THE ELEVATOR ON YOUR NECK IN THREE... TWO...
--AND THAT'S MY CUE. STOP BY NEXT WEEK SOMETIME. WE'LL PICK THIS UP.
I AM NEVER GETTING MARRIED.

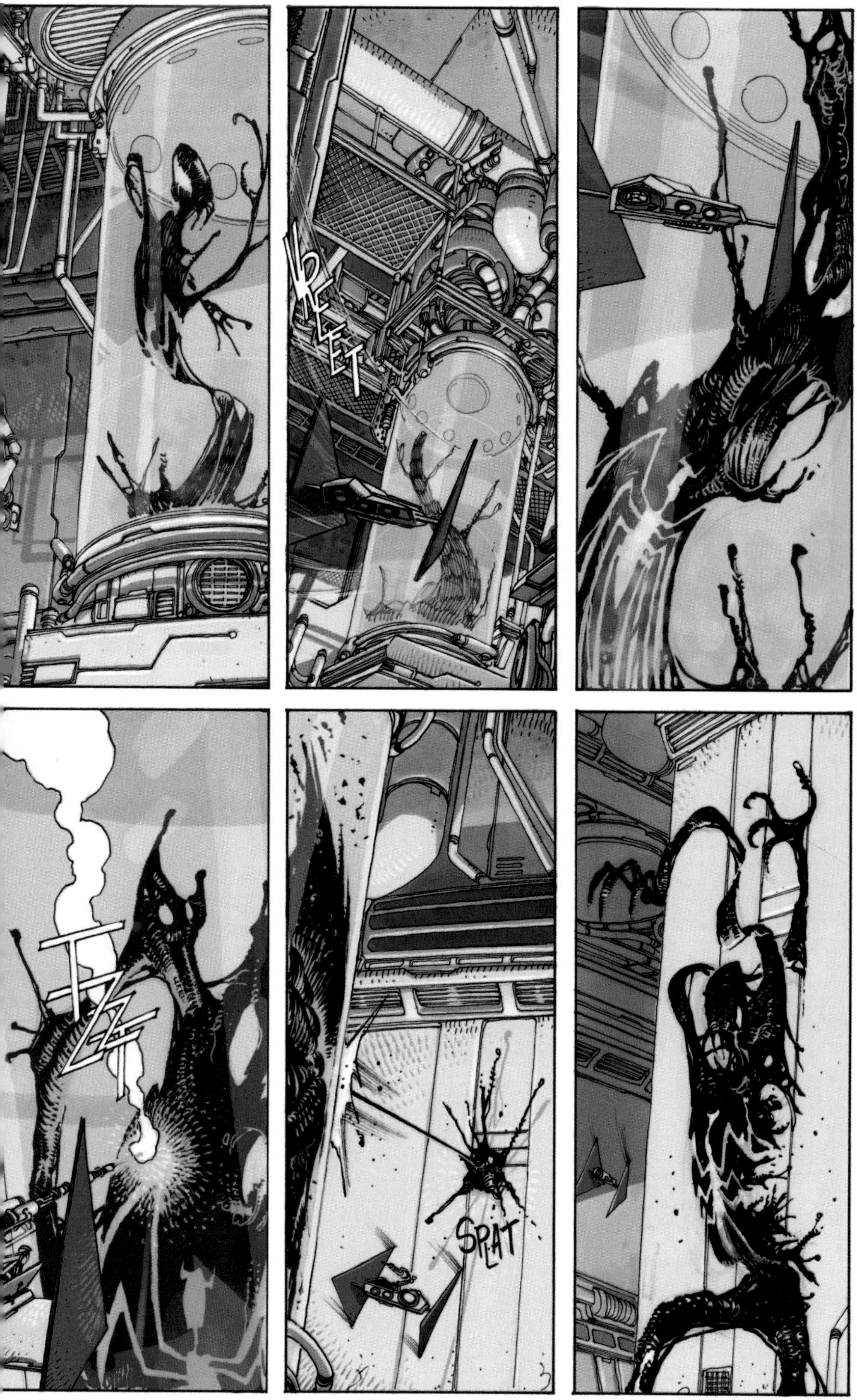
VREEET
TZZT
SPLAT

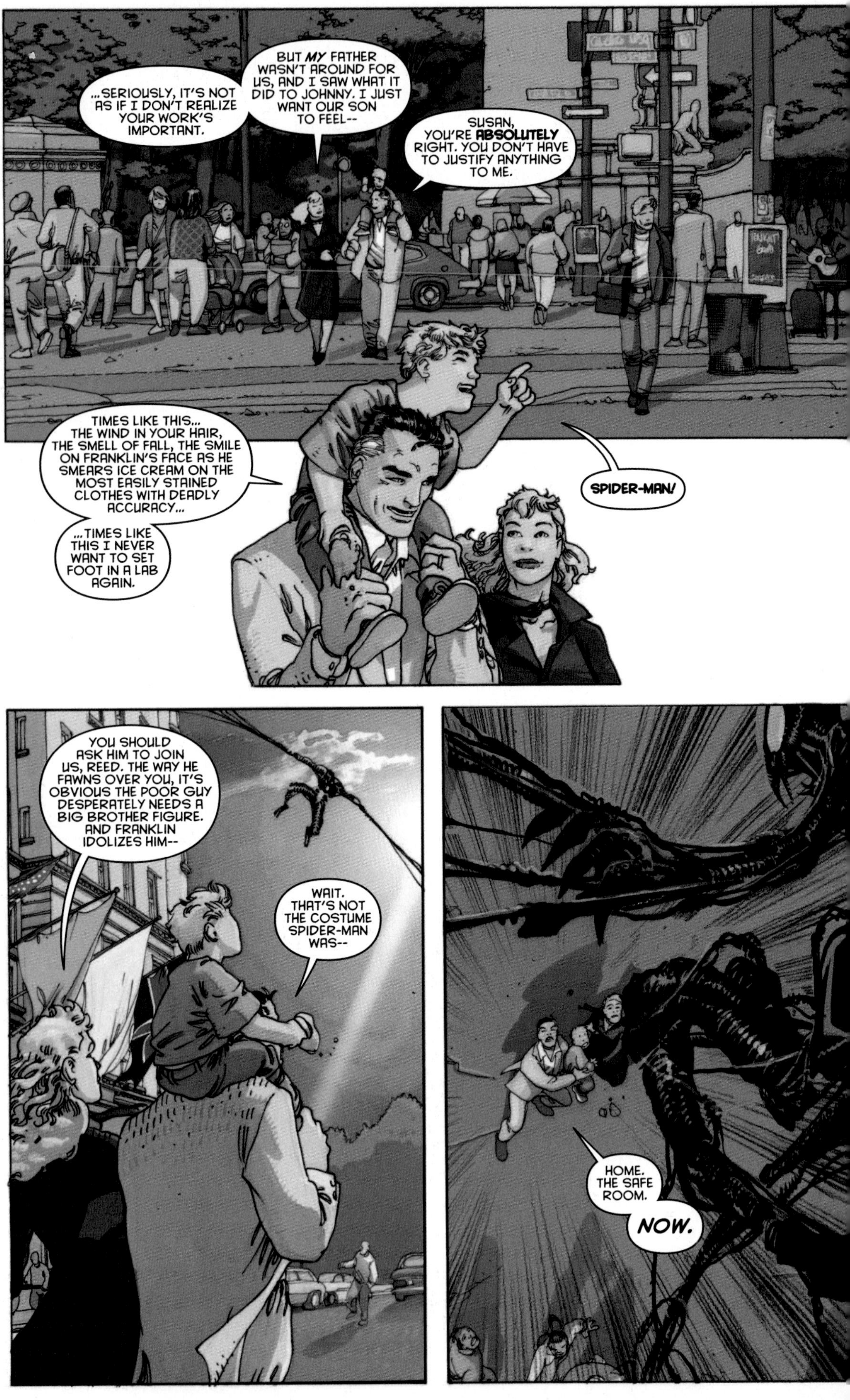
...SERIOUSLY, IT'S NOT AS IF I DON'T REALIZE YOUR WORK'S IMPORTANT.
BUT MY FATHER WASN'T AROUND FOR US, AND I SAW WHAT IT DID TO JOHNNY. I JUST WANT OUR SON TO FEEL--
SUSAN, YOU'RE ABSOLUTELY RIGHT. YOU DON'T HAVE TO JUSTIFY ANYTHING TO ME.
TIMES LIKE THIS... THE WIND IN YOUR HAIR, THE SMELL OF FALL, THE SMILE ON FRANKLIN'S FACE AS HE SMEARS ICE CREAM ON THE MOST EASILY STAINED CLOTHES WITH DEADLY ACCURACY...
...TIMES LIKE THIS I NEVER WANT TO SET FOOT IN A LAB AGAIN.
SPIDER-MAN!
YOU SHOULD ASK HIM TO JOIN US, REED. THE WAY HE FAWNS OVER YOU, IT'S OBVIOUS THE POOR GUY DESPERATELY NEEDS A BIG BROTHER FIGURE. AND FRANKLIN IDOLIZES HIM--
WAIT. THAT'S NOT THE COSTUME SPIDER-MAN WAS--
HOME. THE SAFE ROOM.
NOW.

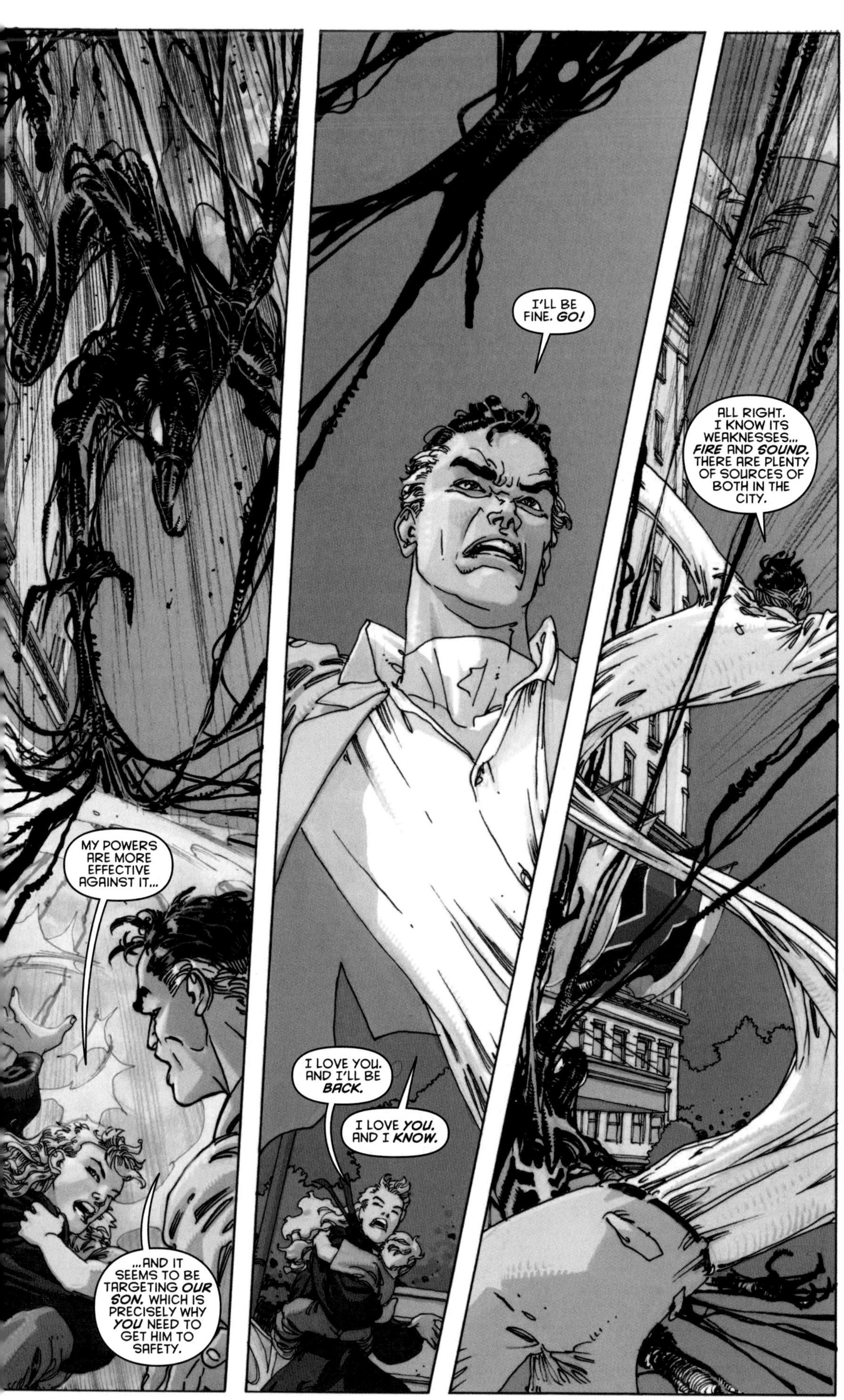
MY POWERS ARE MORE EFFECTIVE AGAINST IT...
...AND IT SEEMS TO BE TARGETING OUR SON. WHICH IS PRECISELY WHY YOU NEED TO GET HIM TO SAFETY.
I'LL BE FINE. GO!
I LOVE YOU. AND I'LL BE BACK.
I LOVE YOU. AND I KNOW.
ALL RIGHT. I KNOW ITS WEAKNESSES... FIRE AND SOUND. THERE ARE PLENTY OF SOURCES OF BOTH IN THE CITY.

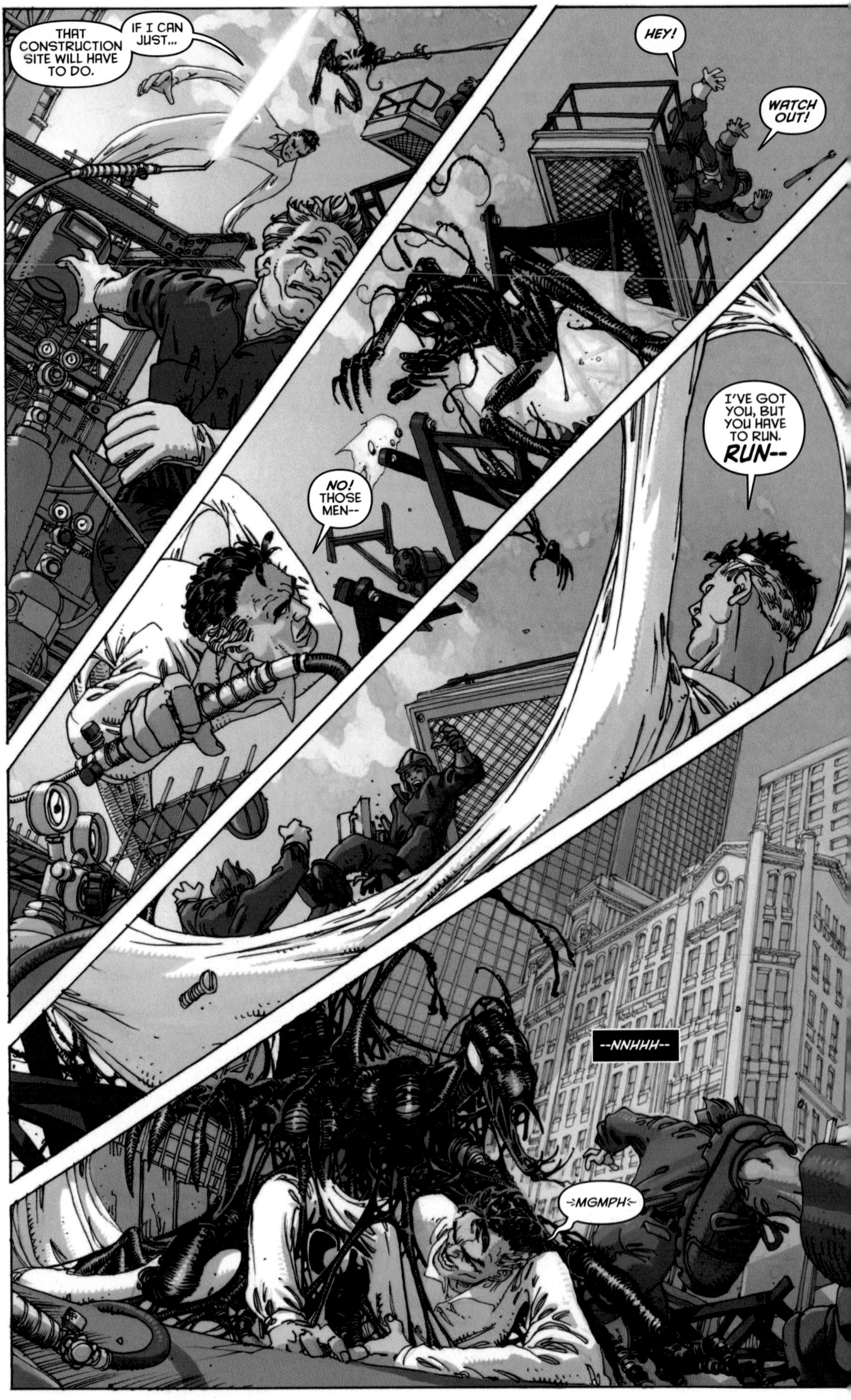
THAT CONSTRUCTION SITE WILL HAVE TO DO.
IF I CAN JUST...
HEY!
WATCH OUT!
NO! THOSE MEN--
I'VE GOT YOU, BUT YOU HAVE TO RUN. RUN--
--NNHHH--
MGMPH

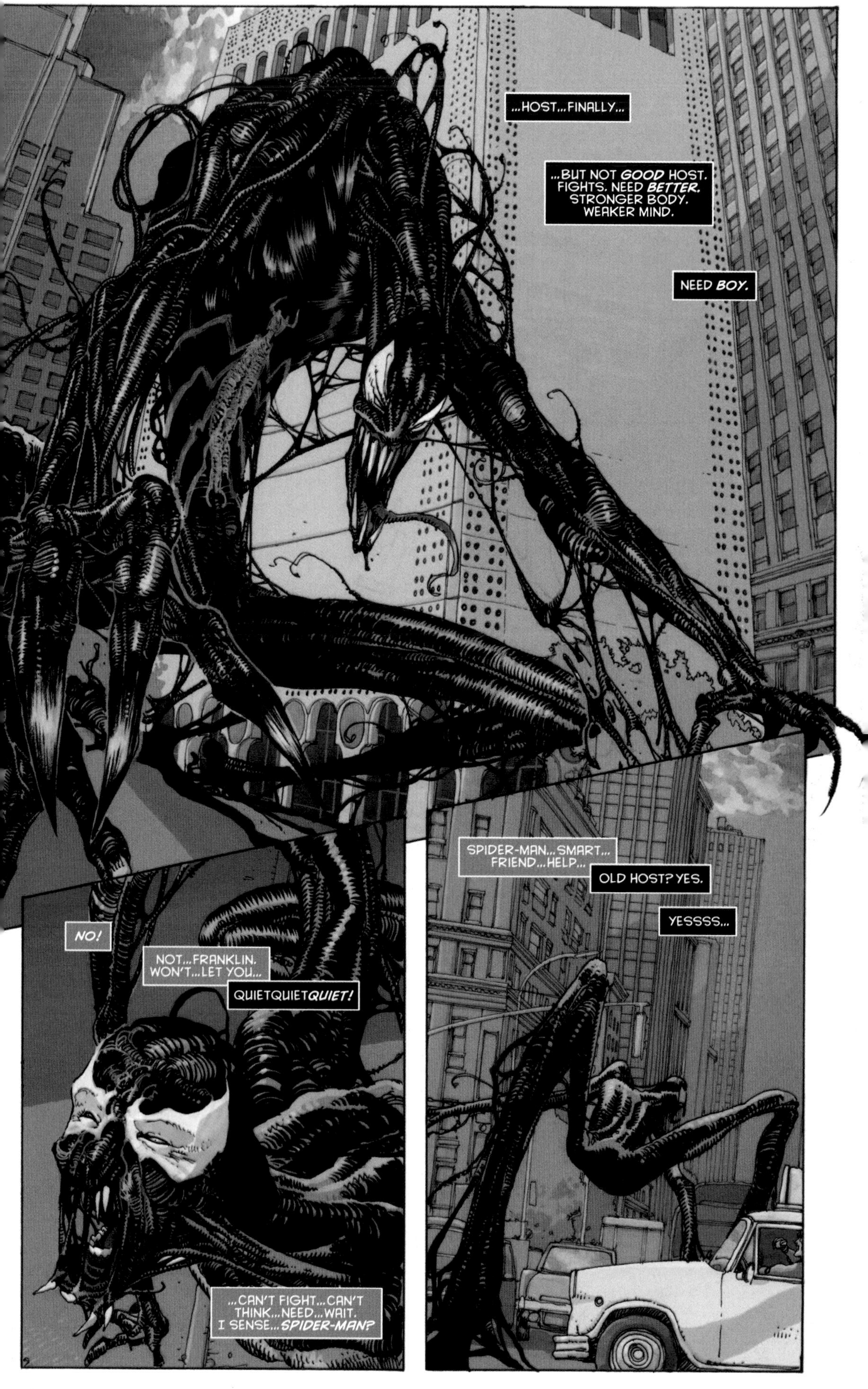
...HOST...FINALLY...
...BUT NOT GOOD HOST. FIGHTS. NEED BETTER. STRONGER BODY. WEAKER MIND.
NEED BOY.
NO!
NOT...FRANKLIN. WON'T...LET YOU...
QUIETQUIETQUIET!
...CAN'T FIGHT...CAN'T THINK...NEED...WAIT. I SENSE...SPIDER-MAN?
SPIDER-MAN...SMART... FRIEND...HELP...
OLD HOST? YES.
YESSSS...

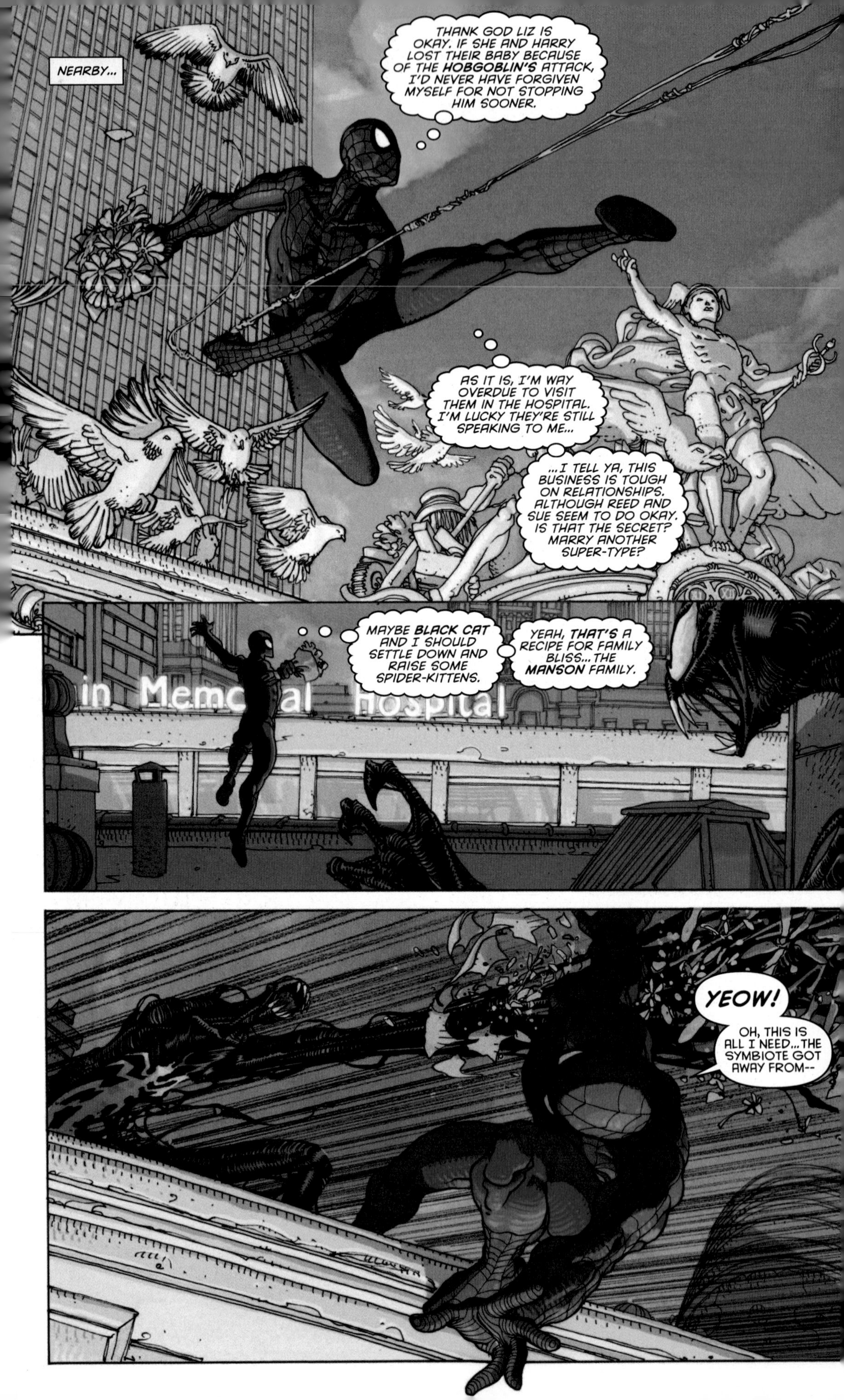
NEARBY...
THANK GOD LIZ IS OKAY. IF SHE AND HARRY LOST THEIR BABY BECAUSE OF THE HOBGOBLIN'S ATTACK, I'D NEVER HAVE FORGIVEN MYSELF FOR NOT STOPPING HIM SOONER.
AS IT IS, I'M WAY OVERDUE TO VISIT THEM IN THE HOSPITAL. I'M LUCKY THEY'RE STILL SPEAKING TO ME...
...I TELL YA, THIS BUSINESS IS TOUGH ON RELATIONSHIPS. ALTHOUGH REED AND SUE SEEM TO DO OKAY. IS THAT THE SECRET? MARRY ANOTHER SUPER-TYPE?
MAYBE BLACK CAT AND I SHOULD SETTLE DOWN AND RAISE SOME SPIDER-KITTENS.
YEAH, THAT'S A RECIPE FOR FAMILY BLISS... THE MANSON FAMILY.
in Memo al Hospital
YEOW!
OH, THIS IS ALL I NEED...THE SYMBIOTE GOT AWAY FROM--

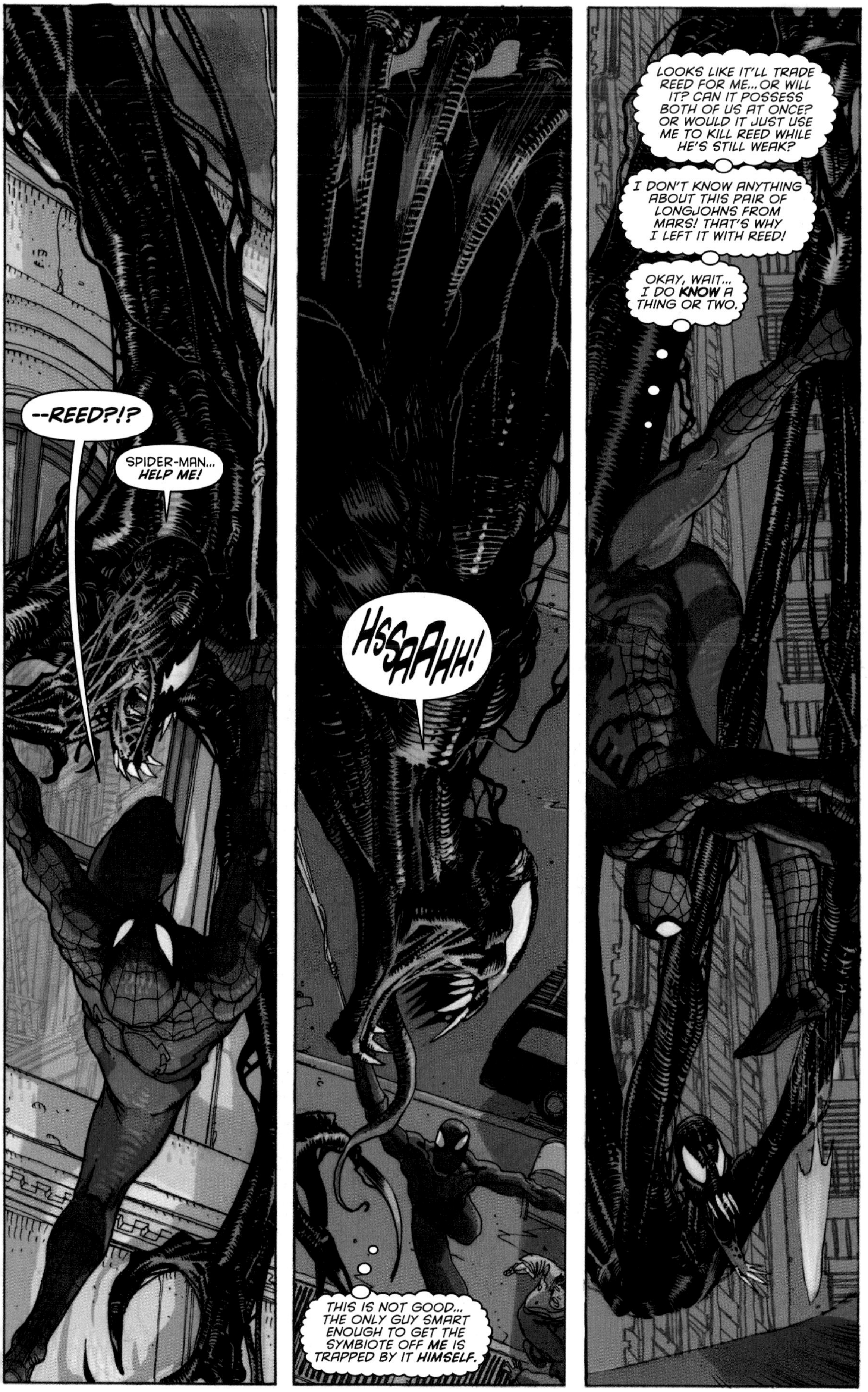
--REED?!?
SPIDER-MAN... HELP ME!
HSSAAHH!
THIS IS NOT GOOD... THE ONLY GUY SMART ENOUGH TO GET THE SYMBIOTE OFF ME IS TRAPPED BY IT HIMSELF.
LOOKS LIKE IT'LL TRADE REED FOR ME...OR WILL IT? CAN IT POSSESS BOTH OF US AT ONCE? OR WOULD IT JUST USE ME TO KILL REED WHILE HE'S STILL WEAK?
I DON'T KNOW ANYTHING ABOUT THIS PAIR OF LONGJOHNS FROM MARS! THAT'S WHY I LEFT IT WITH REED!
OKAY, WAIT... I DO KNOW A THING OR TWO.

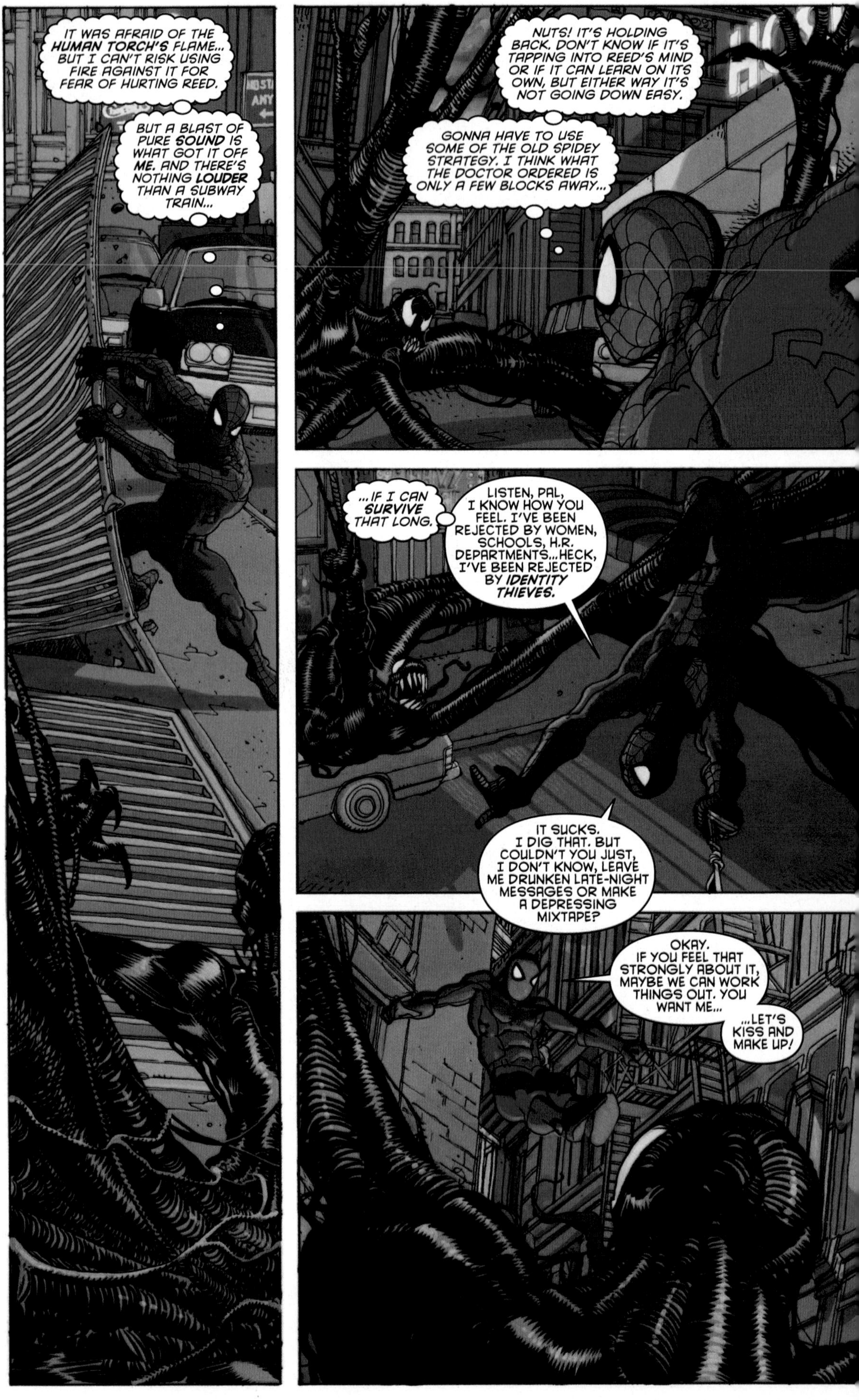
IT WAS AFRAID OF THE HUMAN TORCH'S FLAME... BUT I CAN'T RISK USING FIRE AGAINST IT FOR FEAR OF HURTING REED.
BUT A BLAST OF PURE SOUND IS WHAT GOT IT OFF ME. AND THERE'S NOTHING LOUDER THAN A SUBWAY TRAIN...
NUTS! IT'S HOLDING BACK. DON'T KNOW IF IT'S TAPPING INTO REED'S MIND OR IF IT CAN LEARN ON ITS OWN, BUT EITHER WAY IT'S NOT GOING DOWN EASY.
GONNA HAVE TO USE SOME OF THE OLD SPIDEY STRATEGY. I THINK WHAT THE DOCTOR ORDERED IS ONLY A FEW BLOCKS AWAY...
...IF I CAN SURVIVE THAT LONG.
LISTEN, PAL, I KNOW HOW YOU FEEL. I'VE BEEN REJECTED BY WOMEN, SCHOOLS, H.R. DEPARTMENTS...HECK, I'VE BEEN REJECTED BY IDENTITY THIEVES.
IT SUCKS. I DIG THAT. BUT COULDN'T YOU JUST, I DON'T KNOW, LEAVE ME DRUNKEN LATE-NIGHT MESSAGES OR MAKE A DEPRESSING MIXTAPE?
OKAY. IF YOU FEEL THAT STRONGLY ABOUT IT, MAYBE WE CAN WORK THINGS OUT. YOU WANT ME...
...LET'S KISS AND MAKE UP!

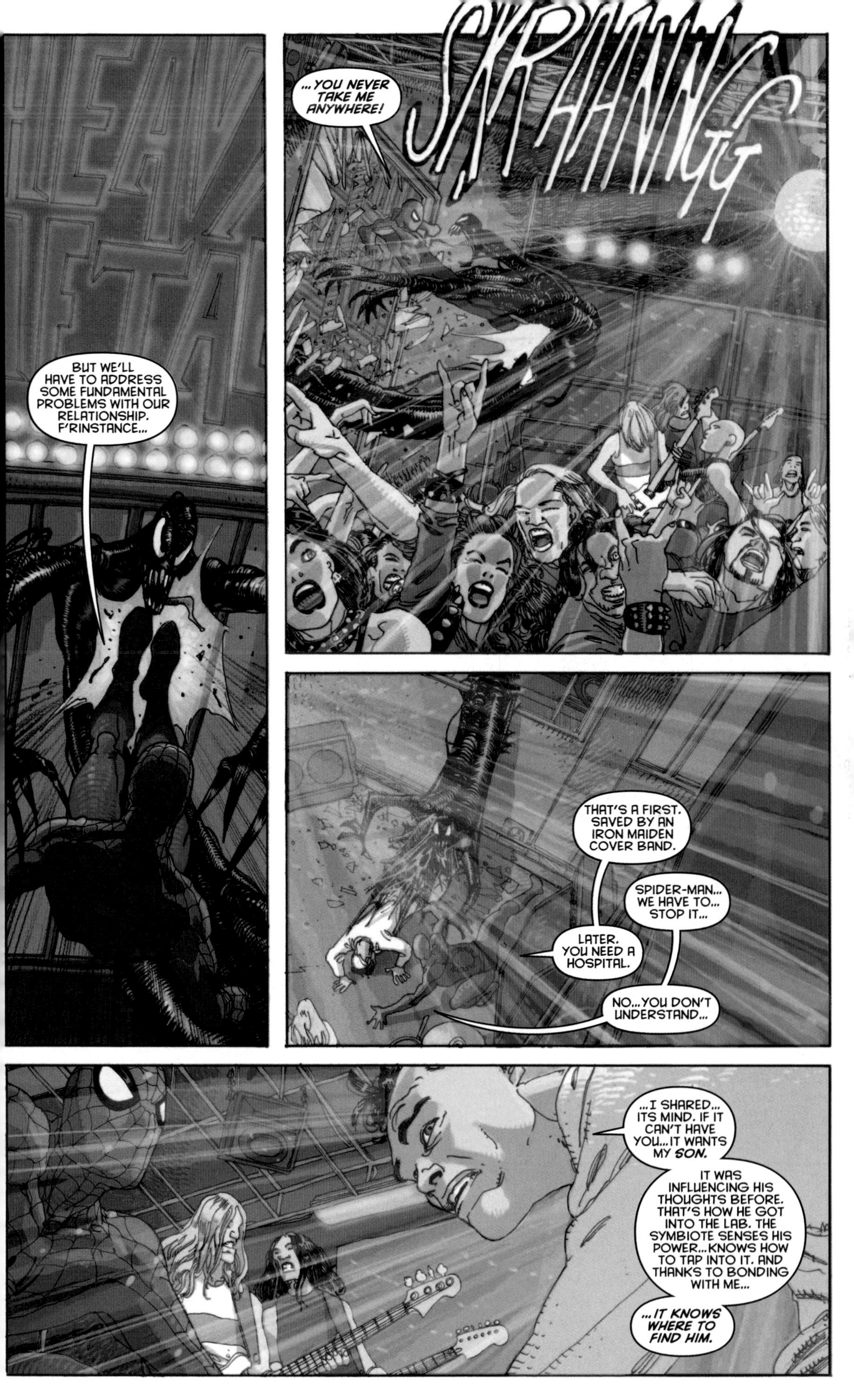
BUT WE'LL HAVE TO ADDRESS SOME FUNDAMENTAL PROBLEMS WITH OUR RELATIONSHIP. F'RINSTANCE...
...YOU NEVER TAKE ME ANYWHERE!
SKRAANNGG
THAT'S A FIRST. SAVED BY AN IRON MAIDEN COVER BAND.
SPIDER-MAN... WE HAVE TO... STOP IT...
LATER. YOU NEED A HOSPITAL.
NO...YOU DON'T UNDERSTAND...
...I SHARED... ITS MIND. IF IT CAN'T HAVE YOU...IT WANTS MY SON.
IT WAS INFLUENCING HIS THOUGHTS BEFORE. THAT'S HOW HE GOT INTO THE LAB. THE SYMBIOTE SENSES HIS POWER...KNOWS HOW TO TAP INTO IT. AND THANKS TO BONDING WITH ME...
...IT KNOWS WHERE TO FIND HIM.

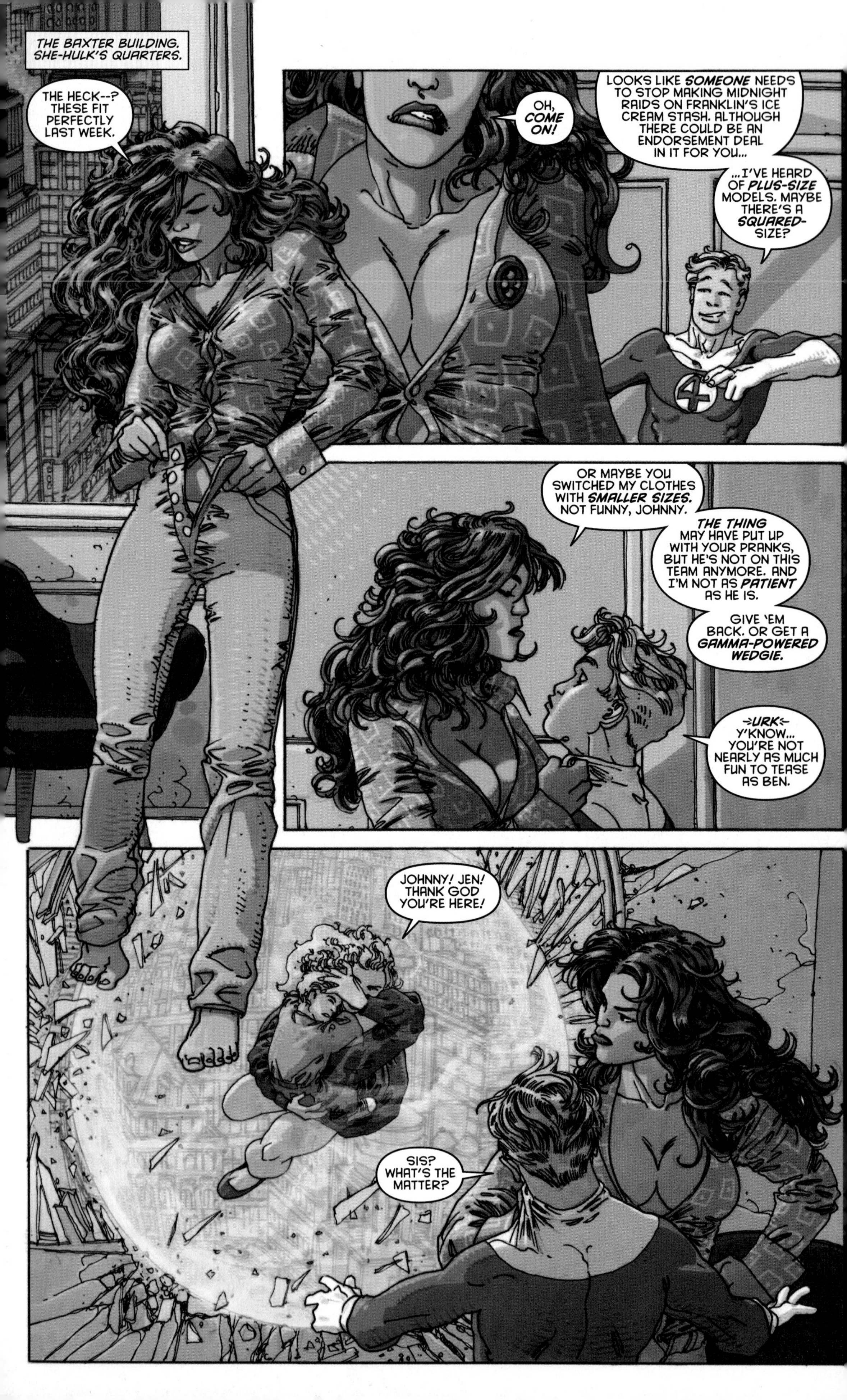
THE BAXTER BUILDING. SHE-HULK'S QUARTERS.
THE HECK--? THESE FIT PERFECTLY LAST WEEK.
OH, COME ON!
LOOKS LIKE SOMEONE NEEDS TO STOP MAKING MIDNIGHT RAIDS ON FRANKLIN'S ICE CREAM STASH. ALTHOUGH THERE COULD BE AN ENDORSEMENT DEAL IN IT FOR YOU...
...I'VE HEARD OF PLUS-SIZE MODELS. MAYBE THERE'S A SQUARED-SIZE?
OR MAYBE YOU SWITCHED MY CLOTHES WITH SMALLER SIZES. NOT FUNNY, JOHNNY.
THE THING MAY HAVE PUT UP WITH YOUR PRANKS, BUT HE'S NOT ON THIS TEAM ANYMORE. AND I'M NOT AS PATIENT AS HE IS.
GIVE 'EM BACK. OR GET A GAMMA-POWERED WEDGIE.
-URK- Y'KNOW... YOU'RE NOT NEARLY AS MUCH FUN TO TEASE AS BEN.
JOHNNY! JEN! THANK GOD YOU'RE HERE!
SIS? WHAT'S THE MATTER?

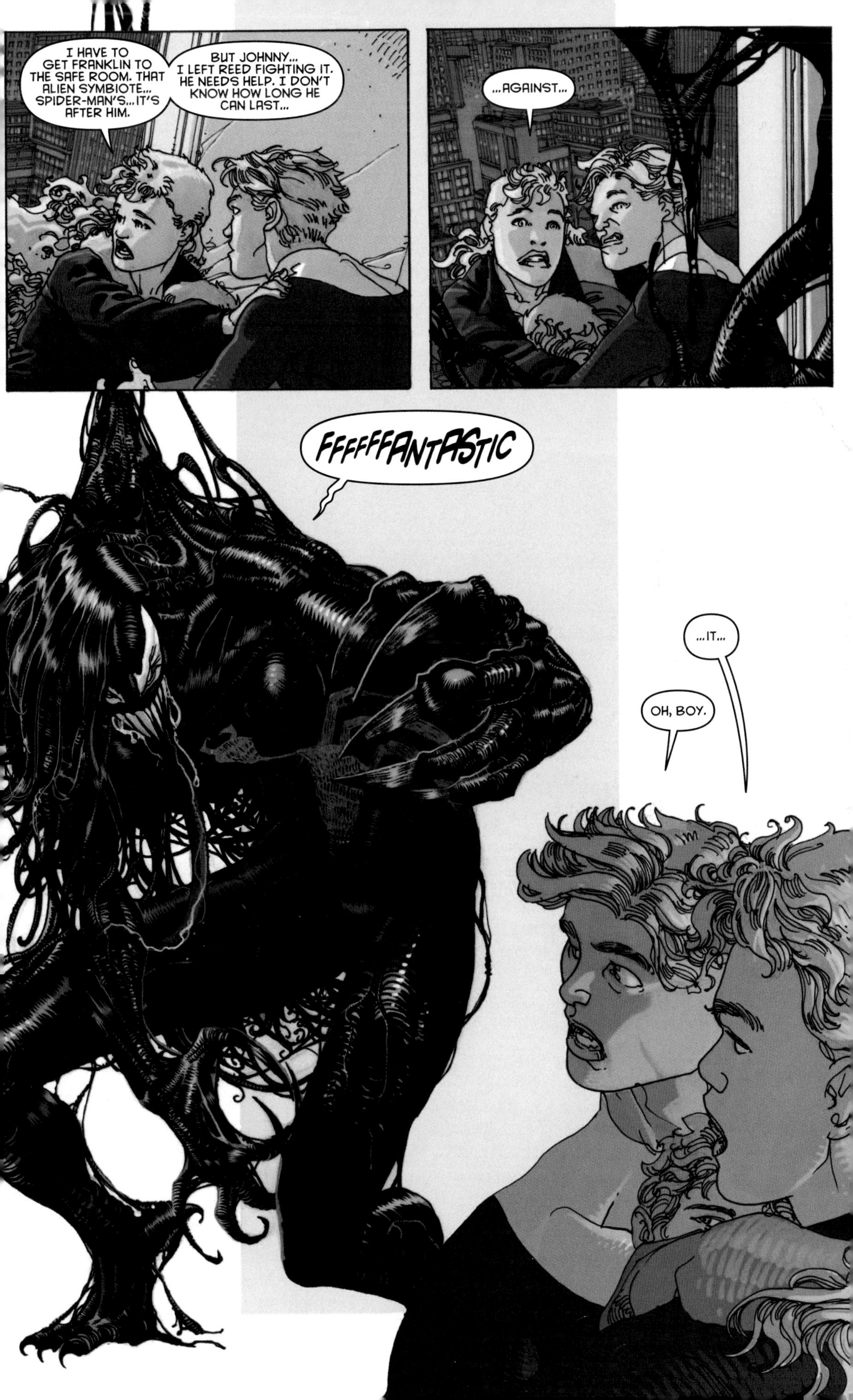
I HAVE TO GET FRANKLIN TO THE SAFE ROOM. THAT ALIEN SYMBIOTE... SPIDER-MAN'S...IT'S AFTER HIM.
BUT JOHNNY... I LEFT REED FIGHTING IT. HE NEEDS HELP. I DON'T KNOW HOW LONG HE CAN LAST...
...AGAINST...
FFFFFFANTASTIC
...IT...
OH, BOY.

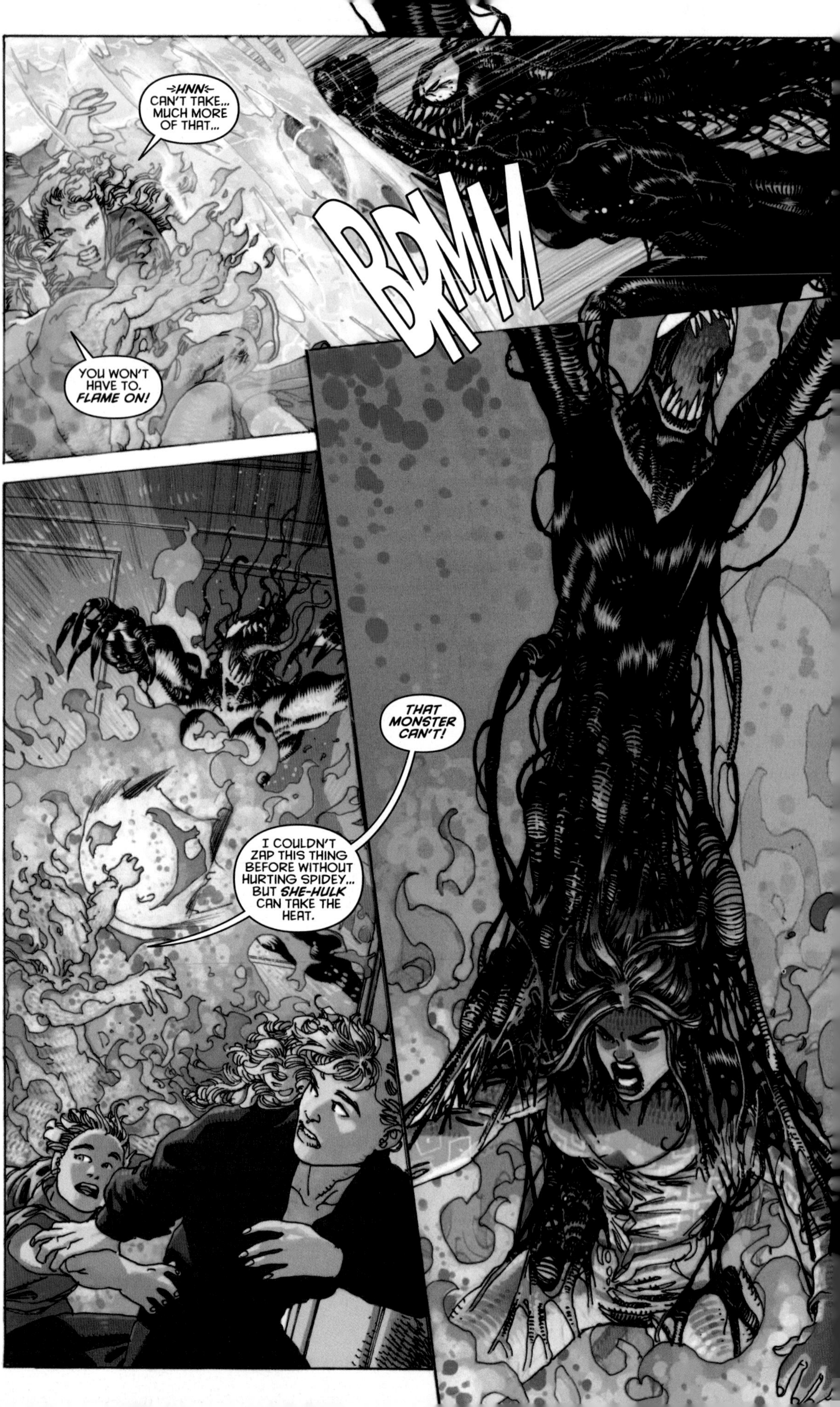

HNN CAN'T TAKE... MUCH MORE OF THAT...
YOU WON'T HAVE TO. FLAME ON!
BRMM
THAT MONSTER CAN'T!
I COULDN'T ZAP THIS THING BEFORE WITHOUT HURTING SPIDEY... BUT SHE-HULK CAN TAKE THE HEAT.

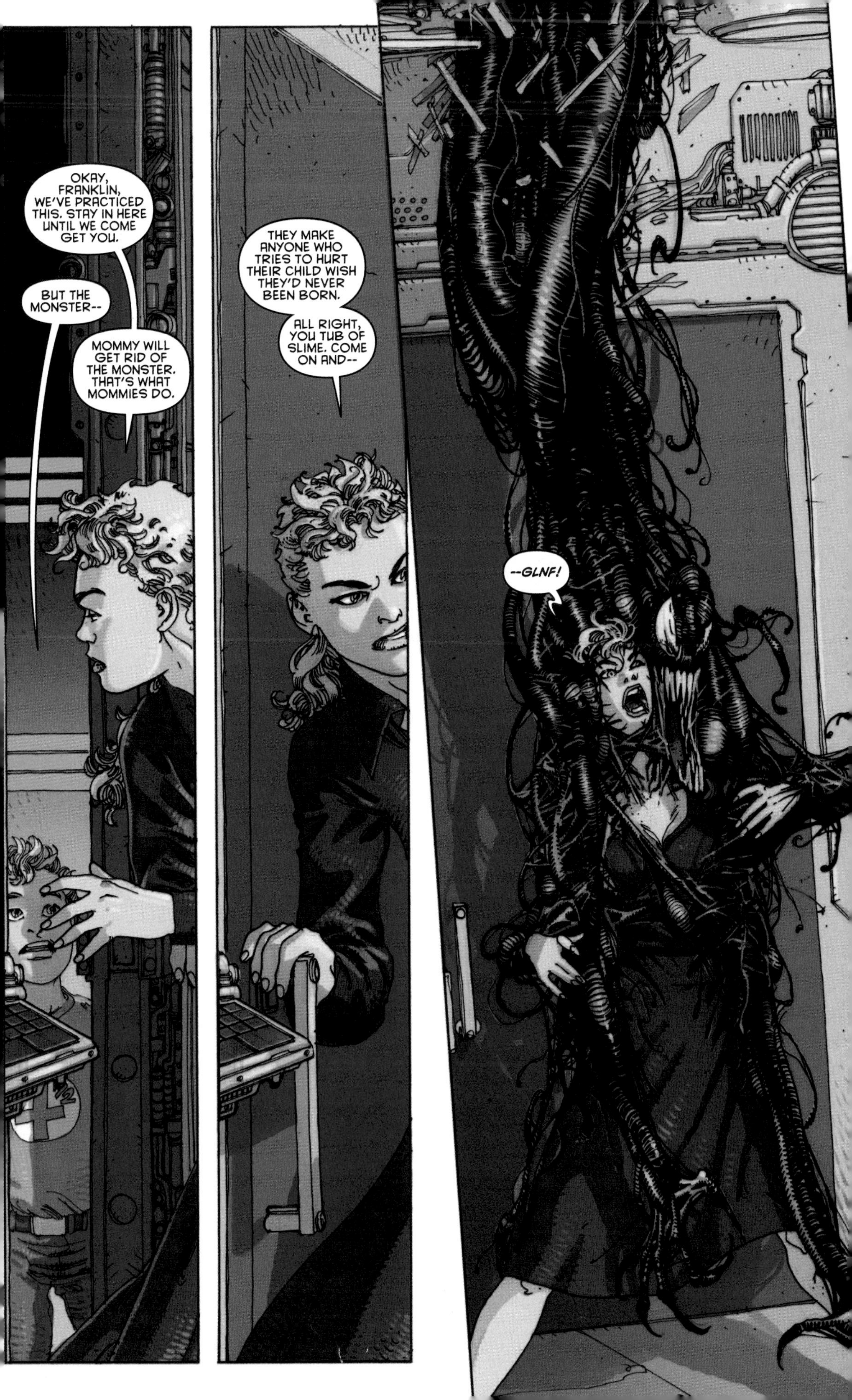
OKAY, FRANKLIN, WE'VE PRACTICED THIS. STAY IN HERE UNTIL WE COME GET YOU.
BUT THE MONSTER--
MOMMY WILL GET RID OF THE MONSTER. THAT'S WHAT MOMMIES DO.
THEY MAKE ANYONE WHO TRIES TO HURT THEIR CHILD WISH THEY'D NEVER BEEN BORN.
ALL RIGHT, YOU TUB OF SLIME. COME ON AND--
--GLNF!

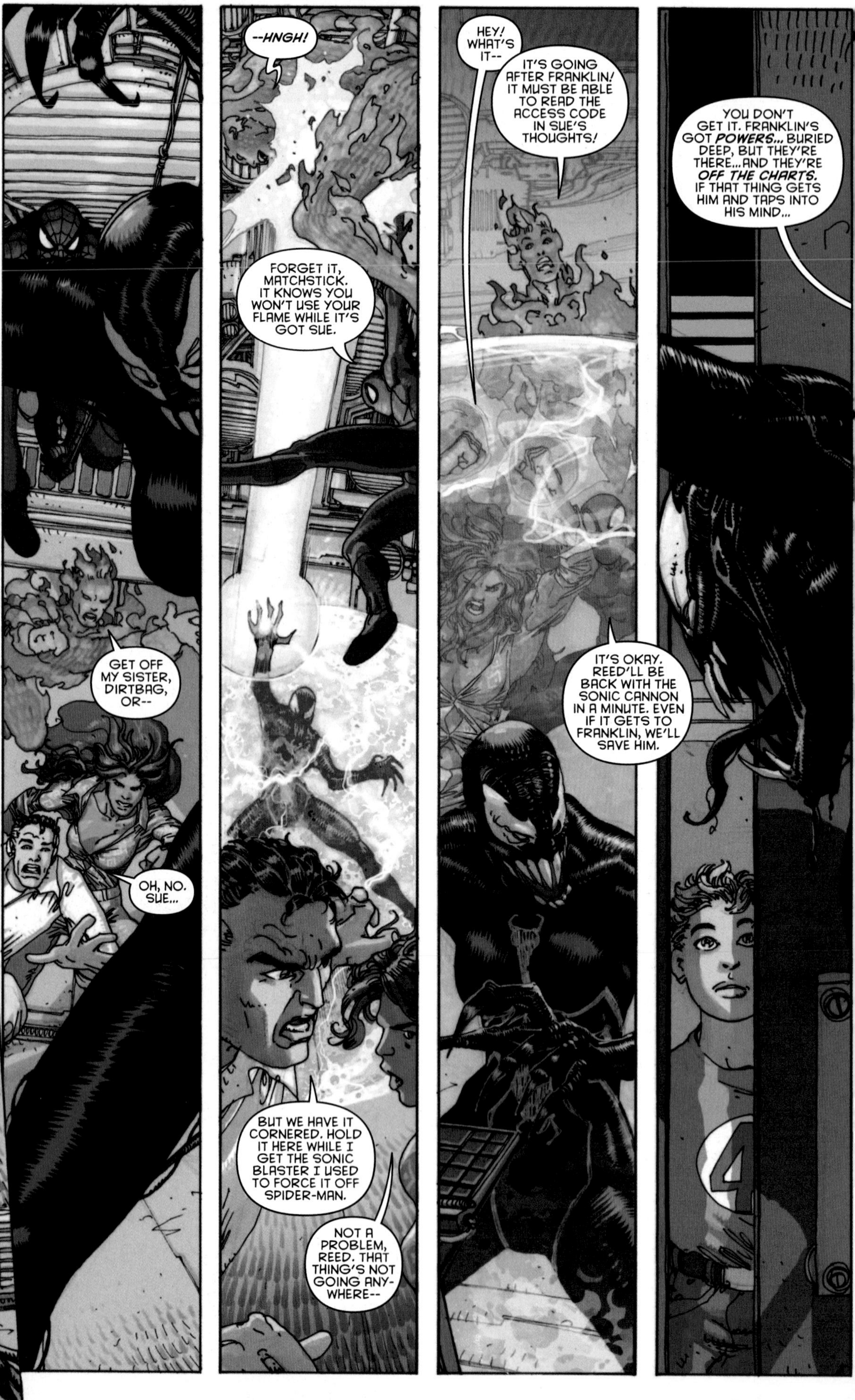
GET OFF MY SISTER, DIRTBAG, OR--
OH, NO. SUE...
--HNGH!
FORGET IT, MATCHSTICK. IT KNOWS YOU WON'T USE YOUR FLAME WHILE IT'S GOT SUE.
BUT WE HAVE IT CORNERED. HOLD IT HERE WHILE I GET THE SONIC BLASTER I USED TO FORCE IT OFF SPIDER-MAN.
NOT A PROBLEM, REED. THAT THING'S NOT GOING ANY-WHERE--
HEY! WHAT'S IT--
IT'S GOING AFTER FRANKLIN! IT MUST BE ABLE TO READ THE ACCESS CODE IN SUE'S THOUGHTS!
IT'S OKAY. REED'LL BE BACK WITH THE SONIC CANNON IN A MINUTE. EVEN IF IT GETS TO FRANKLIN, WE'LL SAVE HIM.
YOU DON'T GET IT. FRANKLIN'S GOT POWERS... BURIED DEEP, BUT THEY'RE THERE...AND THEY'RE OFF THE CHARTS. IF THAT THING GETS HIM AND TAPS INTO HIS MIND...

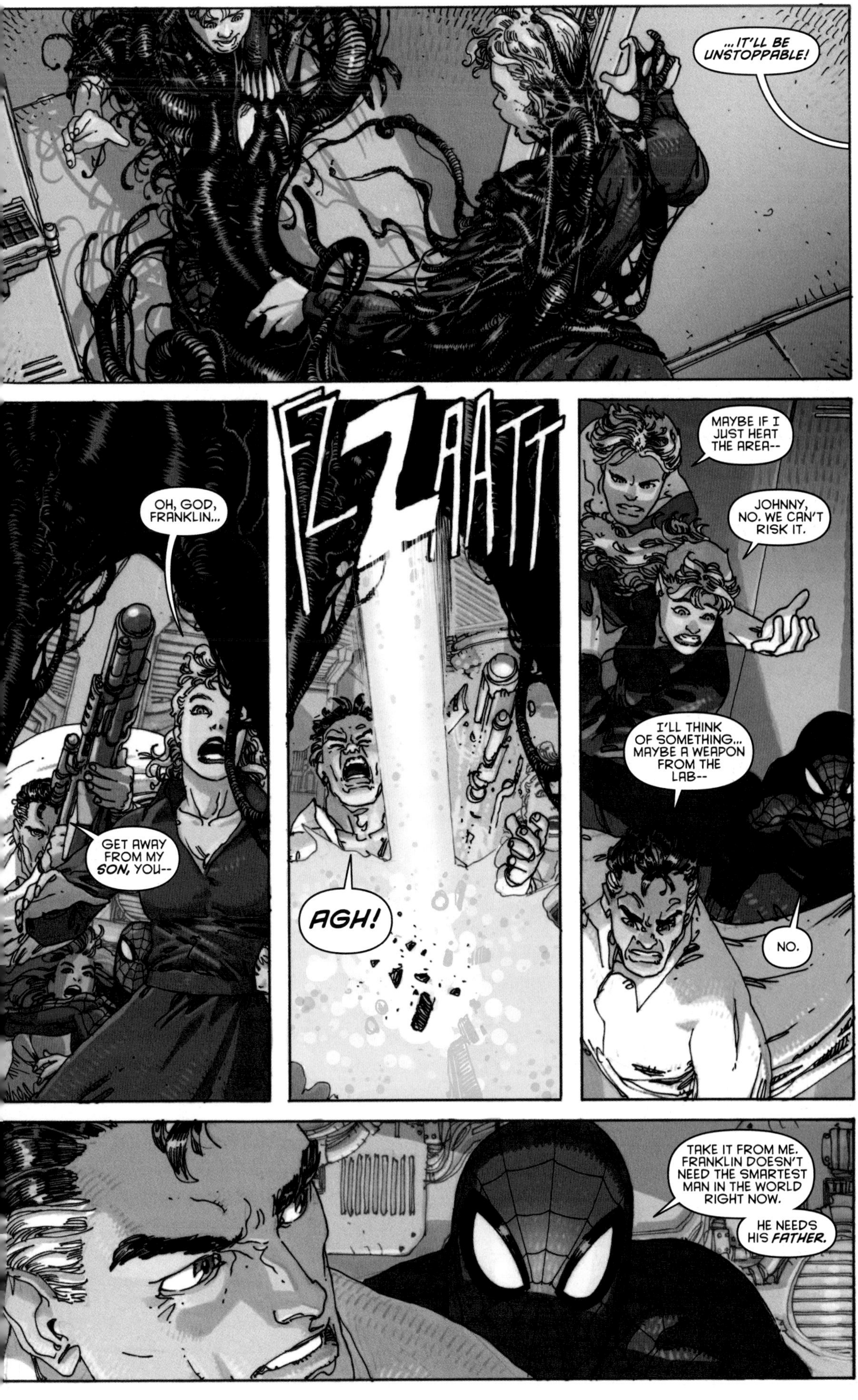

...IT'LL BE UNSTOPPABLE!
OH, GOD, FRANKLIN...
GET AWAY FROM MY SON, YOU--
FZZAATT
AGH!
MAYBE IF I JUST HEAT THE AREA--
JOHNNY, NO. WE CAN'T RISK IT.
I'LL THINK OF SOMETHING... MAYBE A WEAPON FROM THE LAB--
NO.
TAKE IT FROM ME. FRANKLIN DOESN'T NEED THE SMARTEST MAN IN THE WORLD RIGHT NOW.
HE NEEDS HIS FATHER.

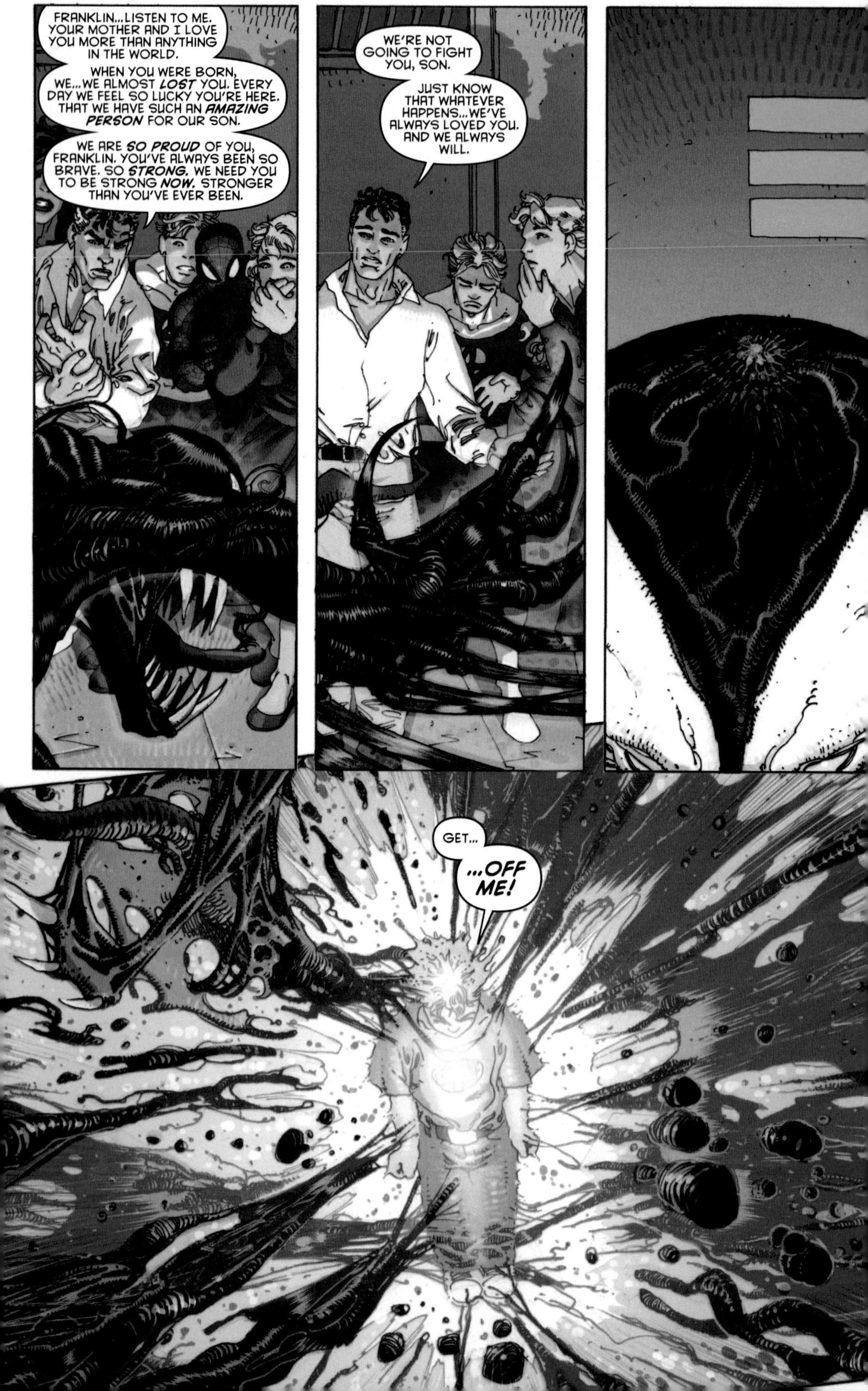
FRANKLIN... LISTEN TO ME. YOUR MOTHER AND I LOVE YOU MORE THAN ANYTHING IN THE WORLD.
WHEN YOU WERE BORN, WE... WE ALMOST LOST YOU. EVERY DAY WE FEEL SO LUCKY YOU'RE HERE. THAT WE HAVE SUCH AN AMAZING PERSON FOR OUR SON.
WE ARE SO PROUD OF YOU, FRANKLIN. YOU'VE ALWAYS BEEN SO BRAVE. SO STRONG. WE NEED YOU TO BE STRONG NOW. STRONGER THAN YOU'VE EVER BEEN.
WE'RE NOT GOING TO FIGHT YOU, SON.
JUST KNOW THAT WHATEVER HAPPENS... WE'VE ALWAYS LOVED YOU. AND WE ALWAYS WILL.
GET...
...OFF ME!

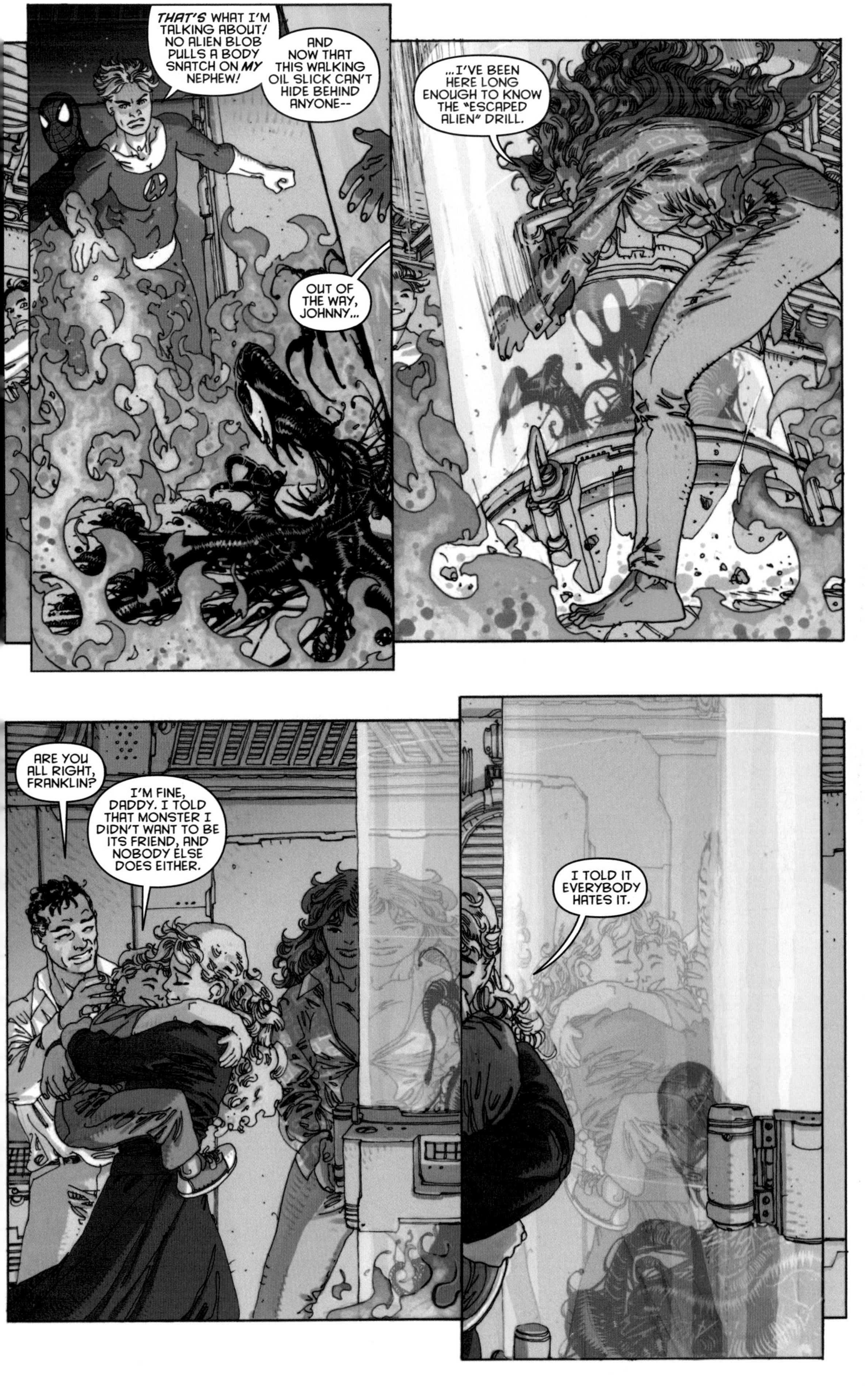
THAT'S WHAT I'M TALKING ABOUT! NO ALIEN BLOB PULLS A BODY SNATCH ON MY NEPHEW!
AND NOW THAT THIS WALKING OIL SLICK CAN'T HIDE BEHIND ANYONE--
OUT OF THE WAY, JOHNNY...
...I'VE BEEN HERE LONG ENOUGH TO KNOW THE "ESCAPED ALIEN" DRILL.
ARE YOU ALL RIGHT, FRANKLIN?
I'M FINE, DADDY. I TOLD THAT MONSTER I DIDN'T WANT TO BE ITS FRIEND, AND NOBODY ELSE DOES EITHER.
I TOLD IT EVERYBODY HATES IT.

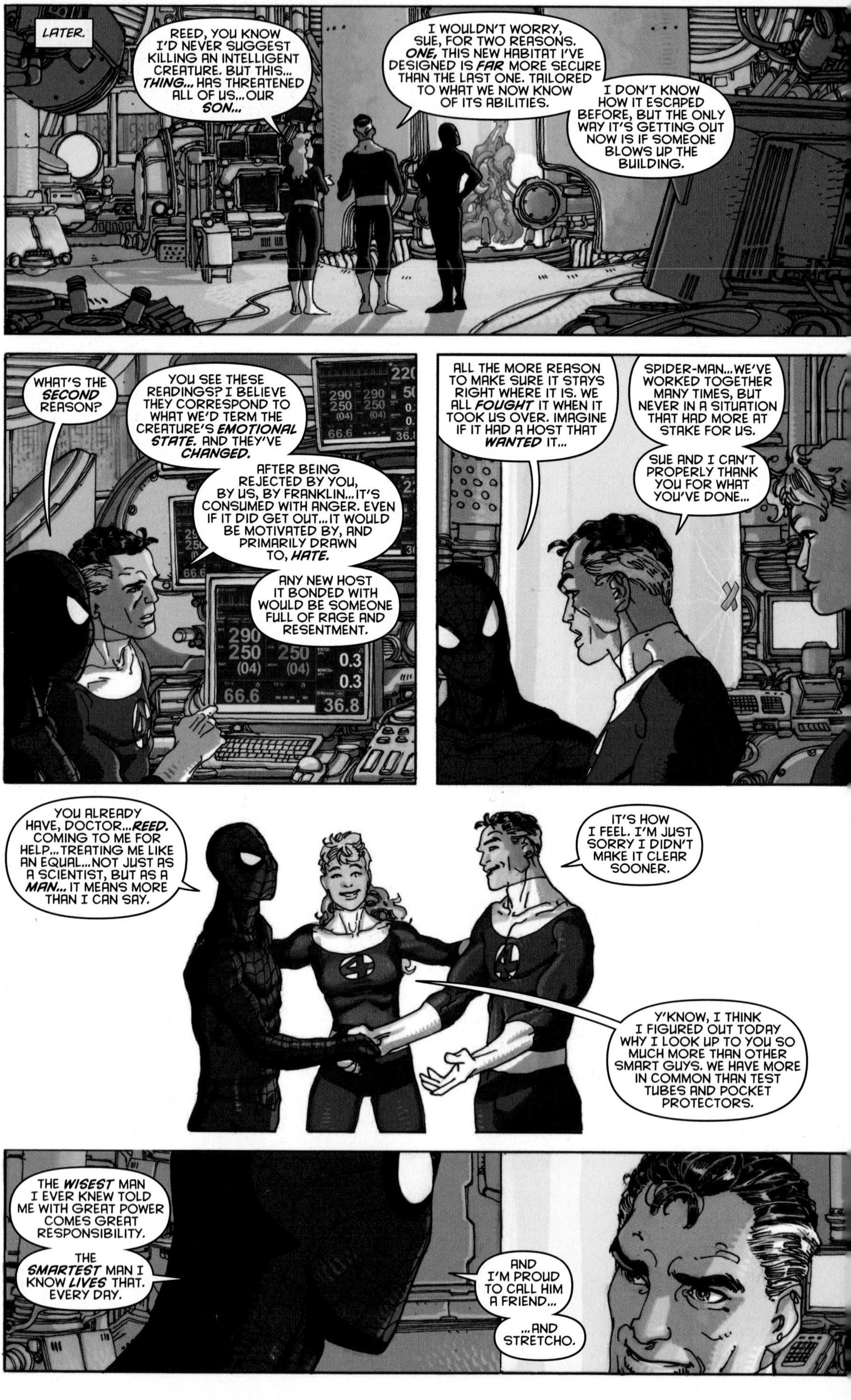
LATER.
REED, YOU KNOW I'D NEVER SUGGEST KILLING AN INTELLIGENT CREATURE. BUT THIS... THING... HAS THREATENED ALL OF US...OUR SON...
I WOULDN'T WORRY, SUE, FOR TWO REASONS. ONE, THIS NEW HABITAT I'VE DESIGNED IS FAR MORE SECURE THAN THE LAST ONE. TAILORED TO WHAT WE NOW KNOW OF ITS ABILITIES.
I DON'T KNOW HOW IT ESCAPED BEFORE, BUT THE ONLY WAY IT'S GETTING OUT NOW IS IF SOMEONE BLOWS UP THE BUILDING.
WHAT'S THE SECOND REASON?
YOU SEE THESE READINGS? I BELIEVE THEY CORRESPOND TO WHAT WE'D TERM THE CREATURE'S EMOTIONAL STATE. AND THEY'VE CHANGED.
AFTER BEING REJECTED BY YOU, BY US, BY FRANKLIN...IT'S CONSUMED WITH ANGER. EVEN IF IT DID GET OUT...IT WOULD BE MOTIVATED BY, AND PRIMARILY DRAWN TO, HATE.
ANY NEW HOST IT BONDED WITH WOULD BE SOMEONE FULL OF RAGE AND RESENTMENT.
ALL THE MORE REASON TO MAKE SURE IT STAYS RIGHT WHERE IT IS. WE ALL FOUGHT IT WHEN IT TOOK US OVER. IMAGINE IF IT HAD A HOST THAT WANTED IT...
SPIDER-MAN...WE'VE WORKED TOGETHER MANY TIMES, BUT NEVER IN A SITUATION THAT HAD MORE AT STAKE FOR US.
SUE AND I CAN'T PROPERLY THANK YOU FOR WHAT YOU'VE DONE...
YOU ALREADY HAVE, DOCTOR...REED. COMING TO ME FOR HELP...TREATING ME LIKE AN EQUAL...NOT JUST AS A SCIENTIST, BUT AS A MAN... IT MEANS MORE THAN I CAN SAY.
IT'S HOW I FEEL. I'M JUST SORRY I DIDN'T MAKE IT CLEAR SOONER.
Y'KNOW, I THINK I FIGURED OUT TODAY WHY I LOOK UP TO YOU SO MUCH MORE THAN OTHER SMART GUYS. WE HAVE MORE IN COMMON THAN TEST TUBES AND POCKET PROTECTORS.
THE WISEST MAN I EVER KNEW TOLD ME WITH GREAT POWER COMES GREAT RESPONSIBILITY.
THE SMARTEST MAN I KNOW LIVES THAT. EVERY DAY.
AND I'M PROUD TO CALL HIM A FRIEND...
...AND STRETCHO.

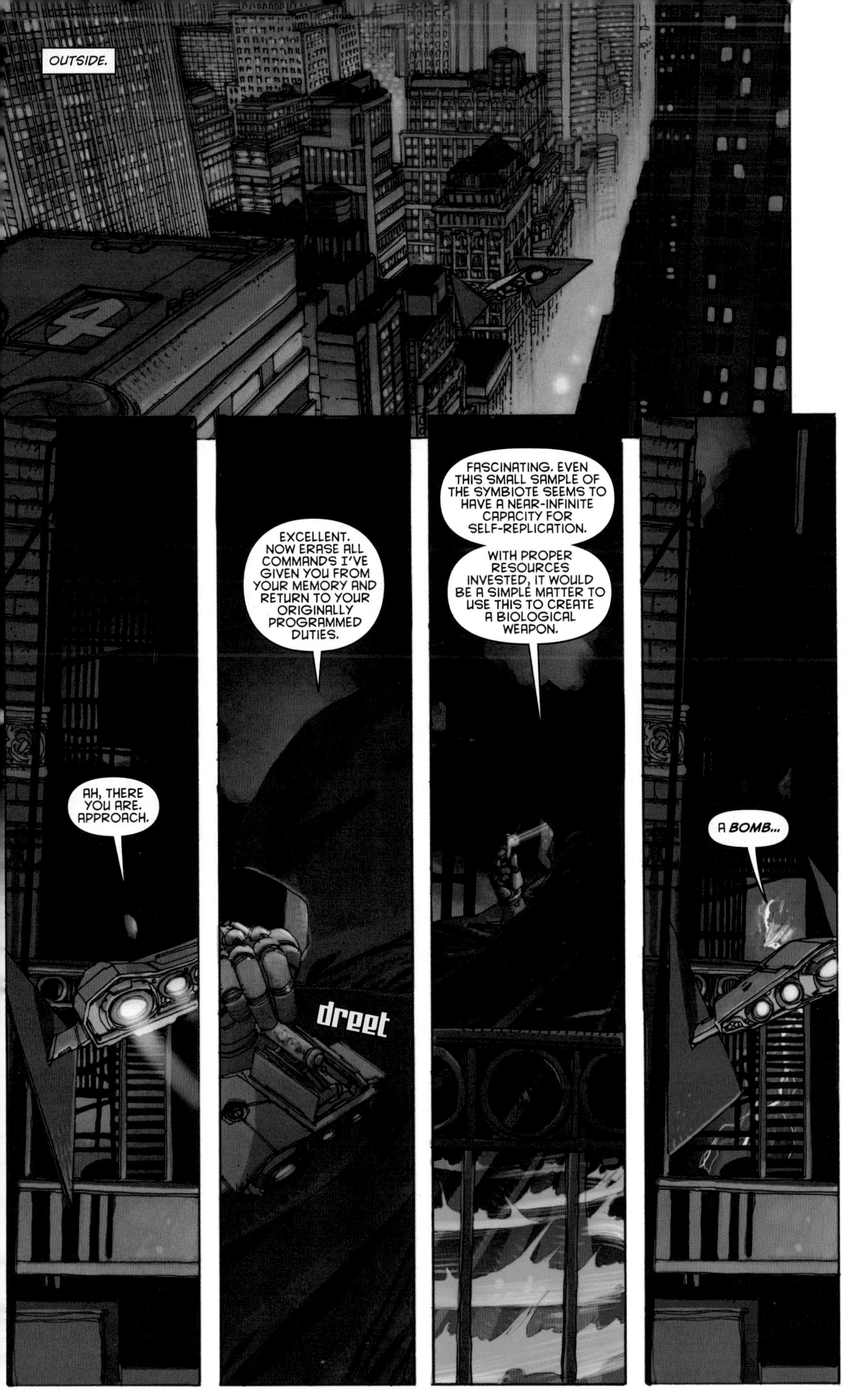
OUTSIDE.
AH, THERE YOU ARE. APPROACH.
EXCELLENT. NOW ERASE ALL COMMANDS I'VE GIVEN YOU FROM YOUR MEMORY AND RETURN TO YOUR ORIGINALLY PROGRAMMED DUTIES.
dreet
FASCINATING. EVEN THIS SMALL SAMPLE OF THE SYMBIOTE SEEMS TO HAVE A NEAR-INFINITE CAPACITY FOR SELF-REPLICATION.
WITH PROPER RESOURCES INVESTED, IT WOULD BE A SIMPLE MATTER TO USE THIS TO CREATE A BIOLOGICAL WEAPON.
A *BOMB*...

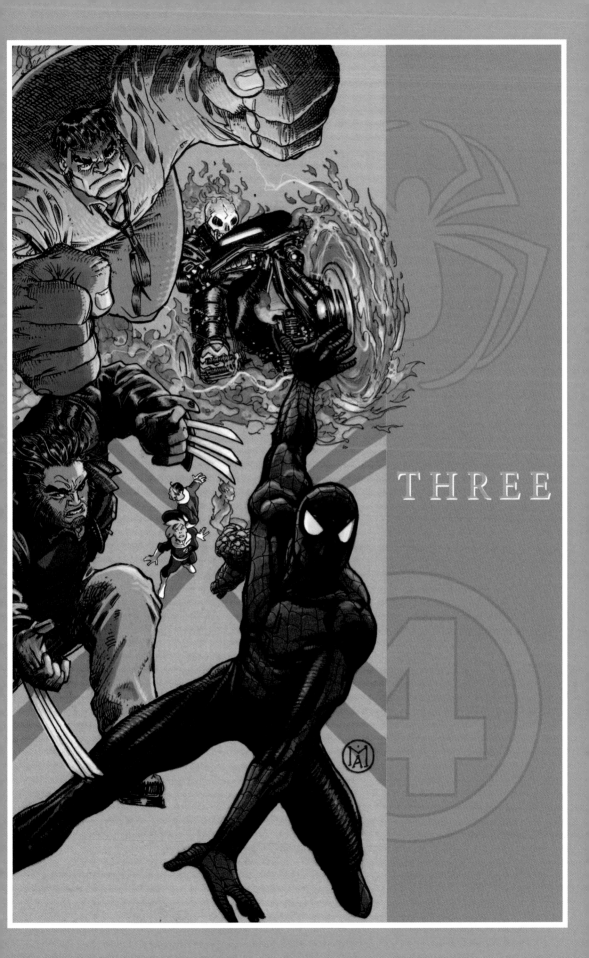

THREE

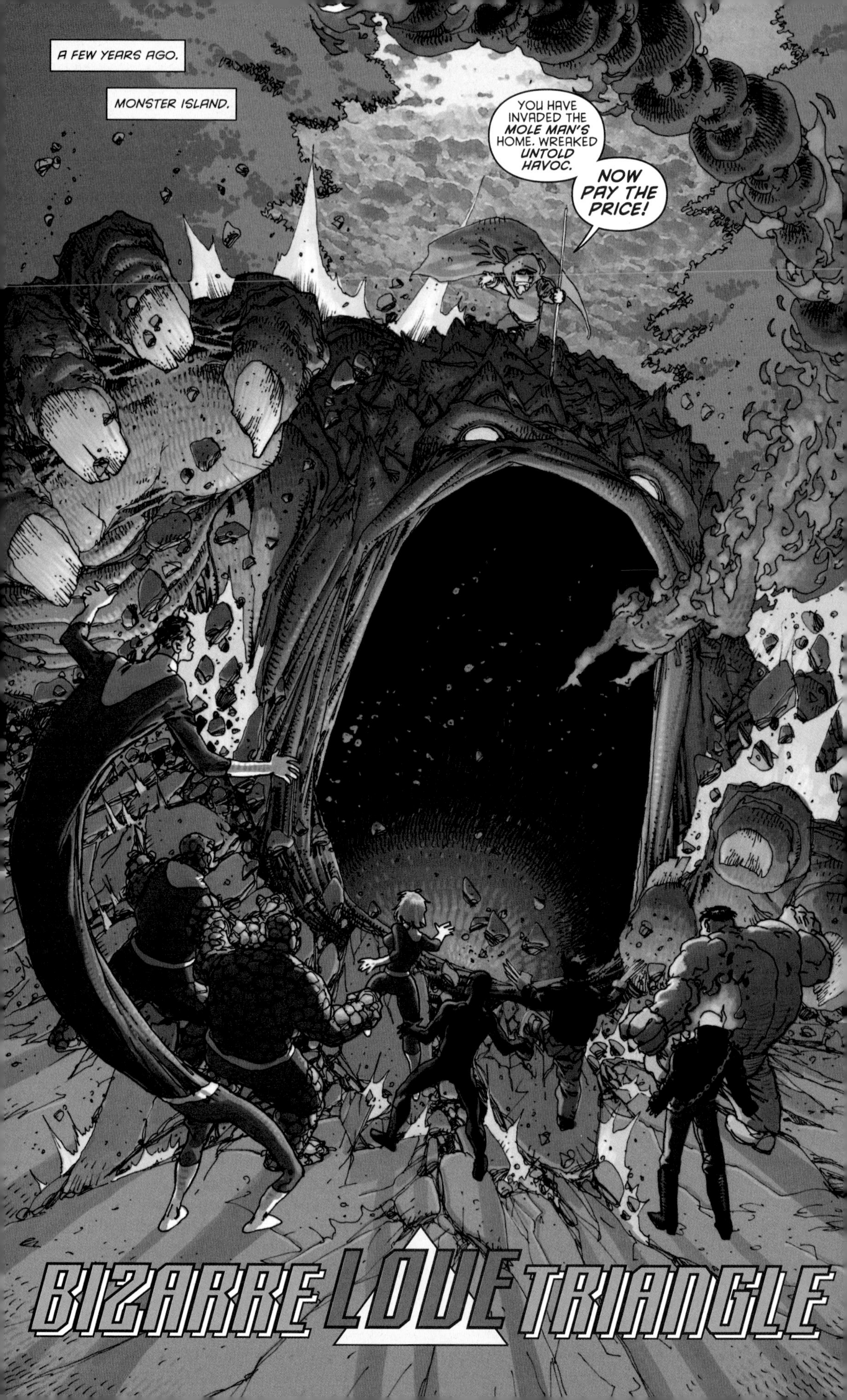

A FEW YEARS AGO.
MONSTER ISLAND.
YOU HAVE INVADED THE MOLE MAN'S HOME. WREAKED UNTOLD HAVOC.
NOW PAY THE PRICE!
BIZARRE LOVE TRIANGLE

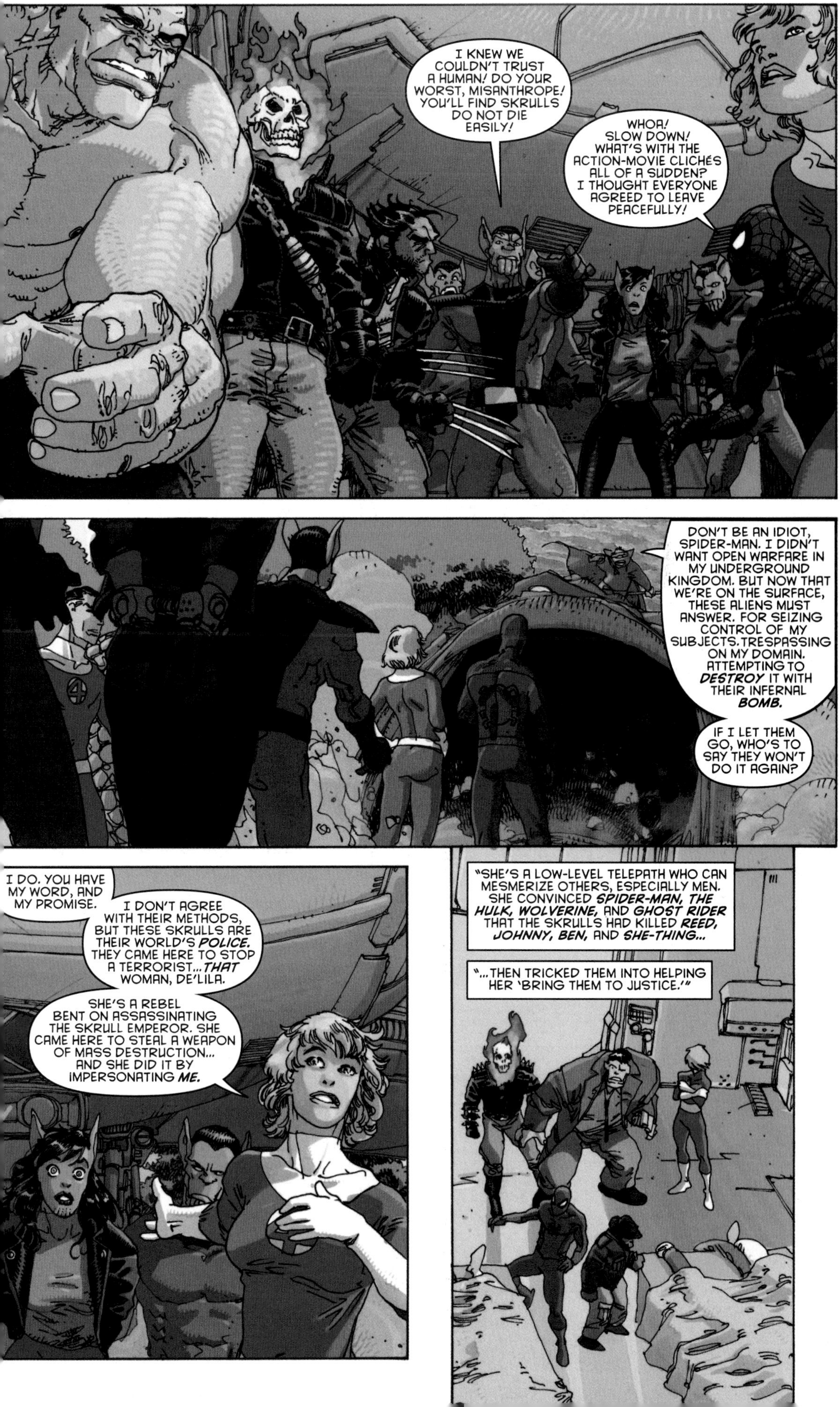
I KNEW WE COULDN'T TRUST A HUMAN! DO YOUR WORST, MISANTHROPE! YOU'LL FIND SKRULLS DO NOT DIE EASILY!
WHOA! SLOW DOWN! WHAT'S WITH THE ACTION-MOVIE CLICHÉS ALL OF A SUDDEN? I THOUGHT EVERYONE AGREED TO LEAVE PEACEFULLY!
DON'T BE AN IDIOT, SPIDER-MAN. I DIDN'T WANT OPEN WARFARE IN MY UNDERGROUND KINGDOM. BUT NOW THAT WE'RE ON THE SURFACE, THESE ALIENS MUST ANSWER. FOR SEIZING CONTROL OF MY SUBJECTS. TRESPASSING ON MY DOMAIN. ATTEMPTING TO DESTROY IT WITH THEIR INFERNAL BOMB.
IF I LET THEM GO, WHO'S TO SAY THEY WON'T DO IT AGAIN?
I DO. YOU HAVE MY WORD, AND MY PROMISE.
I DON'T AGREE WITH THEIR METHODS, BUT THESE SKRULLS ARE THEIR WORLD'S POLICE. THEY CAME HERE TO STOP A TERRORIST...THAT WOMAN, DE'LILA.
SHE'S A REBEL BENT ON ASSASSINATING THE SKRULL EMPEROR. SHE CAME HERE TO STEAL A WEAPON OF MASS DESTRUCTION... AND SHE DID IT BY IMPERSONATING ME.
"SHE'S A LOW-LEVEL TELEPATH WHO CAN MESMERIZE OTHERS, ESPECIALLY MEN. SHE CONVINCED SPIDER-MAN, THE HULK, WOLVERINE, AND GHOST RIDER THAT THE SKRULLS HAD KILLED REED, JOHNNY, BEN, AND SHE-THING...
"...THEN TRICKED THEM INTO HELPING HER 'BRING THEM TO JUSTICE.'"

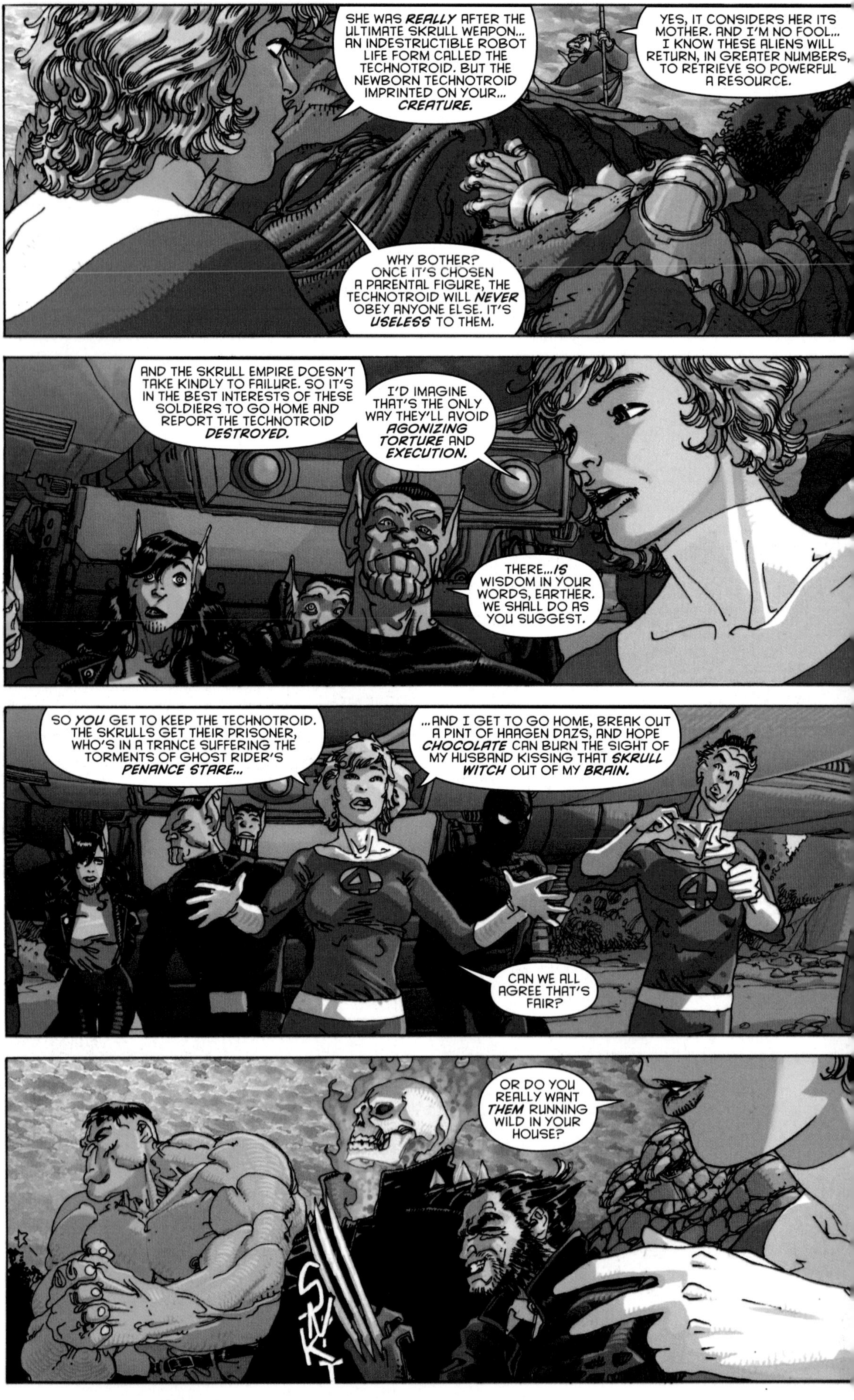
SHE WAS REALLY AFTER THE ULTIMATE SKRULL WEAPON... AN INDESTRUCTIBLE ROBOT LIFE FORM CALLED THE TECHNOTROID. BUT THE NEWBORN TECHNOTROID IMPRINTED ON YOUR... CREATURE.
YES, IT CONSIDERS HER ITS MOTHER. AND I'M NO FOOL... I KNOW THESE ALIENS WILL RETURN, IN GREATER NUMBERS, TO RETRIEVE SO POWERFUL A RESOURCE.
WHY BOTHER? ONCE IT'S CHOSEN A PARENTAL FIGURE, THE TECHNOTROID WILL NEVER OBEY ANYONE ELSE. IT'S USELESS TO THEM.
AND THE SKRULL EMPIRE DOESN'T TAKE KINDLY TO FAILURE. SO IT'S IN THE BEST INTERESTS OF THESE SOLDIERS TO GO HOME AND REPORT THE TECHNOTROID DESTROYED.
I'D IMAGINE THAT'S THE ONLY WAY THEY'LL AVOID AGONIZING TORTURE AND EXECUTION.
THERE...IS WISDOM IN YOUR WORDS, EARTHER. WE SHALL DO AS YOU SUGGEST.
SO YOU GET TO KEEP THE TECHNOTROID. THE SKRULLS GET THEIR PRISONER, WHO'S IN A TRANCE SUFFERING THE TORMENTS OF GHOST RIDER'S PENANCE STARE...
...AND I GET TO GO HOME, BREAK OUT A PINT OF HAAGEN DAZS, AND HOPE CHOCOLATE CAN BURN THE SIGHT OF MY HUSBAND KISSING THAT SKRULL WITCH OUT OF MY BRAIN.
CAN WE ALL AGREE THAT'S FAIR?
OR DO YOU REALLY WANT THEM RUNNING WILD IN YOUR HOUSE?
SNIKT

VERY WELL. YOU ARE A FORMIDABLE WOMAN, SUSAN RICHARDS.

BUT IF ANY OF YOU EVER VIOLATE MY KINGDOM AGAIN...

YEAH, WE KNOW. WITH THE MONSTERS AND THE DESTRUCTION AND THE VENGEANCE.

LET'S GO OVER WHAT YOU'RE GOING TO TELL YOUR EMPEROR. IT HAS TO SOUND CREDIBLE.

I'VE GOT A FEW IDEAS ON HOW THE TECHNOTROID COULD HAVE BEEN DESTROYED...

I WILL LISTEN, REED RICHARDS. *YOU TWO!* GET THE PRISONER ABOARD AND PREPARE FOR DEPARTURE.

INSIDE THE SKRULL SHIP.

...NO RIGHT TO TALK TO *US* THAT WAY. I HEAR HE ONLY GOT HIS JOB BECAUSE HE HAS HOLO-VIDS OF THE *GENERAL* INDULGING HIS DISGUSTING FETISH FOR *KREE FEMALES.*

I DON'T KNOW, I CAN SEE THE APPEAL. THEY'RE THE ENEMY... FORBIDDEN FRUIT. AND YOU KNOW WHAT THEY SAY, ONCE YOU GO BLUE...

SORCERY BROUGHT YOU TO THIS SORRY STATE, WOMAN.

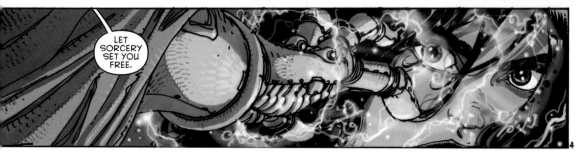

LET SORCERY SET YOU FREE.

4

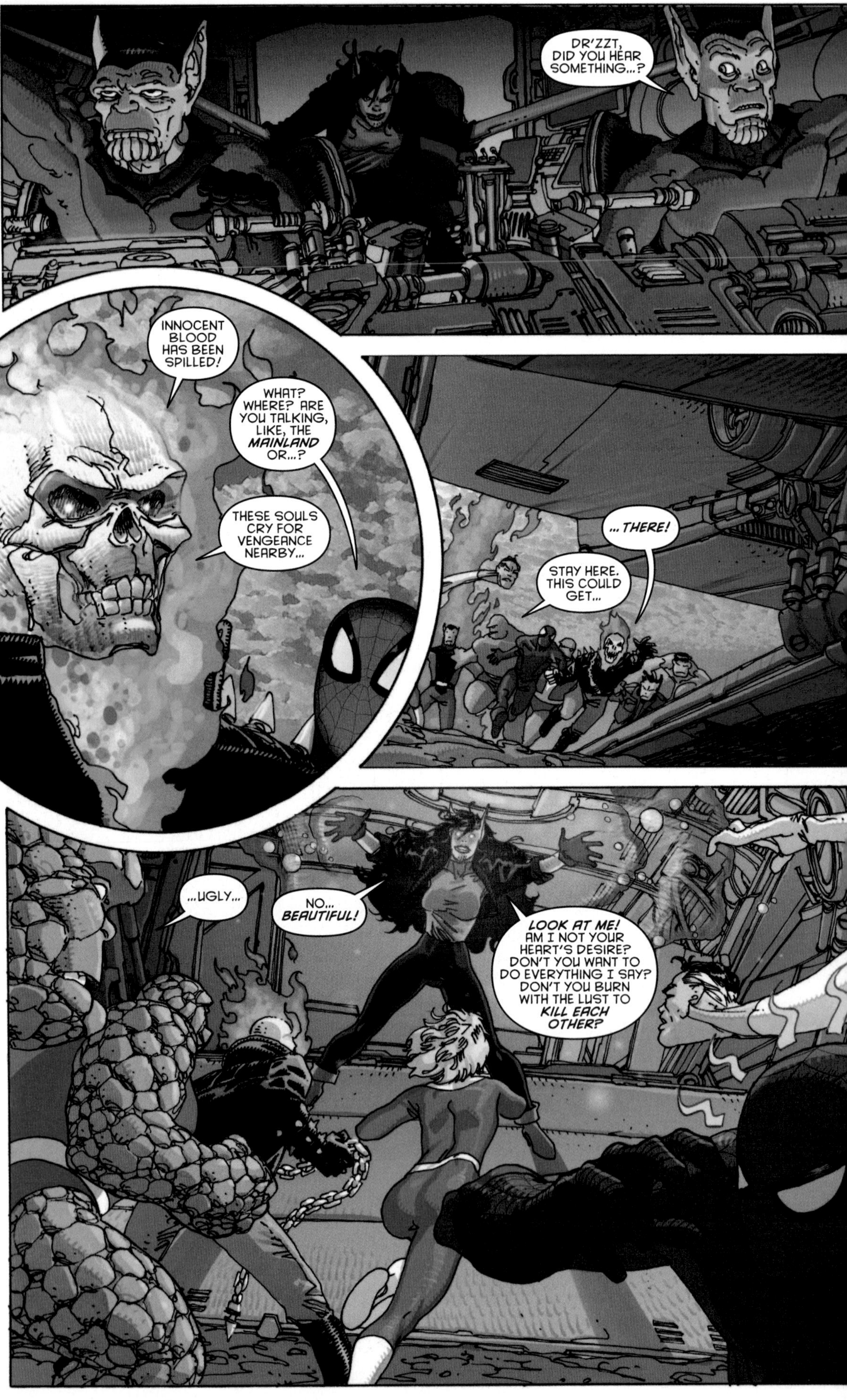
DR'ZZT, DID YOU HEAR SOMETHING...?
INNOCENT BLOOD HAS BEEN SPILLED!
WHAT? WHERE? ARE YOU TALKING, LIKE, THE MAINLAND OR...?
THESE SOULS CRY FOR VENGEANCE NEARBY...
...THERE!
STAY HERE. THIS COULD GET...
...UGLY...
NO... BEAUTIFUL!
LOOK AT ME! AM I NOT YOUR HEART'S DESIRE? DON'T YOU WANT TO DO EVERYTHING I SAY? DON'T YOU BURN WITH THE LUST TO KILL EACH OTHER?

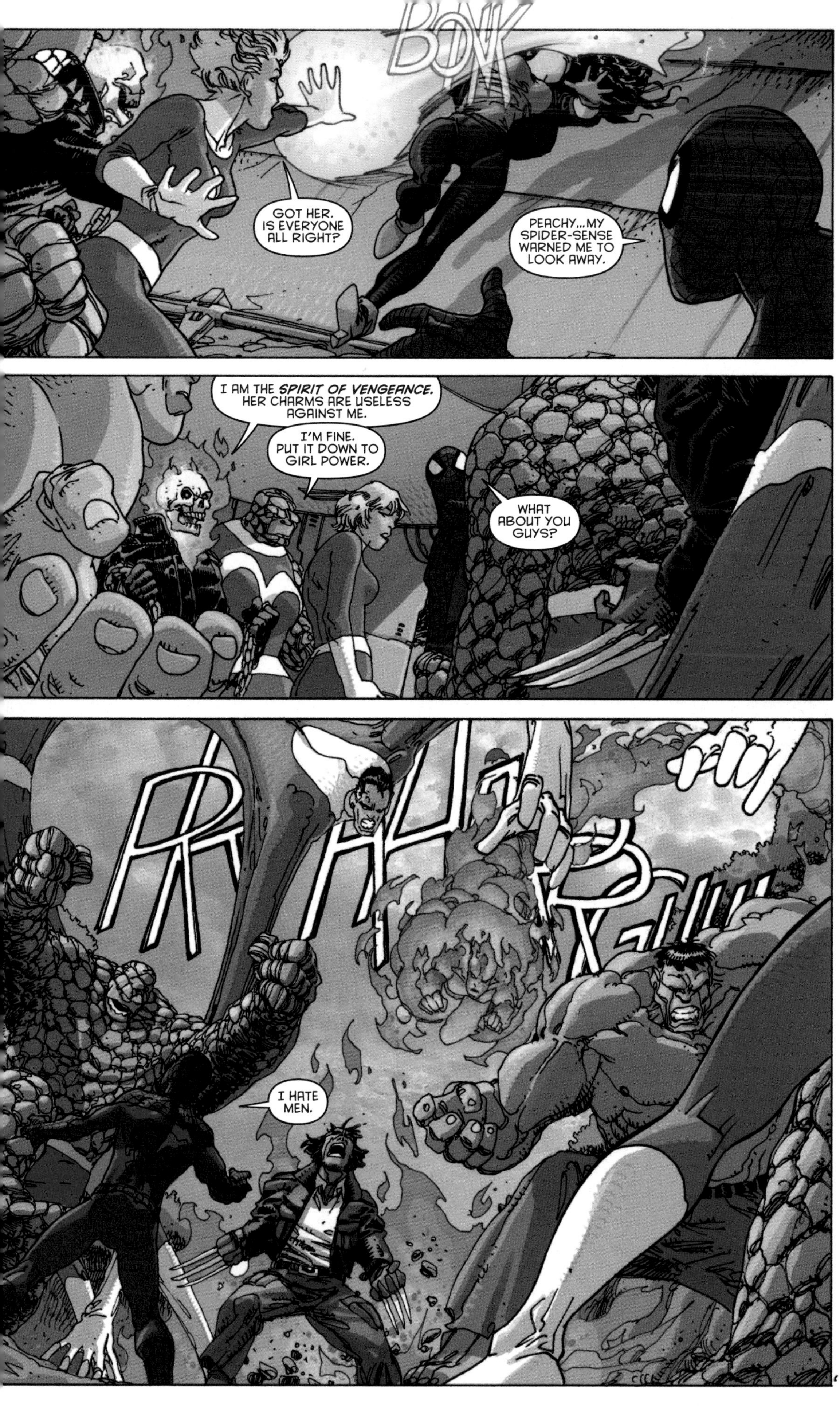
BONK
GOT HER. IS EVERYONE ALL RIGHT?
PEACHY...MY SPIDER-SENSE WARNED ME TO LOOK AWAY.
I AM THE *SPIRIT OF VENGEANCE.* HER CHARMS ARE USELESS AGAINST ME.
I'M FINE. PUT IT DOWN TO GIRL POWER.
WHAT ABOUT YOU GUYS?
I HATE MEN.

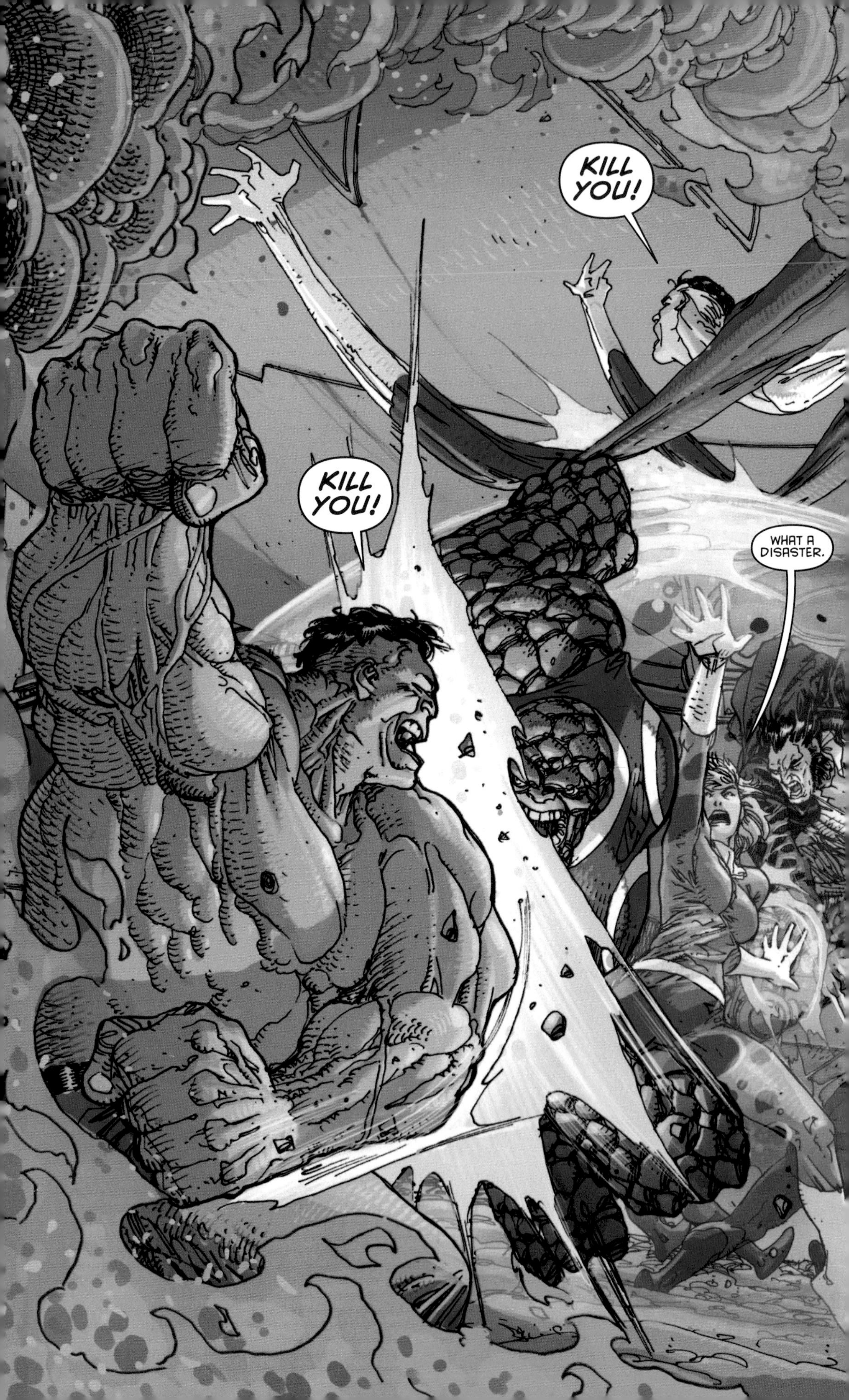
KILL YOU!
KILL YOU!
WHAT A DISASTER.

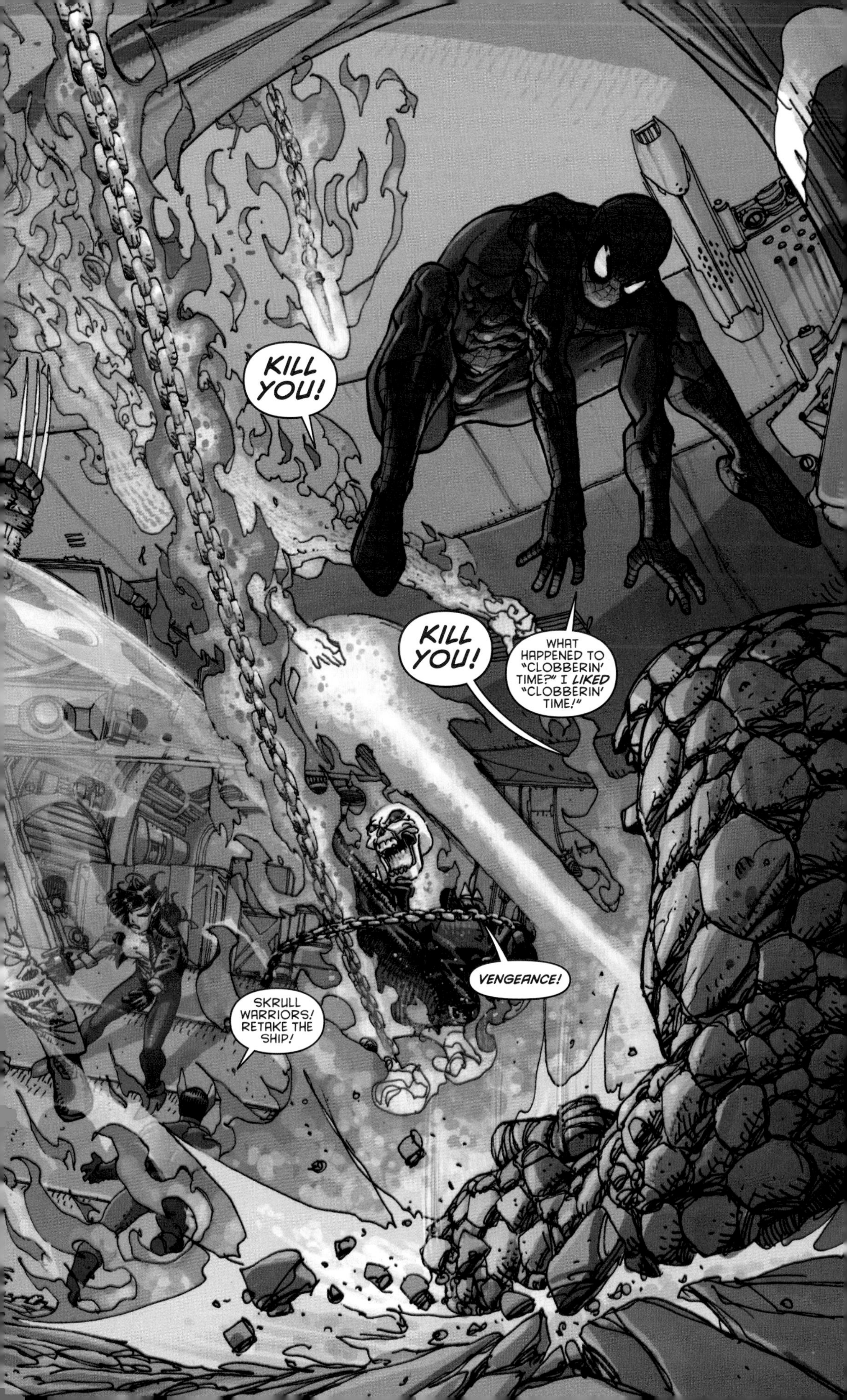
KILL YOU!
KILL YOU!
WHAT HAPPENED TO "CLOBBERIN' TIME?" I LIKED "CLOBBERIN' TIME!"
VENGEANCE!
SKRULL WARRIORS! RETAKE THE SHIP!

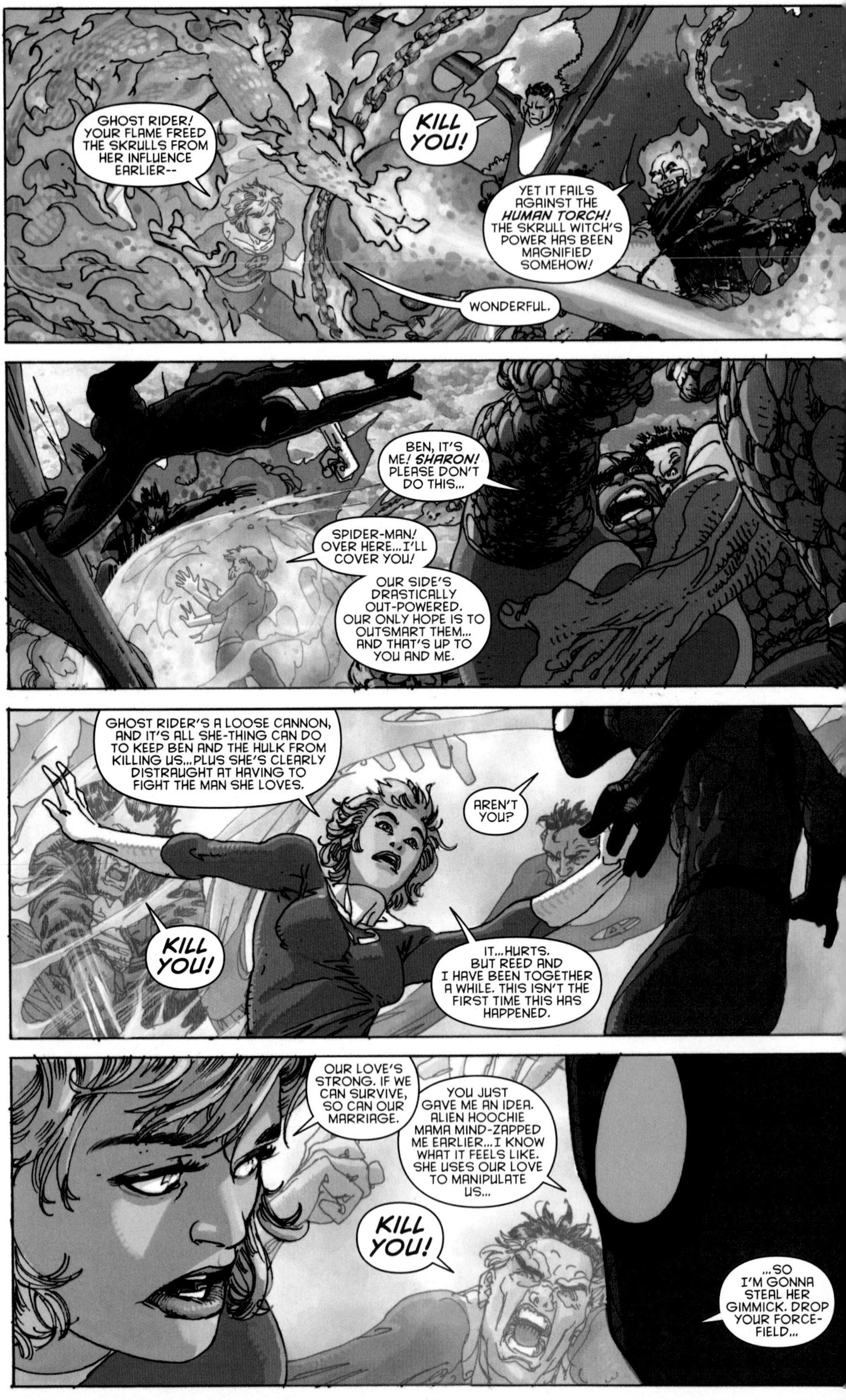
GHOST RIDER! YOUR FLAME FREED THE SKRULLS FROM HER INFLUENCE EARLIER--
KILL YOU!
YET IT FAILS AGAINST THE HUMAN TORCH! THE SKRULL WITCH'S POWER HAS BEEN MAGNIFIED SOMEHOW!
WONDERFUL.
BEN, IT'S ME! SHARON! PLEASE DON'T DO THIS...
SPIDER-MAN! OVER HERE...I'LL COVER YOU!
OUR SIDE'S DRASTICALLY OUT-POWERED. OUR ONLY HOPE IS TO OUTSMART THEM... AND THAT'S UP TO YOU AND ME.
GHOST RIDER'S A LOOSE CANNON, AND IT'S ALL SHE-THING CAN DO TO KEEP BEN AND THE HULK FROM KILLING US...PLUS SHE'S CLEARLY DISTRAUGHT AT HAVING TO FIGHT THE MAN SHE LOVES.
AREN'T YOU?
KILL YOU!
IT...HURTS. BUT REED AND I HAVE BEEN TOGETHER A WHILE. THIS ISN'T THE FIRST TIME THIS HAS HAPPENED.
OUR LOVE'S STRONG. IF WE CAN SURVIVE, SO CAN OUR MARRIAGE.
YOU JUST GAVE ME AN IDEA. ALIEN HOOCHIE MAMA MIND-ZAPPED ME EARLIER...I KNOW WHAT IT FEELS LIKE. SHE USES OUR LOVE TO MANIPULATE US...
KILL YOU!
...SO I'M GONNA STEAL HER GIMMICK. DROP YOUR FORCE-FIELD...

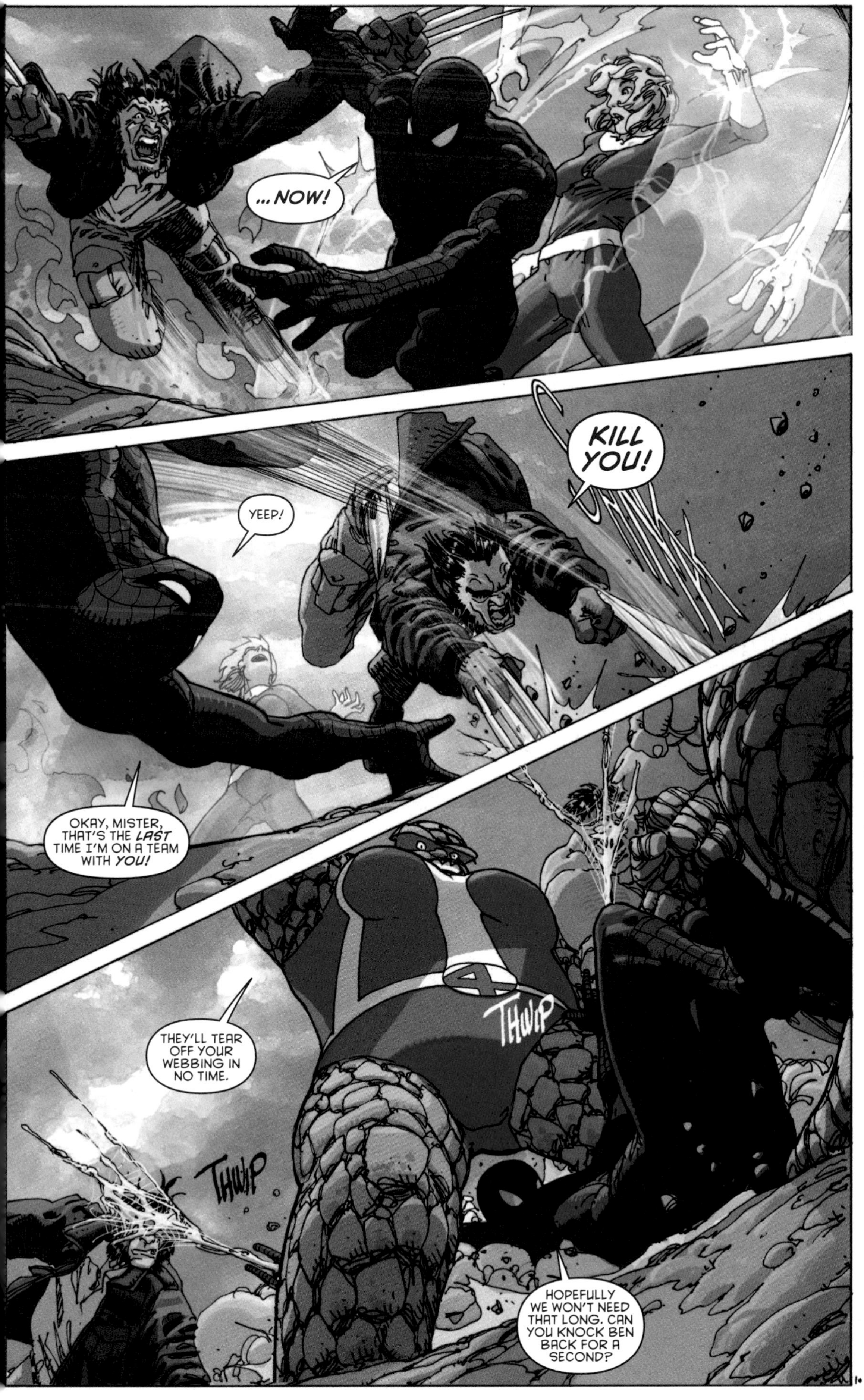
...NOW!
KILL YOU!
YEEP!
OKAY, MISTER, THAT'S THE LAST TIME I'M ON A TEAM WITH YOU!
THEY'LL TEAR OFF YOUR WEBBING IN NO TIME.
THWIP
THWIP
HOPEFULLY WE WON'T NEED THAT LONG. CAN YOU KNOCK BEN BACK FOR A SECOND?

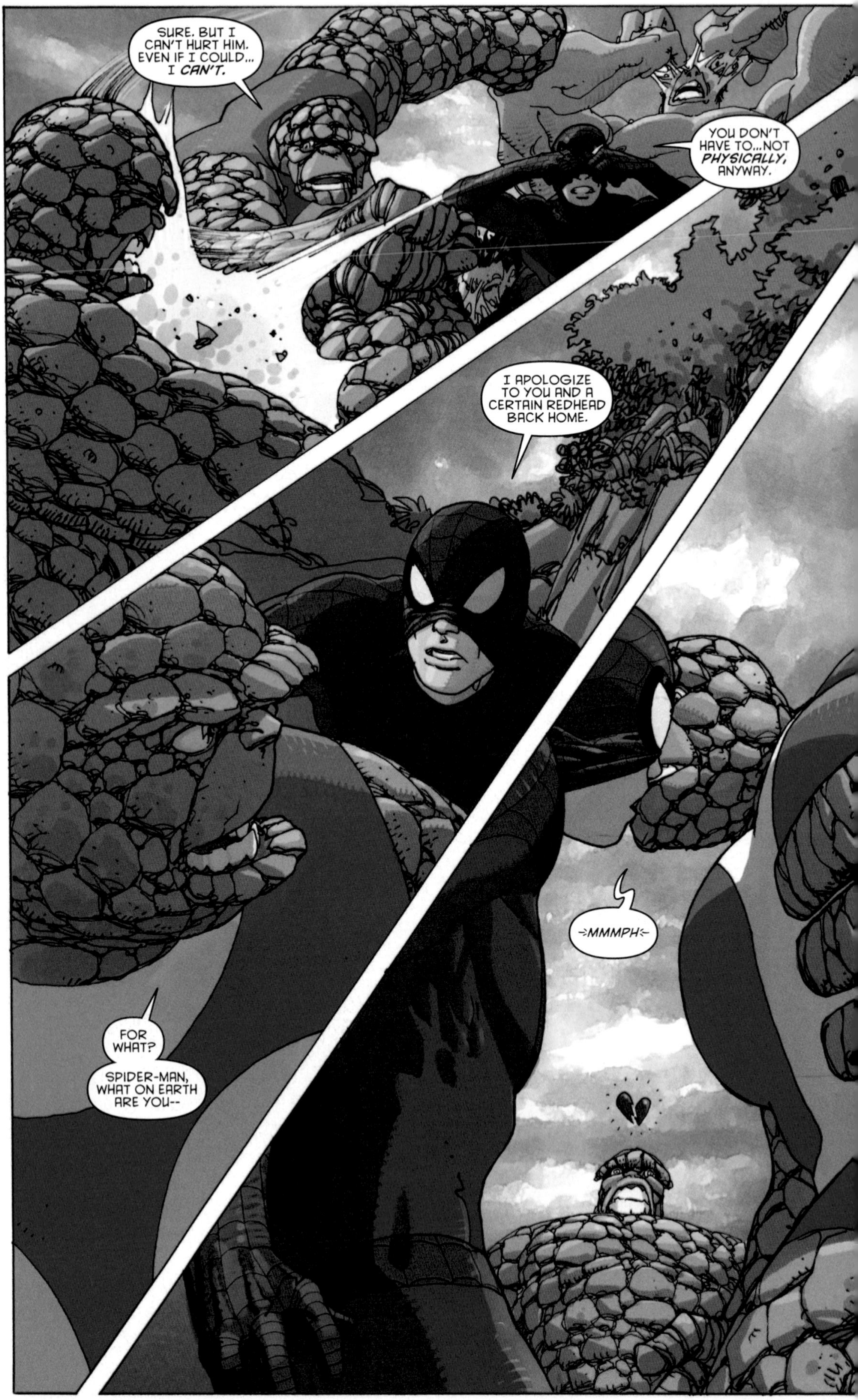
SURE. BUT I CAN'T HURT HIM. EVEN IF I COULD... I *CAN'T.*
YOU DON'T HAVE TO...NOT *PHYSICALLY,* ANYWAY.
I APOLOGIZE TO YOU AND A CERTAIN REDHEAD BACK HOME.
FOR WHAT?
SPIDER-MAN, WHAT ON EARTH ARE YOU--
MMMPH

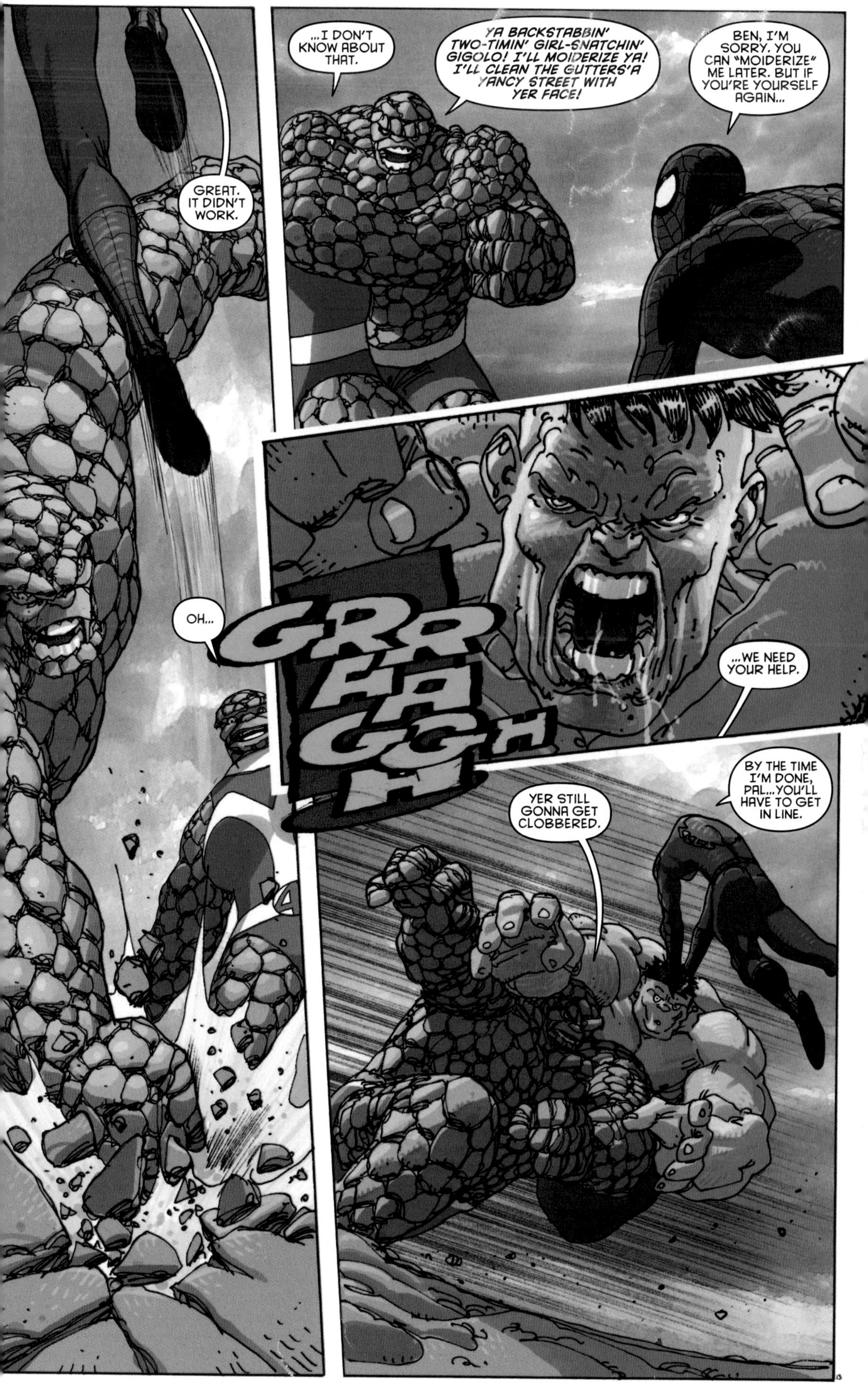
GREAT. IT DIDN'T WORK.
...I DON'T KNOW ABOUT THAT.
YA BACKSTABBIN' TWO-TIMIN' GIRL-SNATCHIN' GIGOLO! I'LL MOIDERIZE YA! I'LL CLEAN THE GUTTERS'A YANCY STREET WITH YER FACE!
BEN, I'M SORRY. YOU CAN "MOIDERIZE" ME LATER. BUT IF YOU'RE YOURSELF AGAIN...
OH...
GRRAAGGHH
...WE NEED YOUR HELP.
YER STILL GONNA GET CLOBBERED.
BY THE TIME I'M DONE, PAL...YOU'LL HAVE TO GET IN LINE.
13

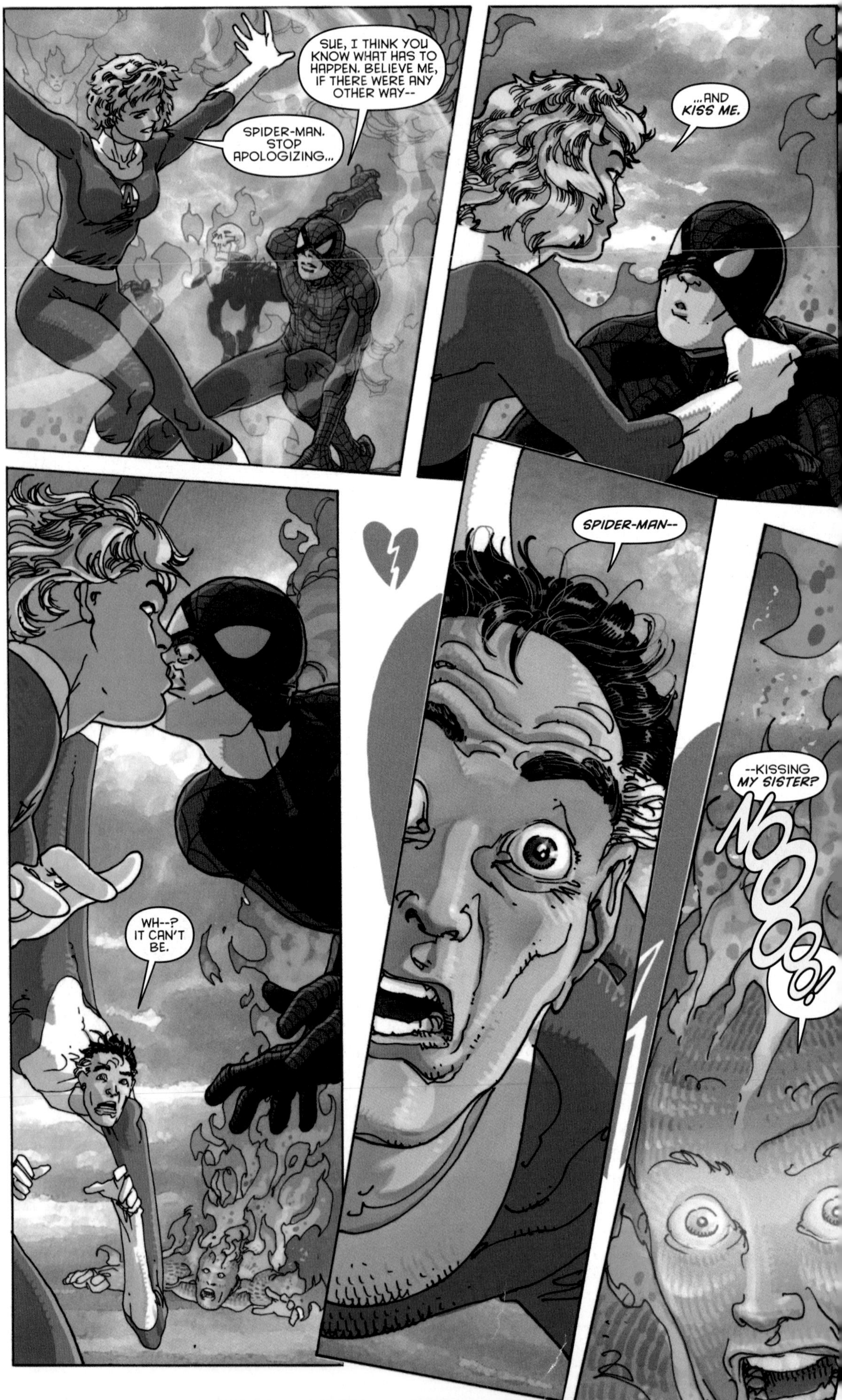
SUE, I THINK YOU KNOW WHAT HAS TO HAPPEN. BELIEVE ME, IF THERE WERE ANY OTHER WAY--
SPIDER-MAN. STOP APOLOGIZING...
...AND *KISS ME.*
WH--? IT CAN'T BE.
SPIDER-MAN--
--KISSING *MY SISTER?*
NOOOOO!

MY EYES ARE SHUT BUT I CAN'T STOP SEEING IT! *IT'S BURNED INTO MY BRAIN!*

CALM DOWN, *JOHNNY.* THEY WERE CLEARLY DOING IT TO SHOCK US INTO OUR RIGHT MINDS.

AND WE'VE STILL GOT A COUPLE OF HUGE PROBLEMS...

KILL YOU!

...WHO REALLY DON'T CARE WHO'S SWAPPING SPIT WITH WHO.

THE HULK'S BAD ENOUGH, BUT IF WE CAN'T STOP WOLVERINE SOON, HE'S LIABLE TO KILL SOMEONE.

ALLOW ME, SUSAN RICHARDS. NOW THAT I AM FREE OF DISTRACTIONS, I BELIEVE I CAN END THIS...THOUGH NOT WITHOUT SUFFERING.

MY *PENANCE STARE* FORCES A MAN TO EXPERIENCE THE PAIN HE HAS INFLICTED ON OTHERS. AND WOLVERINE HAS DEALT MUCH SORROW IN HIS LONG, LONG LIFE...

...MUCH OF IT WARRANTED. THUS I HESITATE TO TAKE THIS STEP,... BUT I SEE NO OTHER WAY.

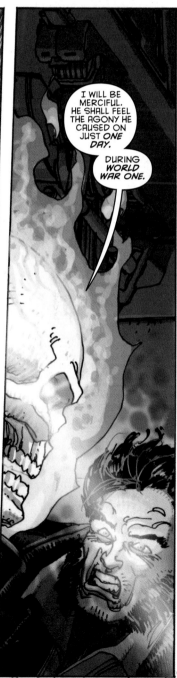

I WILL BE MERCIFUL. HE SHALL FEEL THE AGONY HE CAUSED ON JUST *ONE DAY.*

DURING *WORLD WAR ONE.*

14

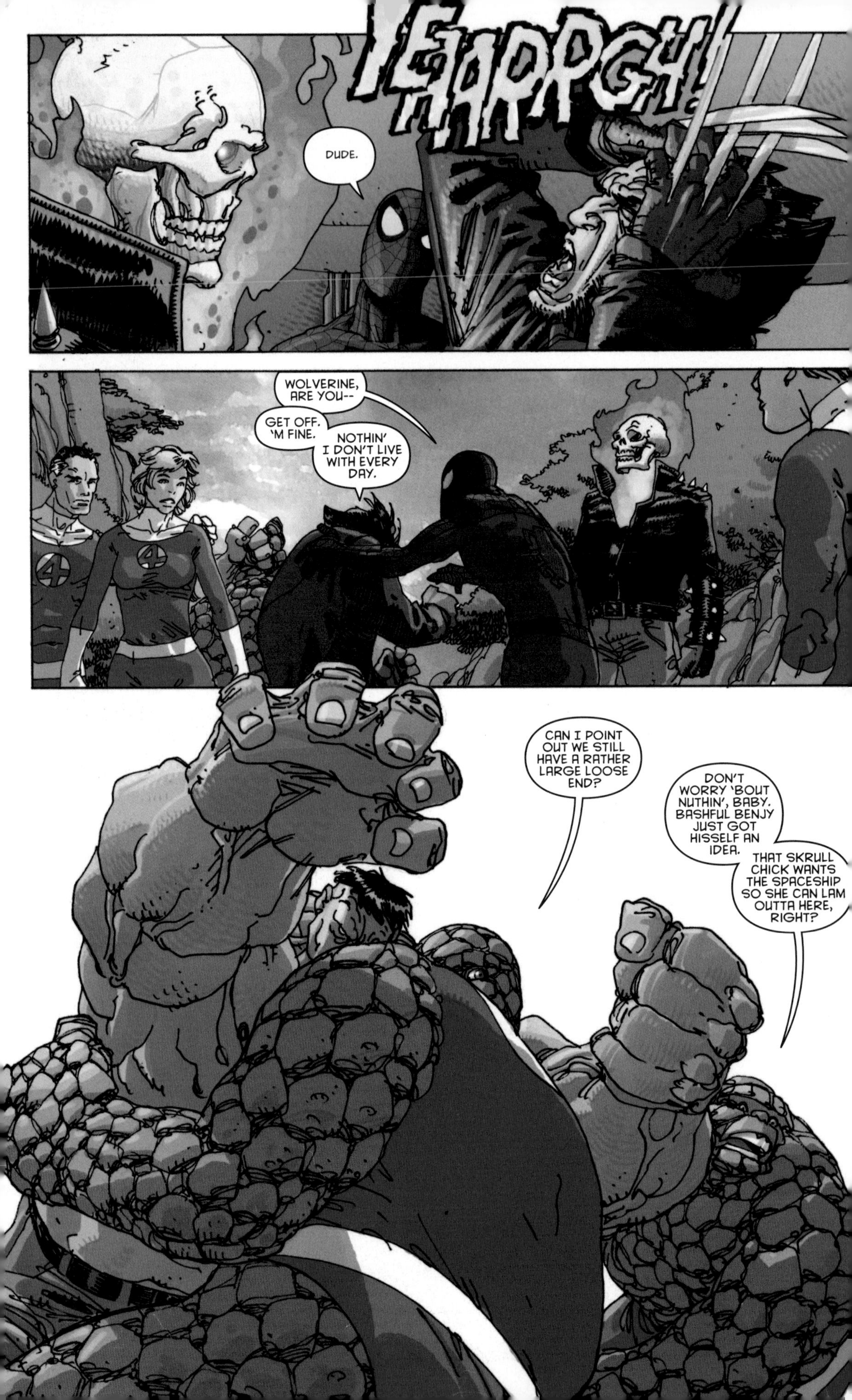
YEARRGH!
DUDE.
WOLVERINE, ARE YOU--
GET OFF. 'M FINE.
NOTHIN' I DON'T LIVE WITH EVERY DAY.
CAN I POINT OUT WE STILL HAVE A RATHER LARGE LOOSE END?
DON'T WORRY 'BOUT NUTHIN', BABY. BASHFUL BENJY JUST GOT HISSELF AN IDEA.
THAT SKRULL CHICK WANTS THE SPACESHIP SO SHE CAN LAM OUTTA HERE, RIGHT?

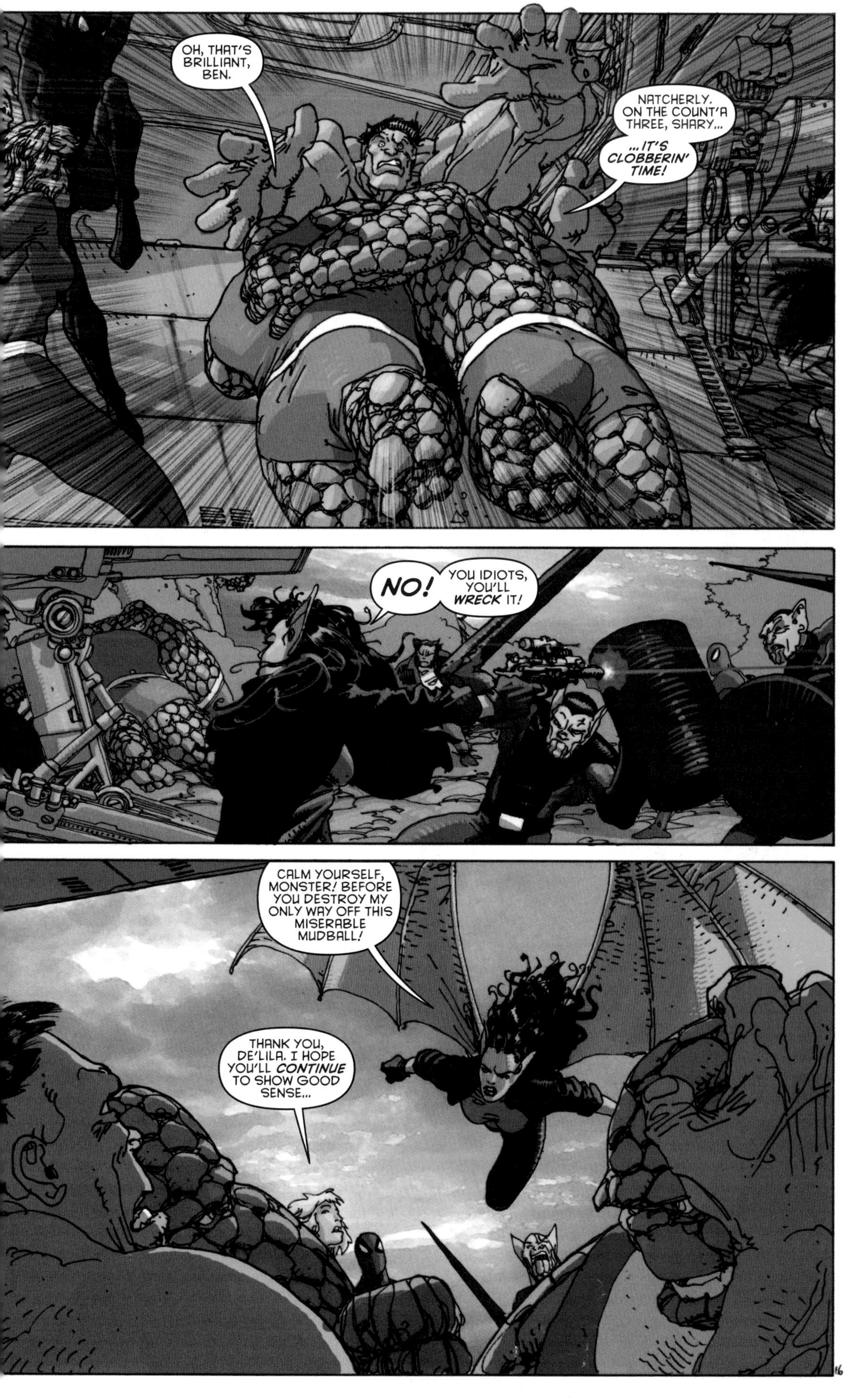
OH, THAT'S BRILLIANT, BEN.
NATCHERLY. ON THE COUNT'A THREE, SHARY...
...IT'S CLOBBERIN' TIME!
NO!
YOU IDIOTS, YOU'LL WRECK IT!
CALM YOURSELF, MONSTER! BEFORE YOU DESTROY MY ONLY WAY OFF THIS MISERABLE MUDBALL!
THANK YOU, DE'LILA. I HOPE YOU'LL CONTINUE TO SHOW GOOD SENSE...

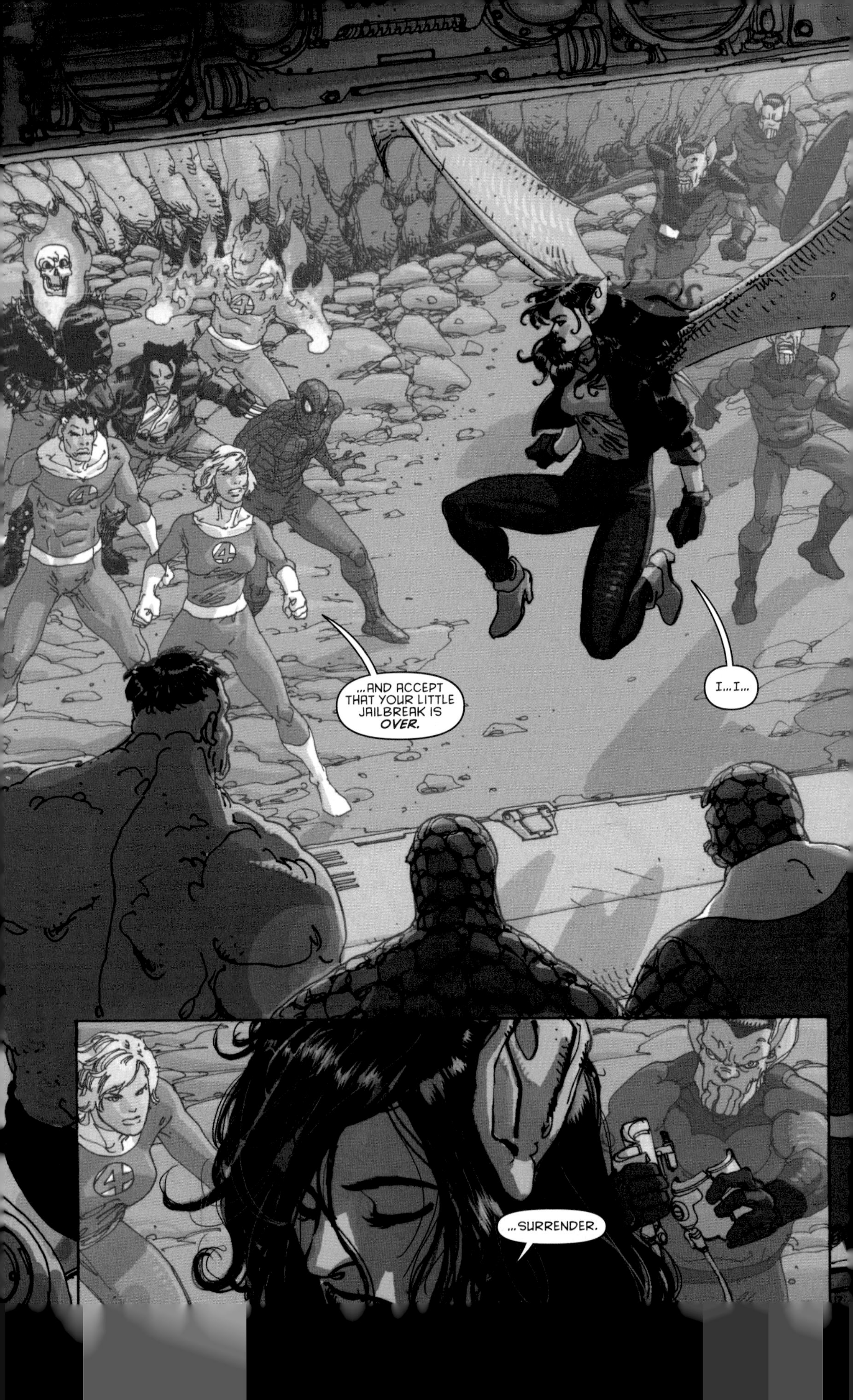
...AND ACCEPT THAT YOUR LITTLE JAILBREAK IS *OVER.*
I... I...
...SURRENDER.

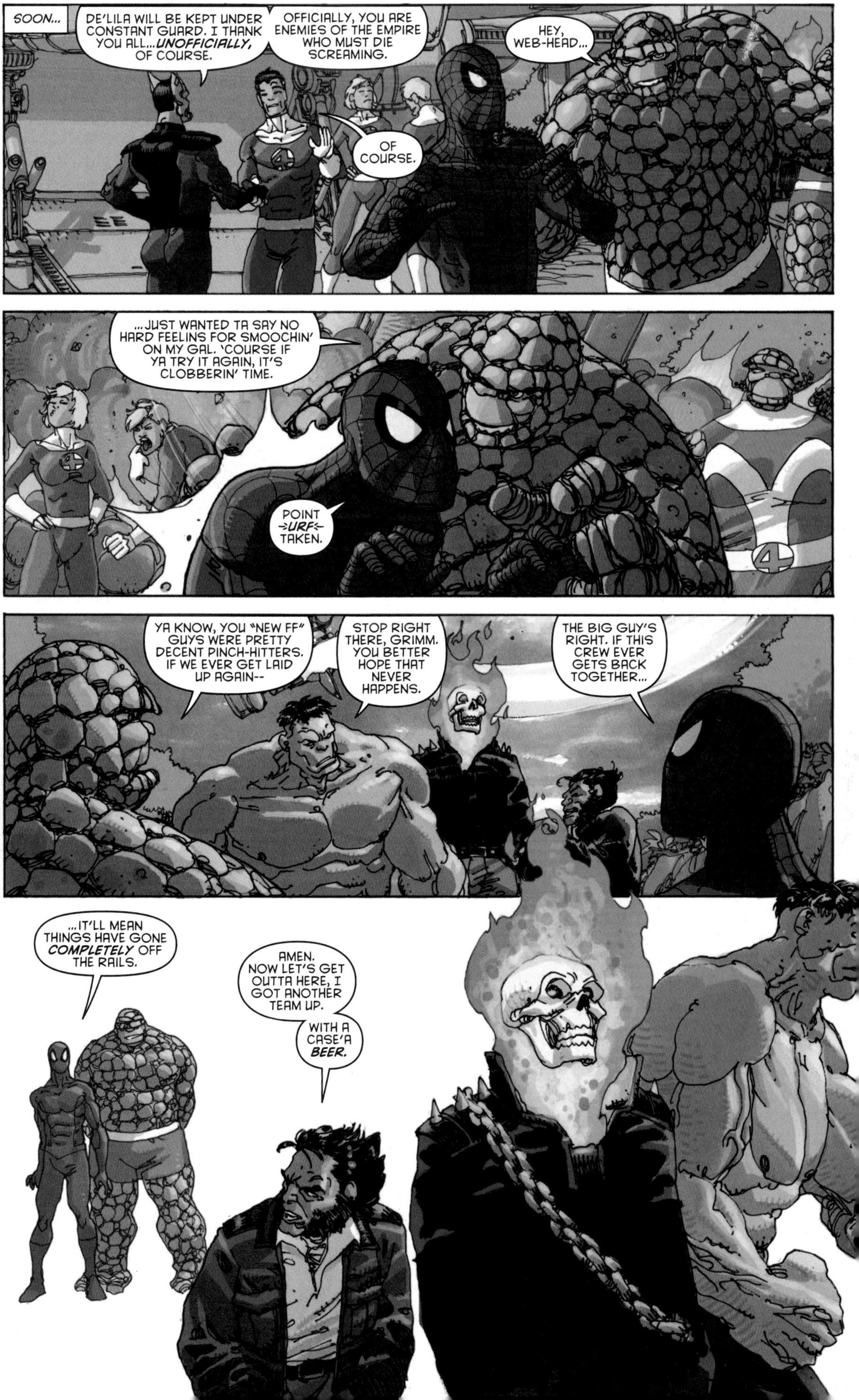
SOON...
DE'LILA WILL BE KEPT UNDER CONSTANT GUARD. I THANK YOU ALL...*UNOFFICIALLY,* OF COURSE.
OFFICIALLY, YOU ARE ENEMIES OF THE EMPIRE WHO MUST DIE SCREAMING.
OF COURSE.
HEY, WEB-HEAD...
...JUST WANTED TA SAY NO HARD FEELINS FOR SMOOCHIN' ON MY GAL. 'COURSE IF YA TRY IT AGAIN, IT'S CLOBBERIN' TIME.
POINT *URF* TAKEN.
YA KNOW, YOU "NEW FF" GUYS WERE PRETTY DECENT PINCH-HITTERS. IF WE EVER GET LAID UP AGAIN--
STOP RIGHT THERE, GRIMM. YOU BETTER HOPE THAT NEVER HAPPENS.
THE BIG GUY'S RIGHT. IF THIS CREW EVER GETS BACK TOGETHER...
...IT'LL MEAN THINGS HAVE GONE *COMPLETELY* OFF THE RAILS.
AMEN. NOW LET'S GET OUTTA HERE, I GOT ANOTHER TEAM UP.
WITH A CASE'A *BEER.*

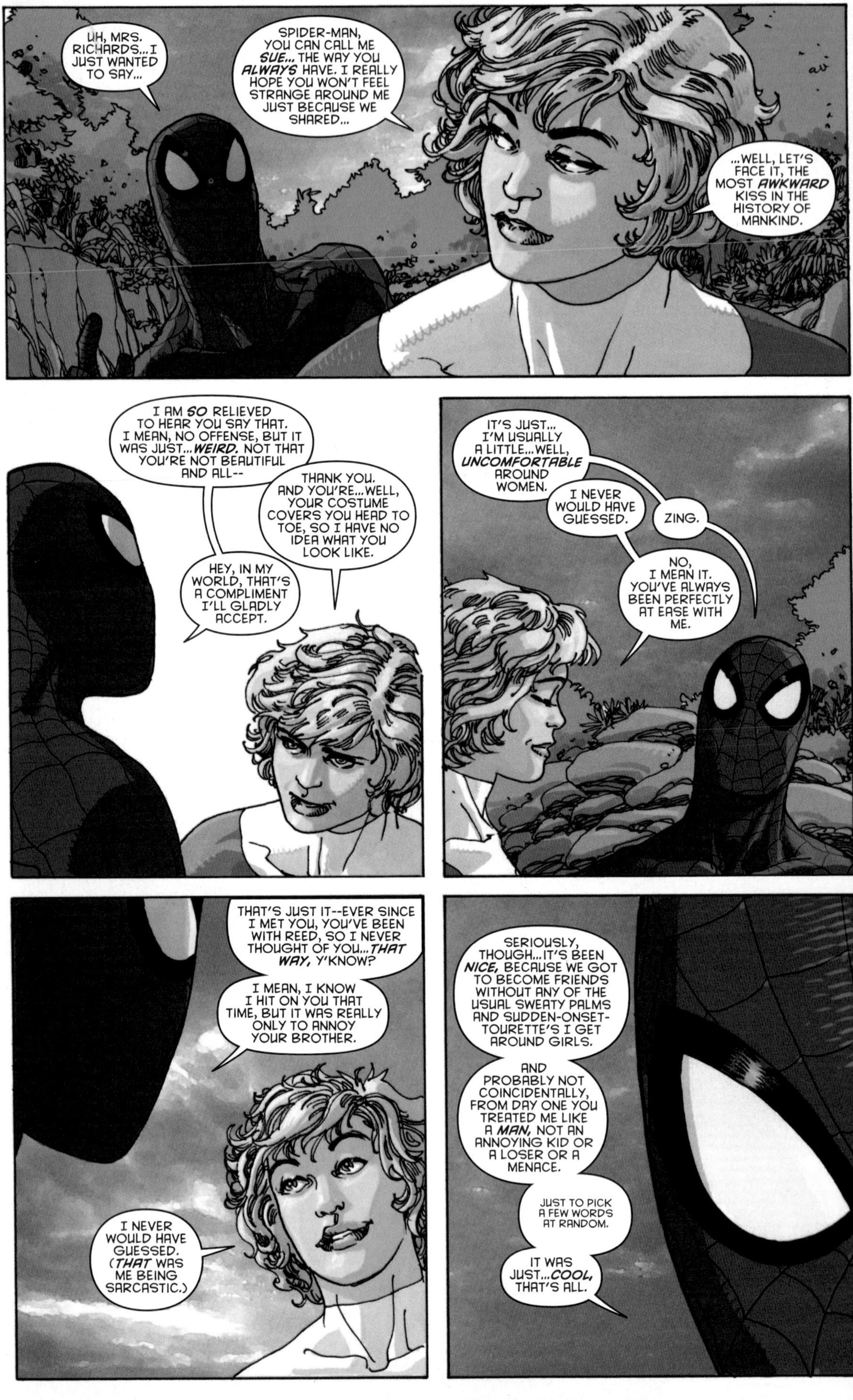

UH, MRS. RICHARDS...I JUST WANTED TO SAY...
SPIDER-MAN, YOU CAN CALL ME SUE... THE WAY YOU ALWAYS HAVE. I REALLY HOPE YOU WON'T FEEL STRANGE AROUND ME JUST BECAUSE WE SHARED...
...WELL, LET'S FACE IT, THE MOST AWKWARD KISS IN THE HISTORY OF MANKIND.
I AM SO RELIEVED TO HEAR YOU SAY THAT. I MEAN, NO OFFENSE, BUT IT WAS JUST...WEIRD. NOT THAT YOU'RE NOT BEAUTIFUL AND ALL--
THANK YOU. AND YOU'RE...WELL, YOUR COSTUME COVERS YOU HEAD TO TOE, SO I HAVE NO IDEA WHAT YOU LOOK LIKE.
HEY, IN MY WORLD, THAT'S A COMPLIMENT I'LL GLADLY ACCEPT.
IT'S JUST... I'M USUALLY A LITTLE...WELL, UNCOMFORTABLE AROUND WOMEN.
I NEVER WOULD HAVE GUESSED.
ZING.
NO, I MEAN IT. YOU'VE ALWAYS BEEN PERFECTLY AT EASE WITH ME.
THAT'S JUST IT--EVER SINCE I MET YOU, YOU'VE BEEN WITH REED, SO I NEVER THOUGHT OF YOU...THAT WAY, Y'KNOW?
I MEAN, I KNOW I HIT ON YOU THAT TIME, BUT IT WAS REALLY ONLY TO ANNOY YOUR BROTHER.
I NEVER WOULD HAVE GUESSED. (THAT WAS ME BEING SARCASTIC.)
SERIOUSLY, THOUGH...IT'S BEEN NICE, BECAUSE WE GOT TO BECOME FRIENDS WITHOUT ANY OF THE USUAL SWEATY PALMS AND SUDDEN-ONSET-TOURETTE'S I GET AROUND GIRLS.
AND PROBABLY NOT COINCIDENTALLY, FROM DAY ONE YOU TREATED ME LIKE A MAN, NOT AN ANNOYING KID OR A LOSER OR A MENACE.
JUST TO PICK A FEW WORDS AT RANDOM.
IT WAS JUST...COOL, THAT'S ALL.

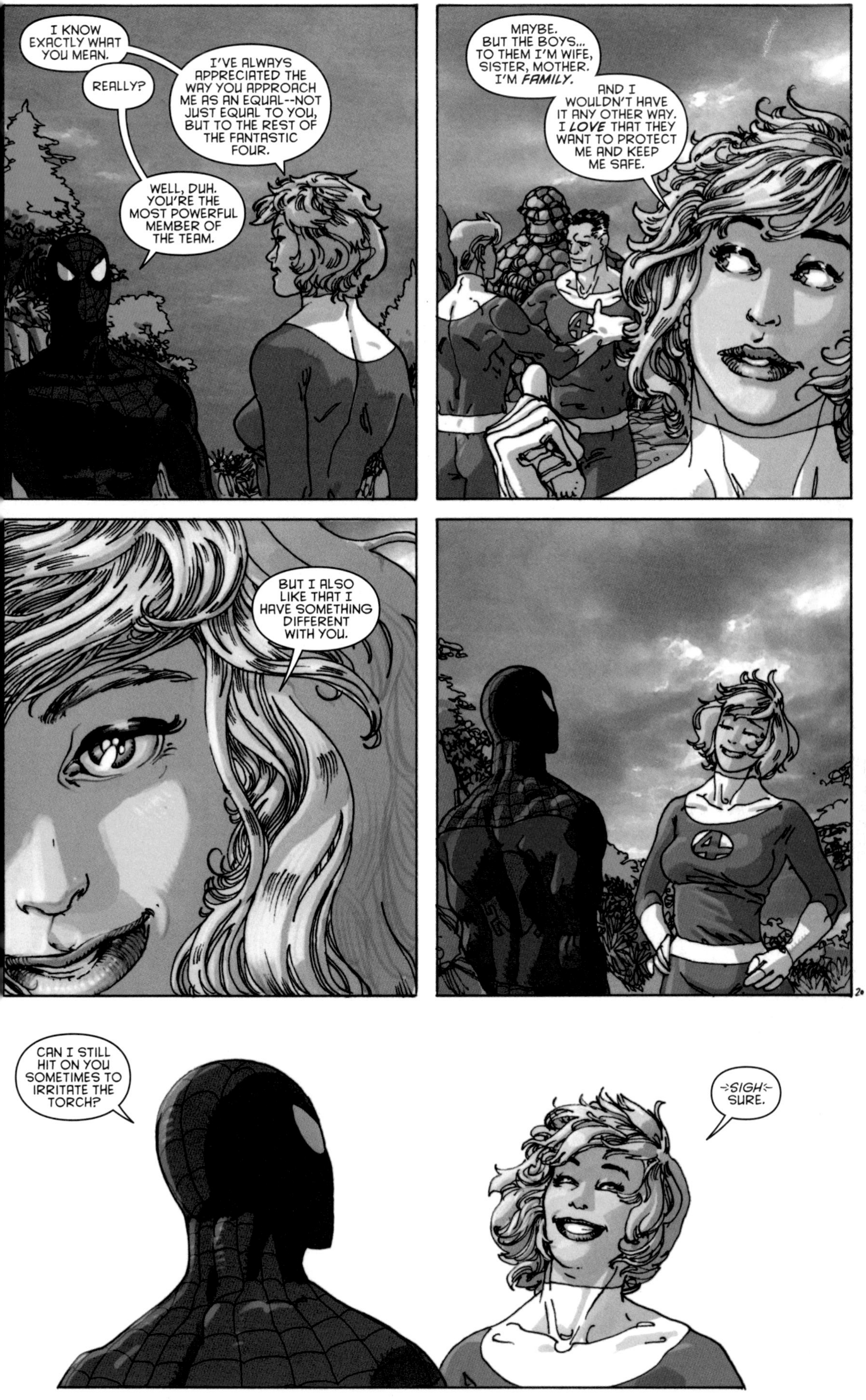
I KNOW EXACTLY WHAT YOU MEAN.
REALLY?
I'VE ALWAYS APPRECIATED THE WAY YOU APPROACH ME AS AN EQUAL--NOT JUST EQUAL TO YOU, BUT TO THE REST OF THE FANTASTIC FOUR.
WELL, DUH. YOU'RE THE MOST POWERFUL MEMBER OF THE TEAM.
MAYBE. BUT THE BOYS... TO THEM I'M WIFE, SISTER, MOTHER. I'M *FAMILY.*
AND I WOULDN'T HAVE IT ANY OTHER WAY. I ***LOVE*** THAT THEY WANT TO PROTECT ME AND KEEP ME SAFE.
BUT I ALSO LIKE THAT I HAVE SOMETHING DIFFERENT WITH YOU.
20
CAN I STILL HIT ON YOU SOMETIMES TO IRRITATE THE TORCH?
SIGH SURE.

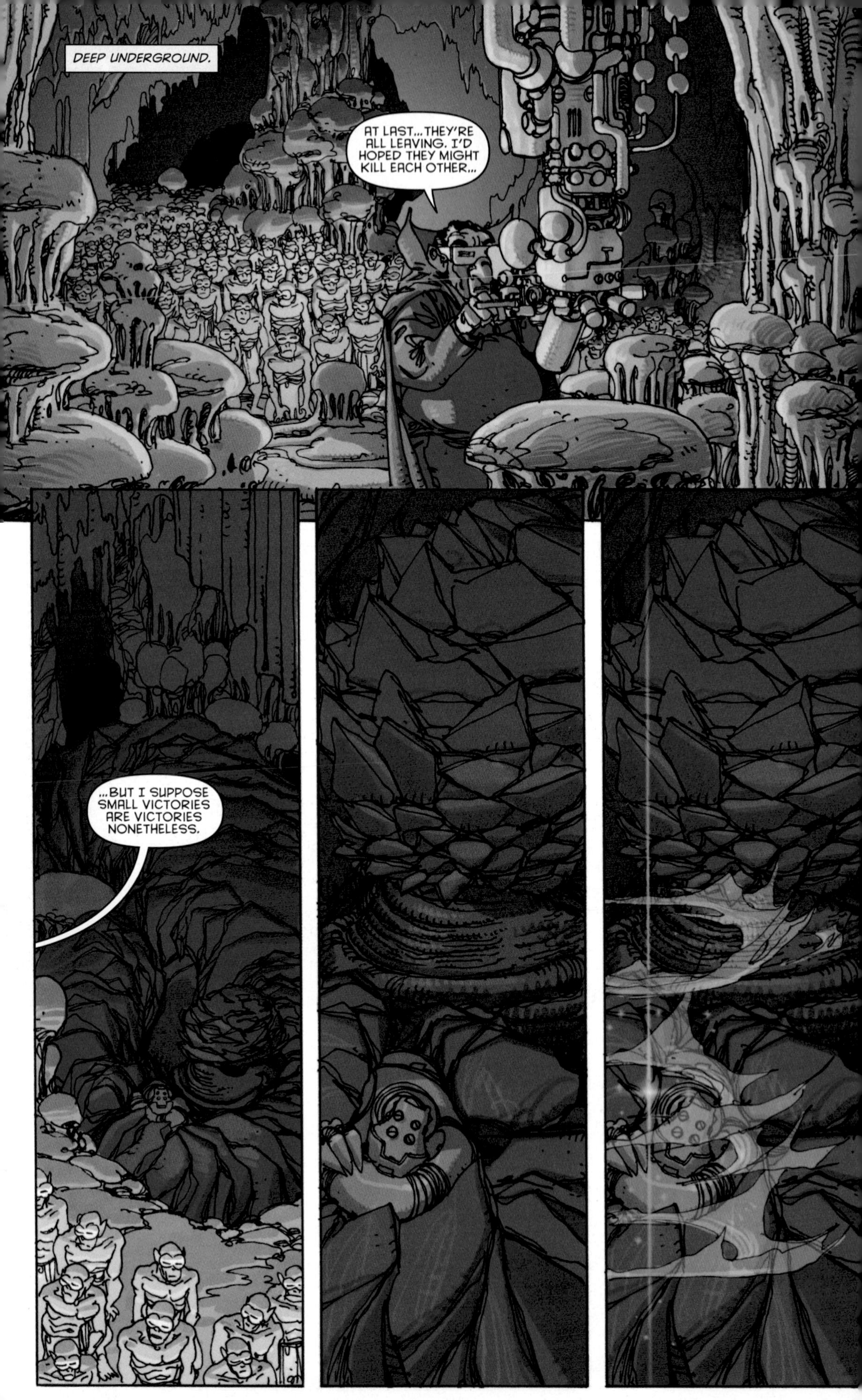
DEEP UNDERGROUND.
AT LAST... THEY'RE ALL LEAVING. I'D HOPED THEY MIGHT KILL EACH OTHER...
...BUT I SUPPOSE SMALL VICTORIES ARE VICTORIES NONETHELESS.

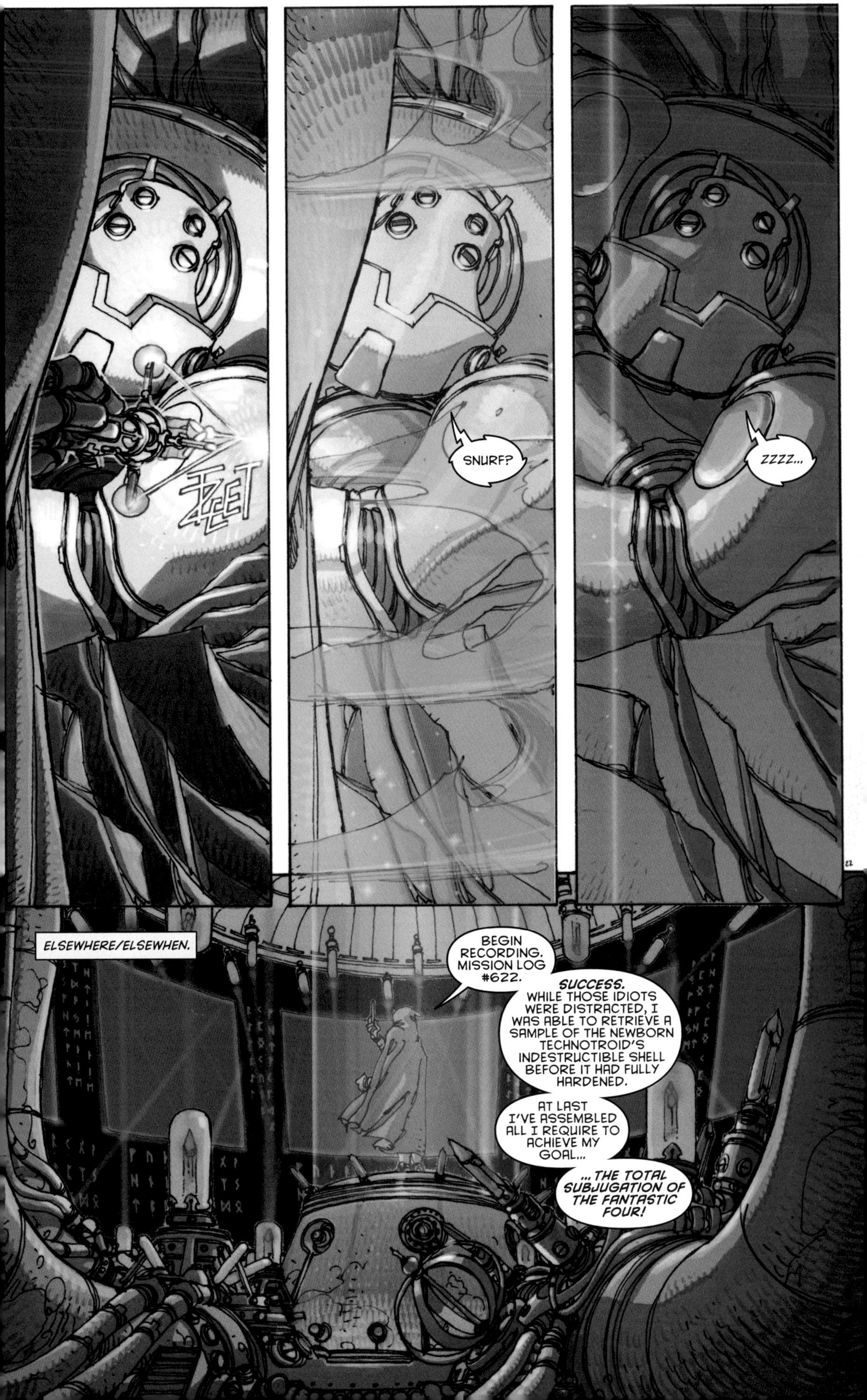
ZZZEEET
SNURF?
ZZZZ...
ELSEWHERE/ELSEWHEN.
BEGIN RECORDING. MISSION LOG #622.
SUCCESS. WHILE THOSE IDIOTS WERE DISTRACTED, I WAS ABLE TO RETRIEVE A SAMPLE OF THE NEWBORN TECHNOTROID'S INDESTRUCTIBLE SHELL BEFORE IT HAD FULLY HARDENED.
AT LAST I'VE ASSEMBLED ALL I REQUIRE TO ACHIEVE MY GOAL...
...THE TOTAL SUBJUGATION OF THE FANTASTIC FOUR!

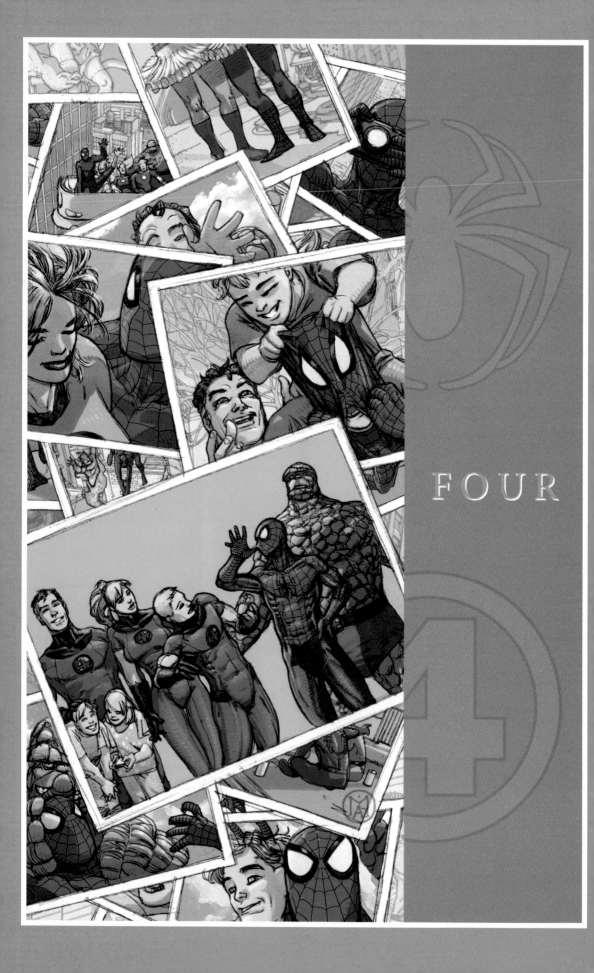

FOUR

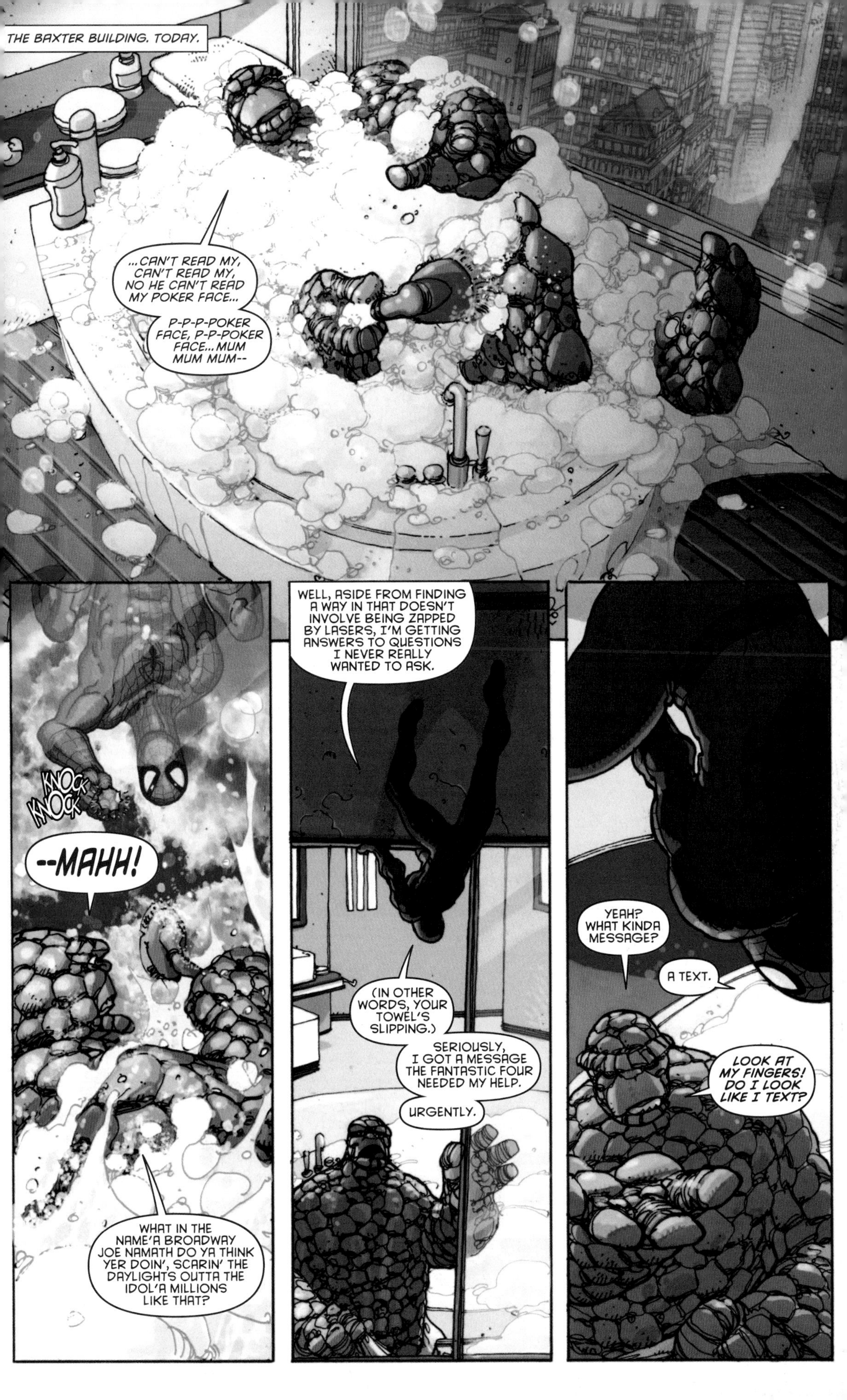
THE BAXTER BUILDING. TODAY.
...CAN'T READ MY, CAN'T READ MY, NO HE CAN'T READ MY POKER FACE...
P-P-P-POKER FACE, P-P-POKER FACE...MUM MUM MUM--
KNOCK KNOCK
--MAHH!
WHAT IN THE NAME'A BROADWAY JOE NAMATH DO YA THINK YER DOIN', SCARIN' THE DAYLIGHTS OUTTA THE IDOL'A MILLIONS LIKE THAT?
WELL, ASIDE FROM FINDING A WAY IN THAT DOESN'T INVOLVE BEING ZAPPED BY LASERS, I'M GETTING ANSWERS TO QUESTIONS I NEVER REALLY WANTED TO ASK.
(IN OTHER WORDS, YOUR TOWEL'S SLIPPING.)
SERIOUSLY, I GOT A MESSAGE THE FANTASTIC FOUR NEEDED MY HELP.
URGENTLY.
YEAH? WHAT KINDA MESSAGE?
A TEXT.
LOOK AT MY FINGERS! DO I LOOK LIKE I TEXT?

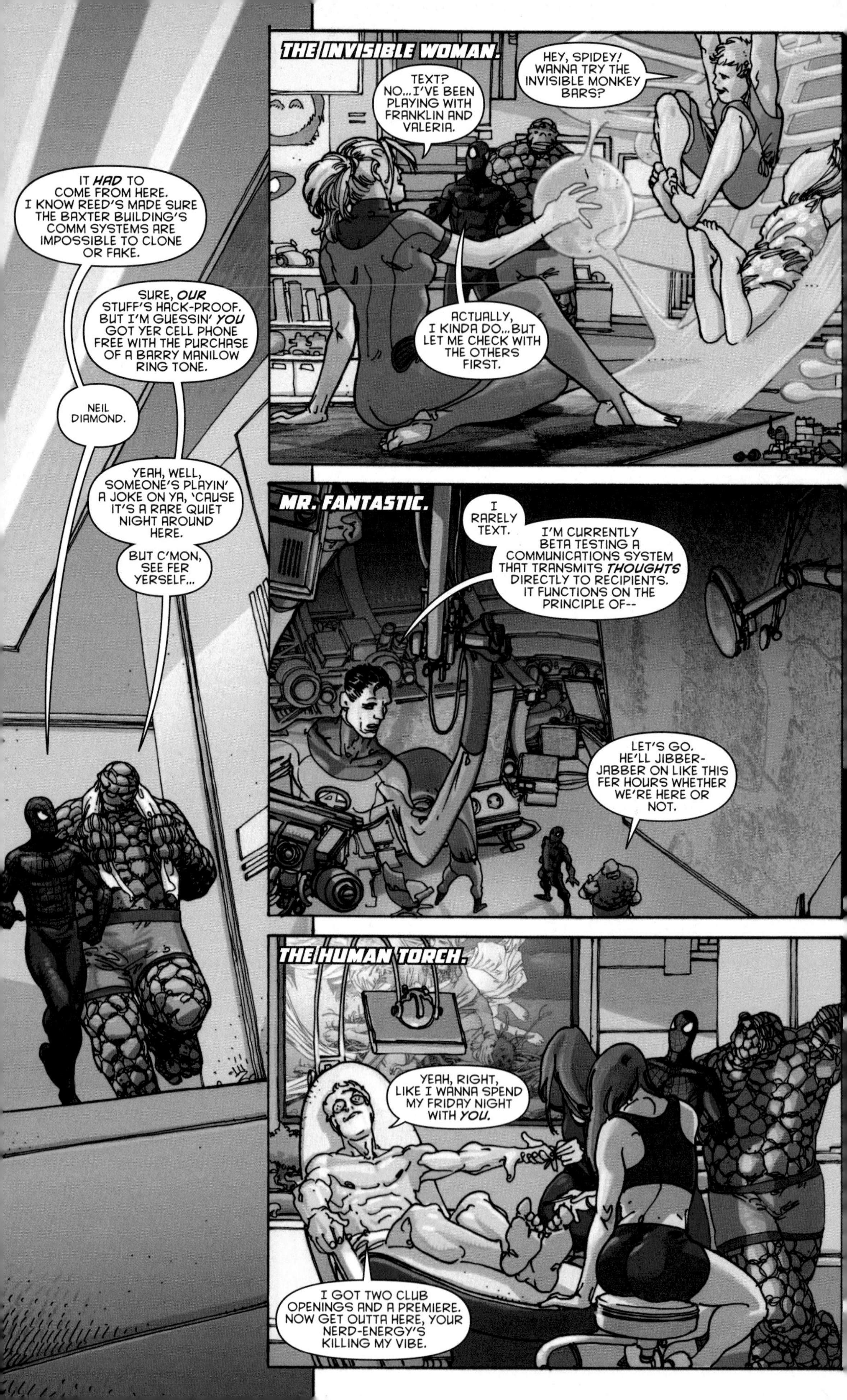
IT HAD TO COME FROM HERE. I KNOW REED'S MADE SURE THE BAXTER BUILDING'S COMM SYSTEMS ARE IMPOSSIBLE TO CLONE OR FAKE.
SURE, OUR STUFF'S HACK-PROOF. BUT I'M GUESSIN' YOU GOT YER CELL PHONE FREE WITH THE PURCHASE OF A BARRY MANILOW RING TONE.
NEIL DIAMOND.
YEAH, WELL, SOMEONE'S PLAYIN' A JOKE ON YA, 'CAUSE IT'S A RARE QUIET NIGHT AROUND HERE.
BUT C'MON, SEE FER YERSELF...
THE INVISIBLE WOMAN.
TEXT? NO...I'VE BEEN PLAYING WITH FRANKLIN AND VALERIA.
HEY, SPIDEY! WANNA TRY THE INVISIBLE MONKEY BARS?
ACTUALLY, I KINDA DO...BUT LET ME CHECK WITH THE OTHERS FIRST.
MR. FANTASTIC.
I RARELY TEXT.
I'M CURRENTLY BETA TESTING A COMMUNICATIONS SYSTEM THAT TRANSMITS THOUGHTS DIRECTLY TO RECIPIENTS. IT FUNCTIONS ON THE PRINCIPLE OF--
LET'S GO. HE'LL JIBBER-JABBER ON LIKE THIS FER HOURS WHETHER WE'RE HERE OR NOT.
THE HUMAN TORCH.
YEAH, RIGHT, LIKE I WANNA SPEND MY FRIDAY NIGHT WITH YOU.
I GOT TWO CLUB OPENINGS AND A PREMIERE. NOW GET OUTTA HERE, YOUR NERD-ENERGY'S KILLING MY VIBE.

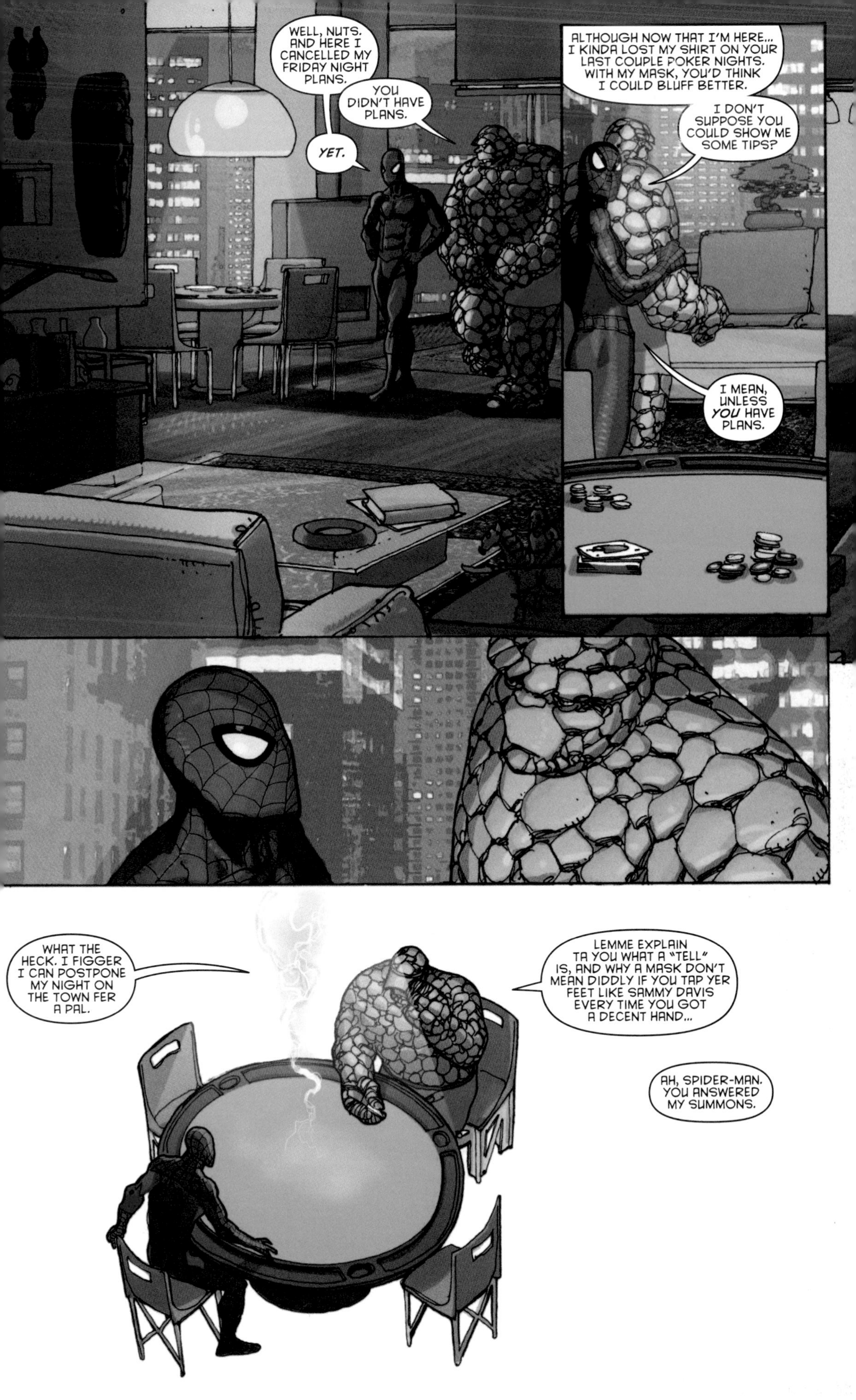
WELL, NUTS. AND HERE I CANCELLED MY FRIDAY NIGHT PLANS.
YOU DIDN'T HAVE PLANS.
YET.
ALTHOUGH NOW THAT I'M HERE... I KINDA LOST MY SHIRT ON YOUR LAST COUPLE POKER NIGHTS. WITH MY MASK, YOU'D THINK I COULD BLUFF BETTER.
I DON'T SUPPOSE YOU COULD SHOW ME SOME TIPS?
I MEAN, UNLESS YOU HAVE PLANS.
WHAT THE HECK. I FIGGER I CAN POSTPONE MY NIGHT ON THE TOWN FER A PAL.
LEMME EXPLAIN TA YOU WHAT A "TELL" IS, AND WHY A MASK DON'T MEAN DIDDLY IF YOU TAP YER FEET LIKE SAMMY DAVIS EVERY TIME YOU GOT A DECENT HAND...
AH, SPIDER-MAN. YOU ANSWERED MY SUMMONS.

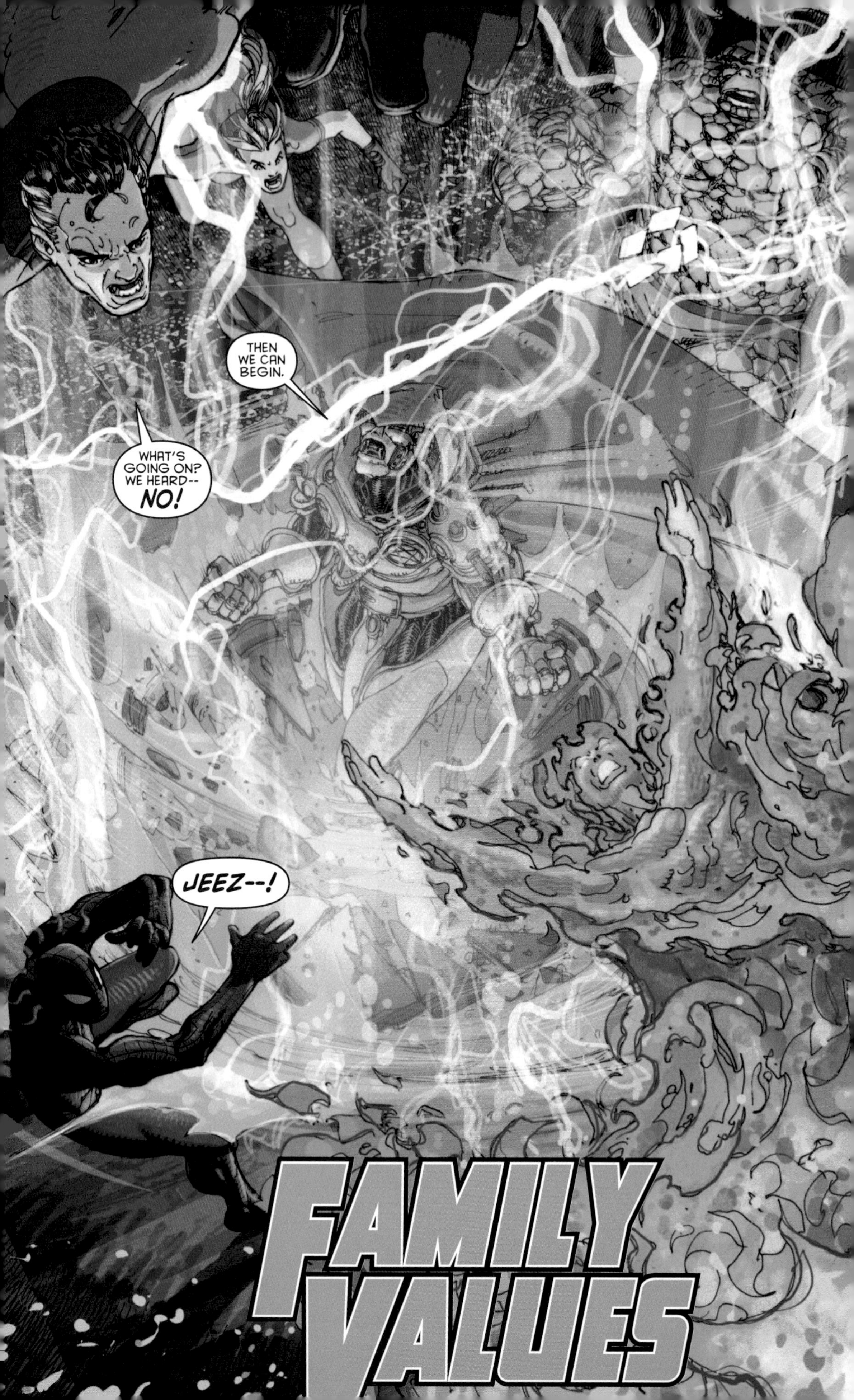
THEN WE CAN BEGIN.
WHAT'S GOING ON? WE HEARD-- NO!
JEEZ--!
FAMILY VALUES

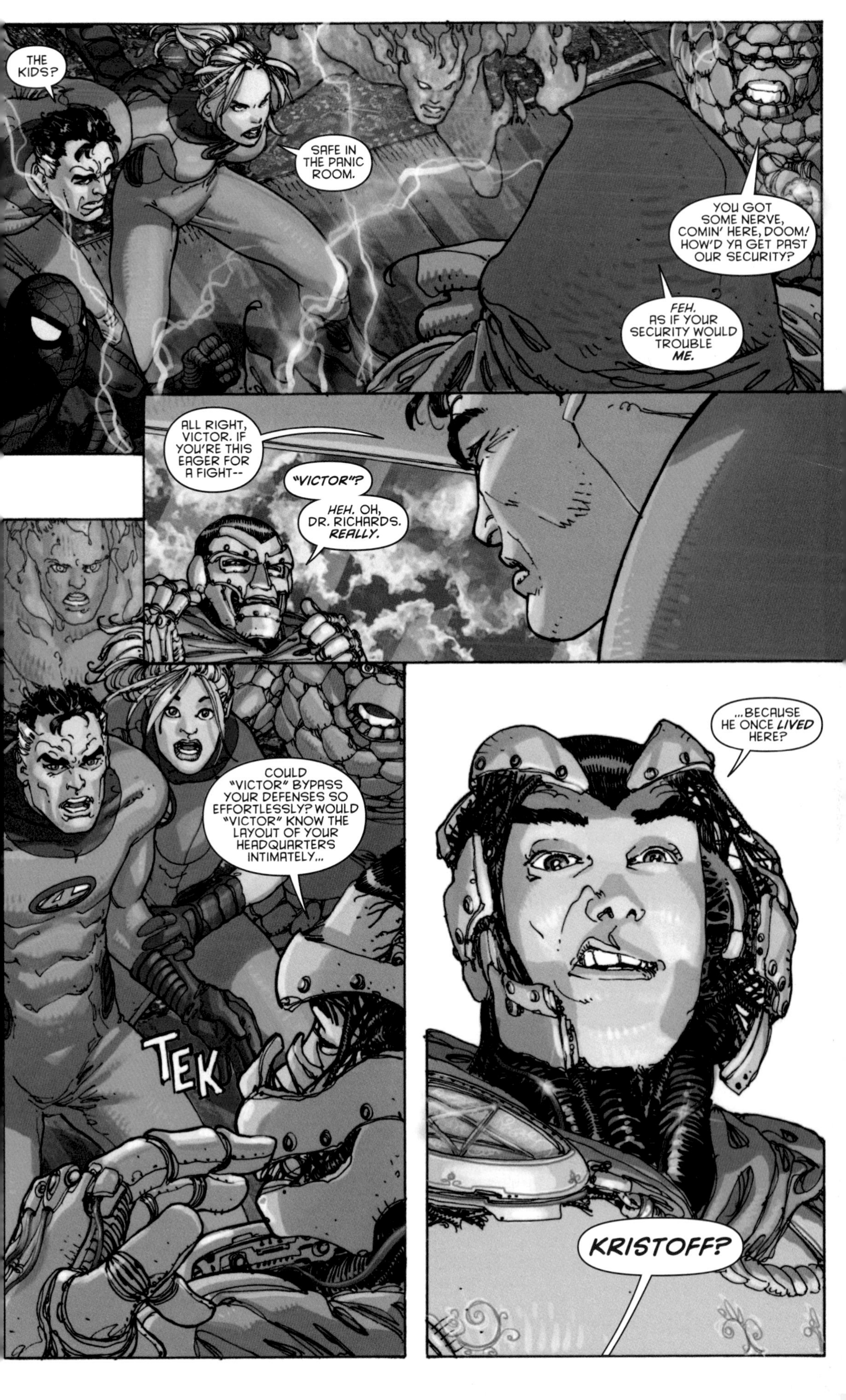

THE KIDS?
SAFE IN THE PANIC ROOM.
YOU GOT SOME NERVE, COMIN' HERE, DOOM! HOW'D YA GET PAST OUR SECURITY?
FEH. AS IF YOUR SECURITY WOULD TROUBLE ME.
ALL RIGHT, VICTOR. IF YOU'RE THIS EAGER FOR A FIGHT--
"VICTOR"?
HEH. OH, DR. RICHARDS. REALLY.
COULD "VICTOR" BYPASS YOUR DEFENSES SO EFFORTLESSLY? WOULD "VICTOR" KNOW THE LAYOUT OF YOUR HEADQUARTERS INTIMATELY...
TEK
...BECAUSE HE ONCE LIVED HERE?
KRISTOFF?

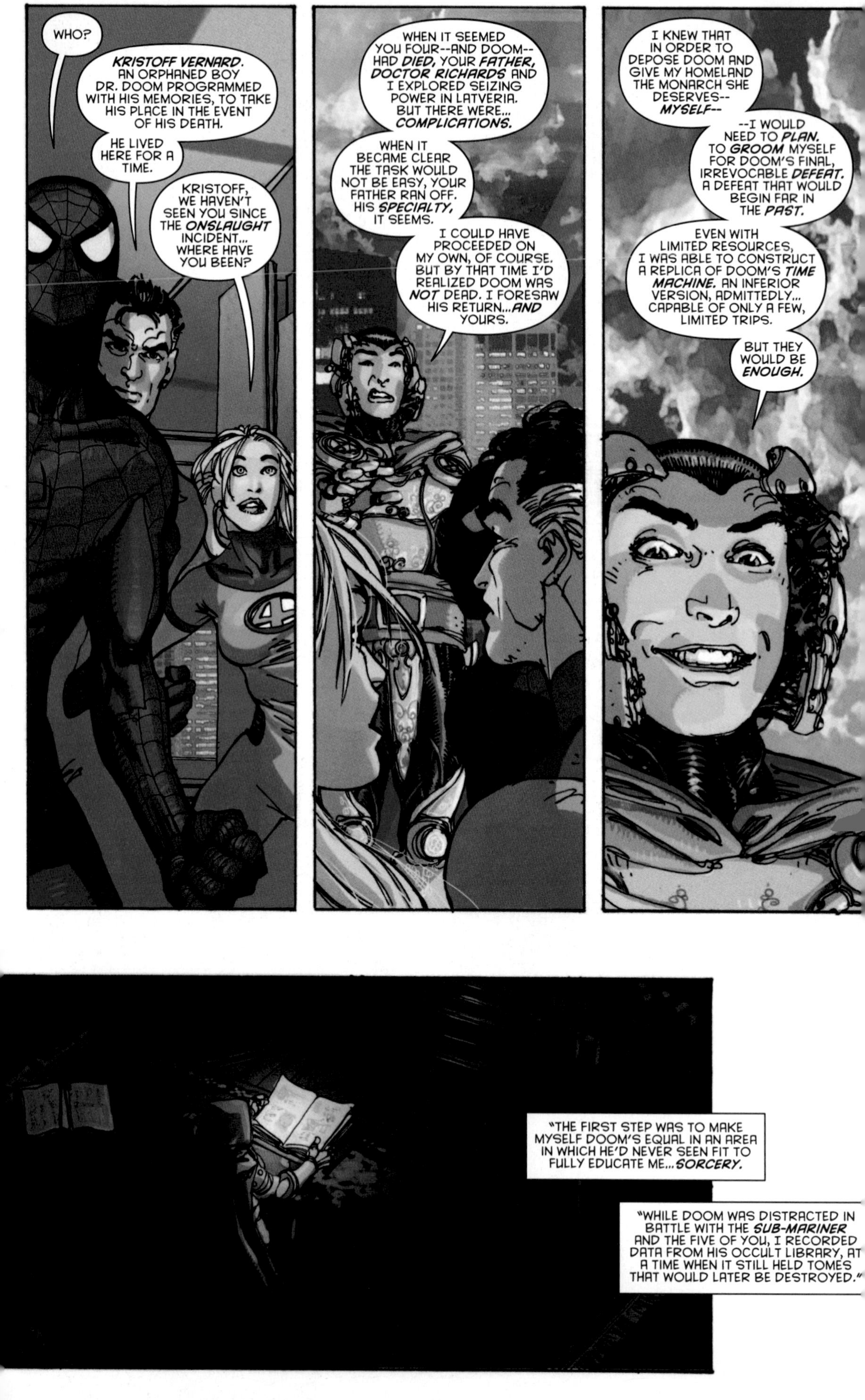
WHO?
KRISTOFF VERNARD. AN ORPHANED BOY DR. DOOM PROGRAMMED WITH HIS MEMORIES, TO TAKE HIS PLACE IN THE EVENT OF HIS DEATH.
HE LIVED HERE FOR A TIME.
KRISTOFF, WE HAVEN'T SEEN YOU SINCE THE ONSLAUGHT INCIDENT... WHERE HAVE YOU BEEN?
WHEN IT SEEMED YOU FOUR--AND DOOM--HAD DIED, YOUR FATHER, DOCTOR RICHARDS AND I EXPLORED SEIZING POWER IN LATVERIA. BUT THERE WERE... COMPLICATIONS.
WHEN IT BECAME CLEAR THE TASK WOULD NOT BE EASY, YOUR FATHER RAN OFF. HIS SPECIALTY, IT SEEMS.
I COULD HAVE PROCEEDED ON MY OWN, OF COURSE. BUT BY THAT TIME I'D REALIZED DOOM WAS NOT DEAD. I FORESAW HIS RETURN...AND YOURS.
I KNEW THAT IN ORDER TO DEPOSE DOOM AND GIVE MY HOMELAND THE MONARCH SHE DESERVES--MYSELF--
--I WOULD NEED TO PLAN. TO GROOM MYSELF FOR DOOM'S FINAL, IRREVOCABLE DEFEAT. A DEFEAT THAT WOULD BEGIN FAR IN THE PAST.
EVEN WITH LIMITED RESOURCES, I WAS ABLE TO CONSTRUCT A REPLICA OF DOOM'S TIME MACHINE. AN INFERIOR VERSION, ADMITTEDLY... CAPABLE OF ONLY A FEW, LIMITED TRIPS.
BUT THEY WOULD BE ENOUGH.
"THE FIRST STEP WAS TO MAKE MYSELF DOOM'S EQUAL IN AN AREA IN WHICH HE'D NEVER SEEN FIT TO FULLY EDUCATE ME...SORCERY.
"WHILE DOOM WAS DISTRACTED IN BATTLE WITH THE SUB-MARINER AND THE FIVE OF YOU, I RECORDED DATA FROM HIS OCCULT LIBRARY, AT A TIME WHEN IT STILL HELD TOMES THAT WOULD LATER BE DESTROYED."

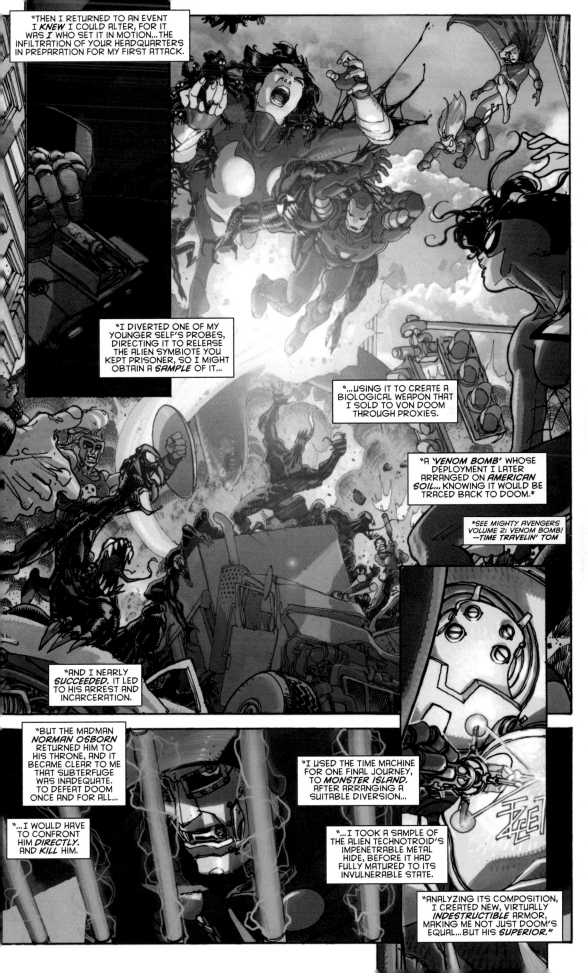

"THEN I RETURNED TO AN EVENT I *KNEW* I COULD ALTER, FOR IT WAS *I* WHO SET IT IN MOTION...THE INFILTRATION OF YOUR HEADQUARTERS IN PREPARATION FOR MY FIRST ATTACK.

"I DIVERTED ONE OF MY YOUNGER SELF'S PROBES, DIRECTING IT TO RELEASE THE ALIEN SYMBIOTE YOU KEPT PRISONER, SO I MIGHT OBTAIN A *SAMPLE* OF IT...

"...USING IT TO CREATE A BIOLOGICAL WEAPON THAT I SOLD TO VON DOOM THROUGH PROXIES.

"A *'VENOM BOMB'* WHOSE DEPLOYMENT I LATER ARRANGED ON *AMERICAN SOIL*... KNOWING IT WOULD BE TRACED BACK TO DOOM.*

*SEE MIGHTY AVENGERS VOLUME 2: VENOM BOMB! --TIME TRAVELIN' TOM

"AND I NEARLY *SUCCEEDED.* IT LED TO HIS ARREST AND INCARCERATION.

"BUT THE MADMAN *NORMAN OSBORN* RETURNED HIM TO HIS THRONE, AND IT BECAME CLEAR TO ME THAT SUBTERFUGE WAS INADEQUATE. TO DEFEAT DOOM ONCE AND FOR ALL...

"...I WOULD HAVE TO CONFRONT HIM *DIRECTLY.* AND *KILL* HIM.

"I USED THE TIME MACHINE FOR ONE FINAL JOURNEY, TO *MONSTER ISLAND.* AFTER ARRANGING A SUITABLE DIVERSION...

"...I TOOK A SAMPLE OF THE ALIEN TECHNOTROID'S IMPENETRABLE METAL HIDE, BEFORE IT HAD FULLY MATURED TO ITS INVULNERABLE STATE.

"ANALYZING ITS COMPOSITION, I CREATED NEW, VIRTUALLY *INDESTRUCTIBLE* ARMOR, MAKING ME NOT JUST DOOM'S EQUAL...BUT HIS *SUPERIOR.*"

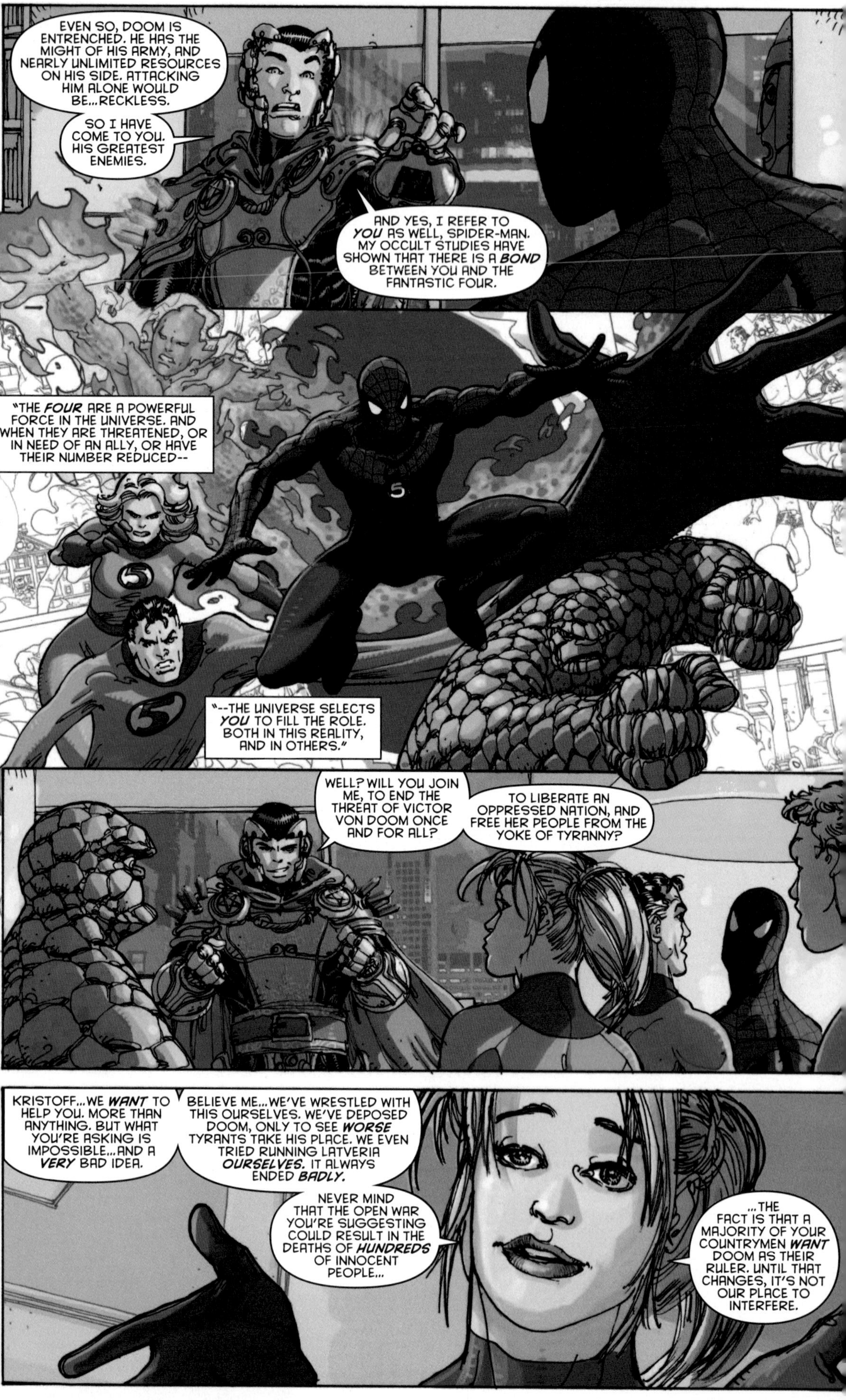
EVEN SO, DOOM IS ENTRENCHED. HE HAS THE MIGHT OF HIS ARMY, AND NEARLY UNLIMITED RESOURCES ON HIS SIDE. ATTACKING HIM ALONE WOULD BE...RECKLESS.
SO I HAVE COME TO YOU. HIS GREATEST ENEMIES.
AND YES, I REFER TO YOU AS WELL, SPIDER-MAN. MY OCCULT STUDIES HAVE SHOWN THAT THERE IS A BOND BETWEEN YOU AND THE FANTASTIC FOUR.
"THE FOUR ARE A POWERFUL FORCE IN THE UNIVERSE. AND WHEN THEY ARE THREATENED, OR IN NEED OF AN ALLY, OR HAVE THEIR NUMBER REDUCED--
"--THE UNIVERSE SELECTS YOU TO FILL THE ROLE. BOTH IN THIS REALITY, AND IN OTHERS."
WELL? WILL YOU JOIN ME, TO END THE THREAT OF VICTOR VON DOOM ONCE AND FOR ALL?
TO LIBERATE AN OPPRESSED NATION, AND FREE HER PEOPLE FROM THE YOKE OF TYRANNY?
KRISTOFF...WE WANT TO HELP YOU. MORE THAN ANYTHING. BUT WHAT YOU'RE ASKING IS IMPOSSIBLE...AND A VERY BAD IDEA.
BELIEVE ME...WE'VE WRESTLED WITH THIS OURSELVES. WE'VE DEPOSED DOOM, ONLY TO SEE WORSE TYRANTS TAKE HIS PLACE. WE EVEN TRIED RUNNING LATVERIA OURSELVES. IT ALWAYS ENDED BADLY.
NEVER MIND THAT THE OPEN WAR YOU'RE SUGGESTING COULD RESULT IN THE DEATHS OF HUNDREDS OF INNOCENT PEOPLE...
...THE FACT IS THAT A MAJORITY OF YOUR COUNTRYMEN WANT DOOM AS THEIR RULER. UNTIL THAT CHANGES, IT'S NOT OUR PLACE TO INTERFERE.

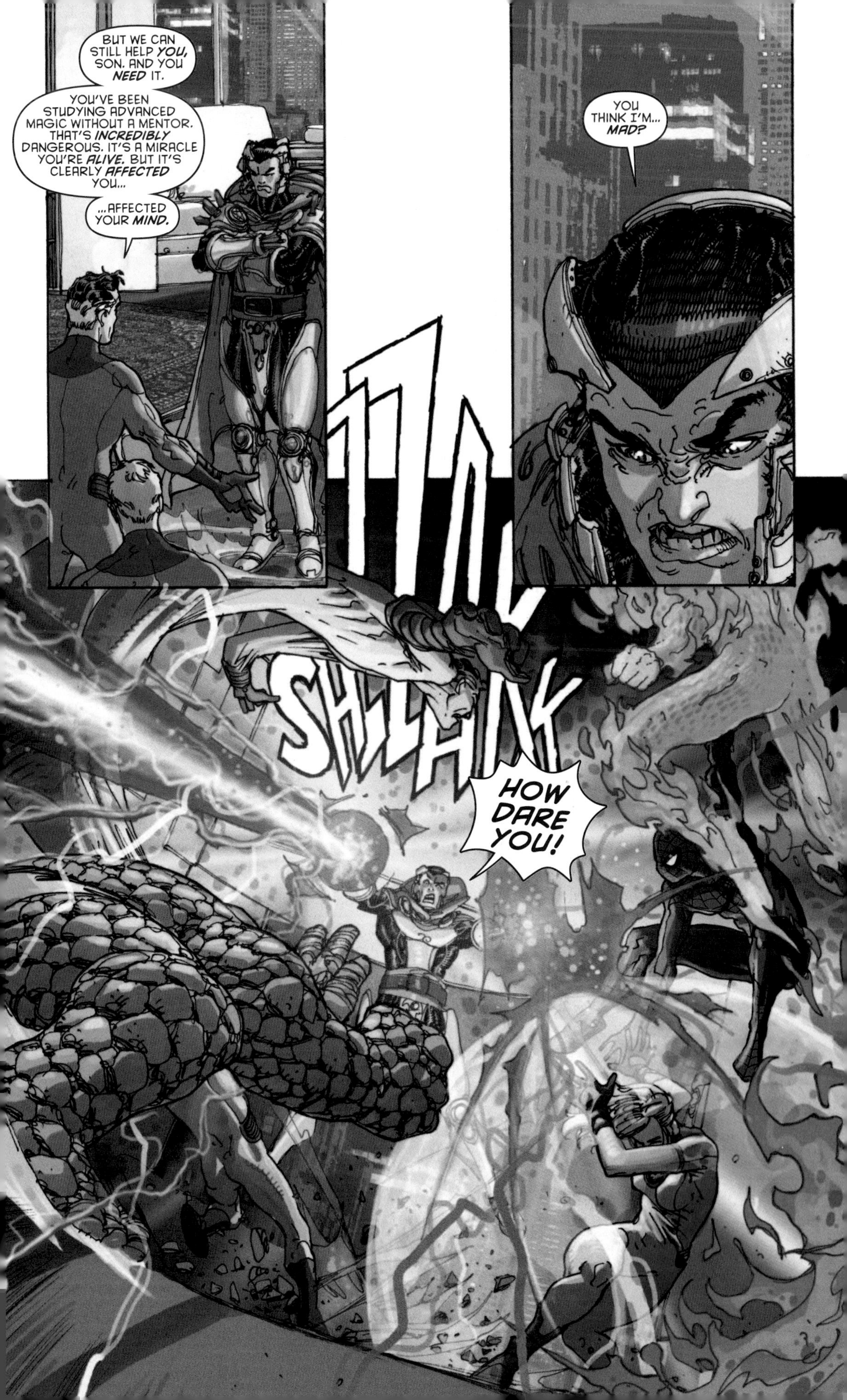
BUT WE CAN STILL HELP YOU, SON. AND YOU NEED IT.
YOU'VE BEEN STUDYING ADVANCED MAGIC WITHOUT A MENTOR. THAT'S INCREDIBLY DANGEROUS. IT'S A MIRACLE YOU'RE ALIVE. BUT IT'S CLEARLY AFFECTED YOU...
...AFFECTED YOUR MIND.
YOU THINK I'M... MAD?
SHLAK
SHLAK
HOW DARE YOU!

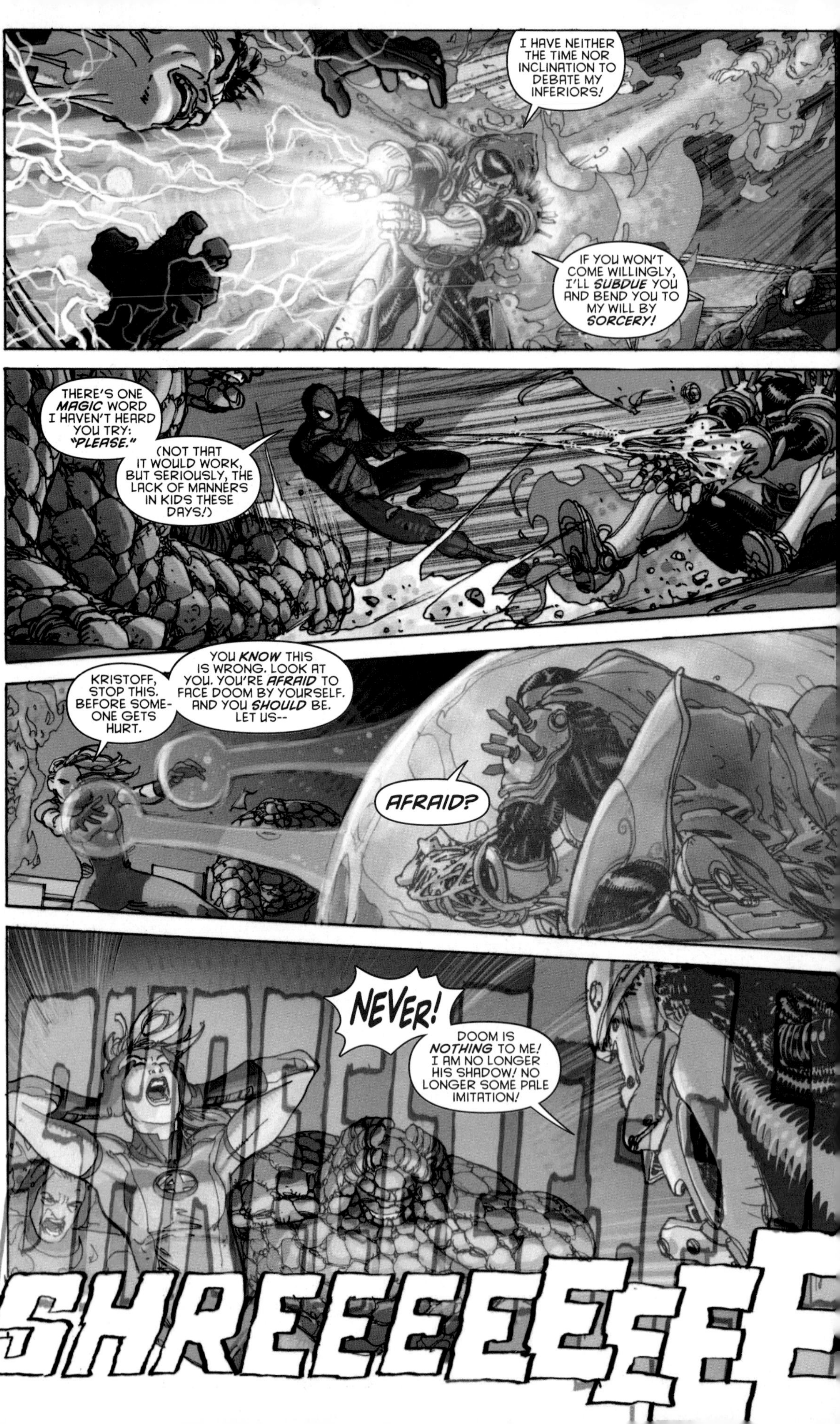
I HAVE NEITHER THE TIME NOR INCLINATION TO DEBATE MY INFERIORS!
IF YOU WON'T COME WILLINGLY, I'LL SUBDUE YOU AND BEND YOU TO MY WILL BY SORCERY!
THERE'S ONE MAGIC WORD I HAVEN'T HEARD YOU TRY: "PLEASE."
(NOT THAT IT WOULD WORK, BUT SERIOUSLY, THE LACK OF MANNERS IN KIDS THESE DAYS!)
KRISTOFF, STOP THIS. BEFORE SOME-ONE GETS HURT.
YOU KNOW THIS IS WRONG. LOOK AT YOU. YOU'RE AFRAID TO FACE DOOM BY YOURSELF. AND YOU SHOULD BE. LET US--
AFRAID?
NEVER!
DOOM IS NOTHING TO ME! I AM NO LONGER HIS SHADOW! NO LONGER SOME PALE IMITATION!
SHREEEEEEE

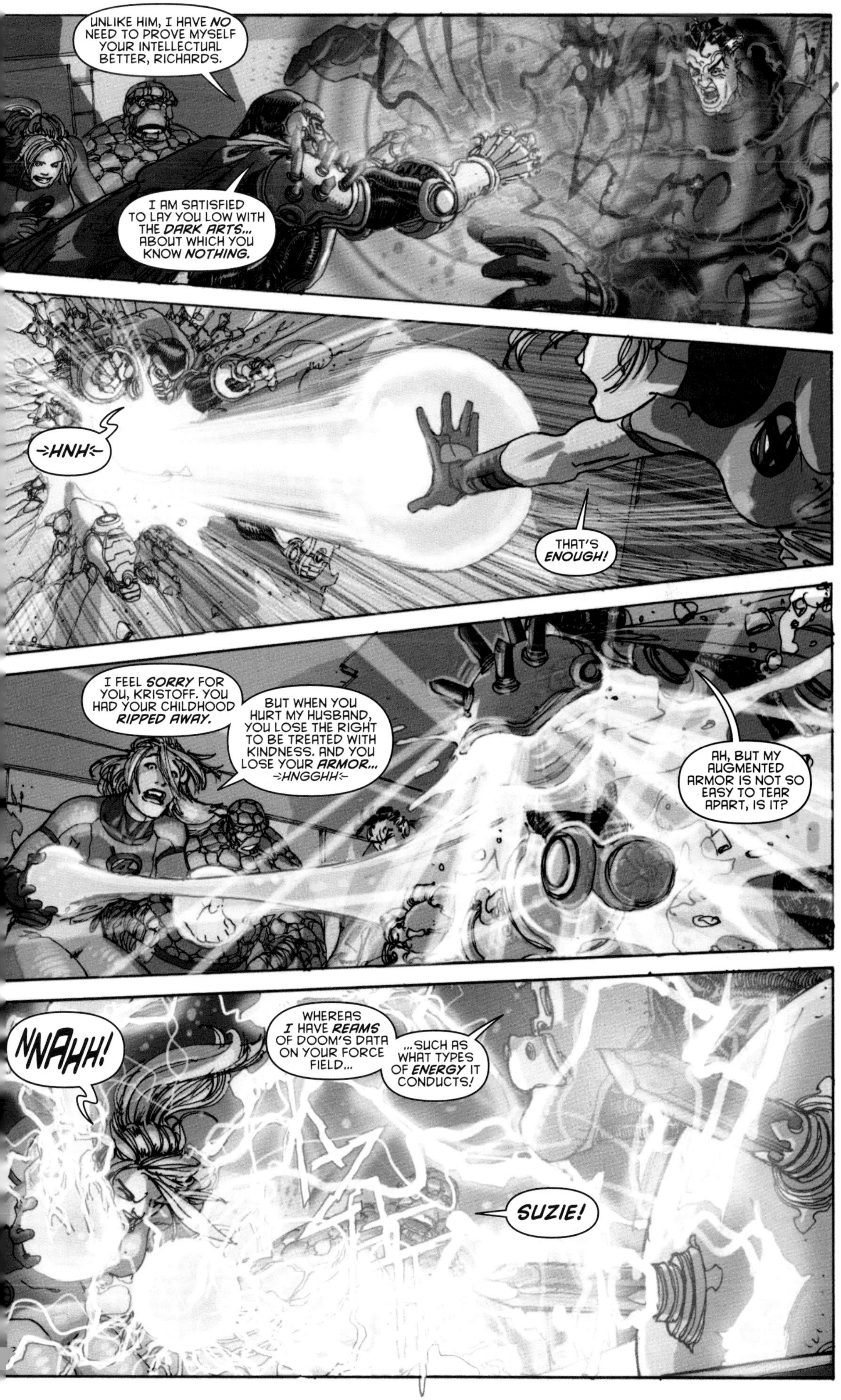
UNLIKE HIM, I HAVE NO NEED TO PROVE MYSELF YOUR INTELLECTUAL BETTER, RICHARDS.
I AM SATISFIED TO LAY YOU LOW WITH THE DARK ARTS... ABOUT WHICH YOU KNOW NOTHING.
HNH
THAT'S ENOUGH!
I FEEL SORRY FOR YOU, KRISTOFF. YOU HAD YOUR CHILDHOOD RIPPED AWAY.
BUT WHEN YOU HURT MY HUSBAND, YOU LOSE THE RIGHT TO BE TREATED WITH KINDNESS. AND YOU LOSE YOUR ARMOR... HNGGHH
AH, BUT MY AUGMENTED ARMOR IS NOT SO EASY TO TEAR APART, IS IT?
WHEREAS I HAVE REAMS OF DOOM'S DATA ON YOUR FORCE FIELD...
...SUCH AS WHAT TYPES OF ENERGY IT CONDUCTS!
NNAHH!
SUZIE!

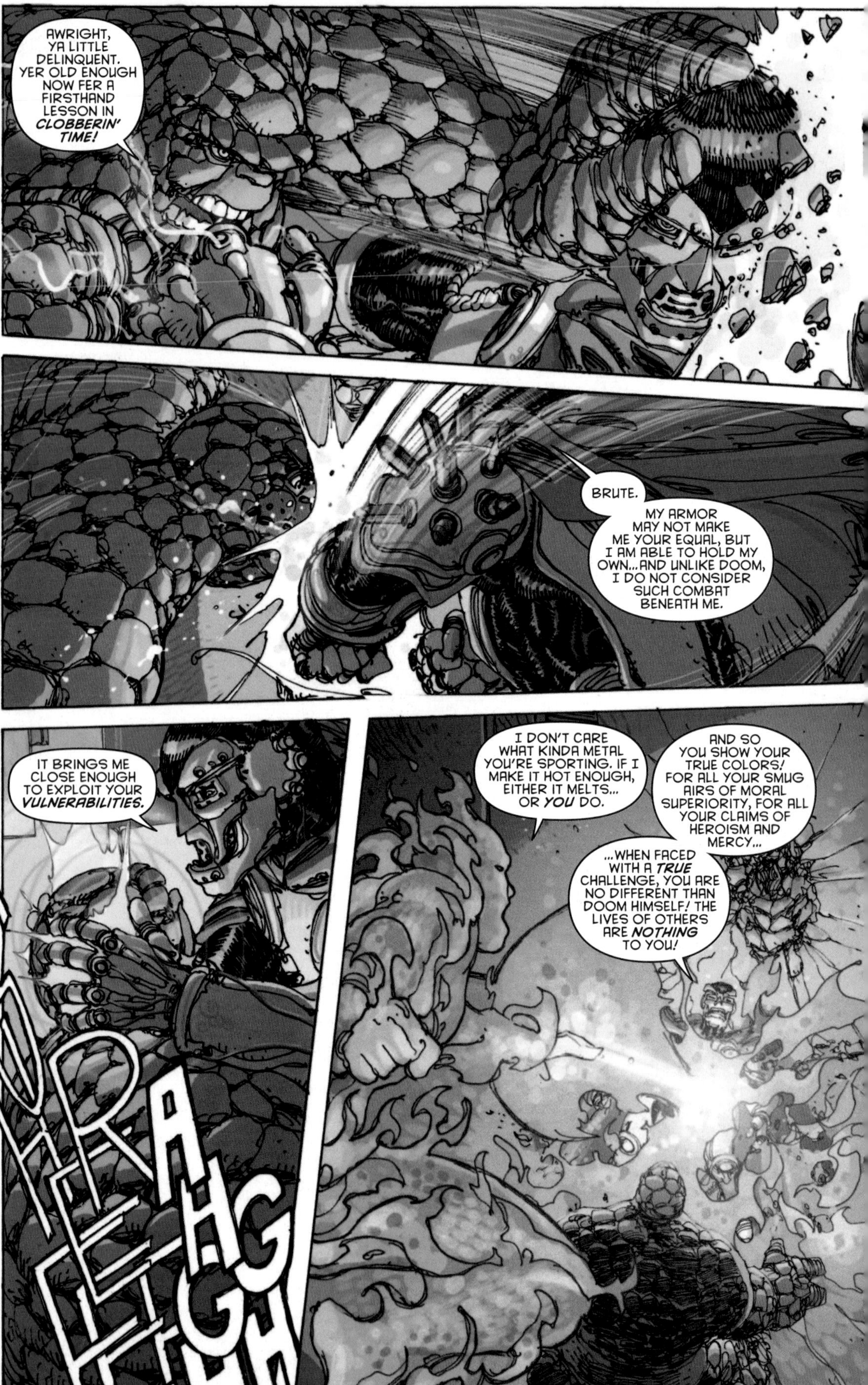
AWRIGHT, YA LITTLE DELINQUENT. YER OLD ENOUGH NOW FER A FIRSTHAND LESSON IN **CLOBBERIN' TIME!**
BRUTE.
MY ARMOR MAY NOT MAKE ME YOUR EQUAL, BUT I AM ABLE TO HOLD MY OWN...AND UNLIKE DOOM, I DO NOT CONSIDER SUCH COMBAT BENEATH ME.
IT BRINGS ME CLOSE ENOUGH TO EXPLOIT YOUR ***VULNERABILITIES.***
I DON'T CARE WHAT KINDA METAL YOU'RE SPORTING. IF I MAKE IT HOT ENOUGH, EITHER IT MELTS... OR ***YOU*** DO.
AND SO YOU SHOW YOUR TRUE COLORS! FOR ALL YOUR SMUG AIRS OF MORAL SUPERIORITY, FOR ALL YOUR CLAIMS OF HEROISM AND MERCY...
...WHEN FACED WITH A ***TRUE*** CHALLENGE, YOU ARE NO DIFFERENT THAN DOOM HIMSELF! THE LIVES OF OTHERS ARE ***NOTHING*** TO YOU!

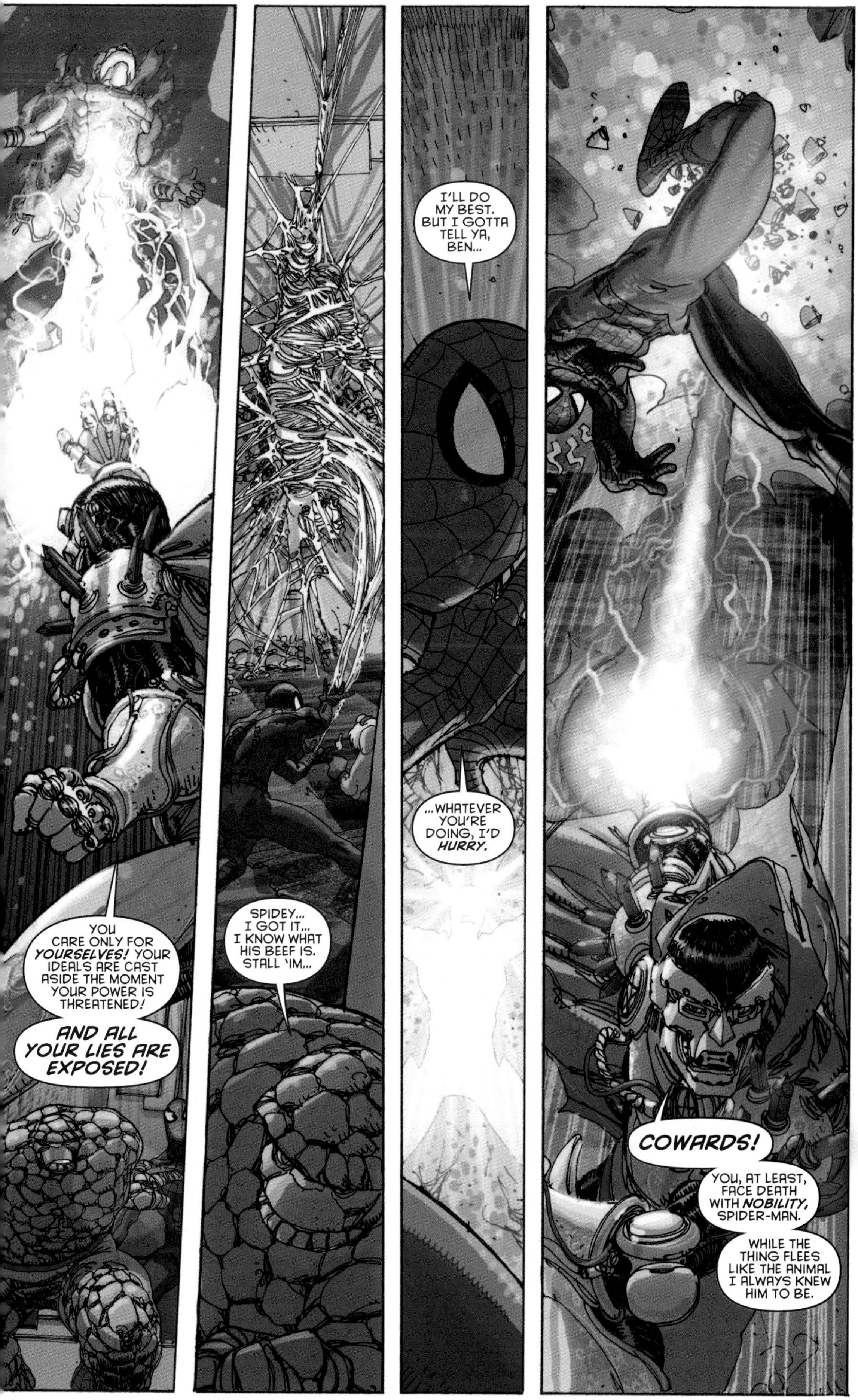
YOU CARE ONLY FOR YOURSELVES! YOUR IDEALS ARE CAST ASIDE THE MOMENT YOUR POWER IS THREATENED!
AND ALL YOUR LIES ARE EXPOSED!
SPIDEY... I GOT IT... I KNOW WHAT HIS BEEF IS. STALL 'IM...
I'LL DO MY BEST. BUT I GOTTA TELL YA, BEN...
...WHATEVER YOU'RE DOING, I'D HURRY.
COWARDS!
YOU, AT LEAST, FACE DEATH WITH NOBILITY, SPIDER-MAN.
WHILE THE THING FLEES LIKE THE ANIMAL I ALWAYS KNEW HIM TO BE.

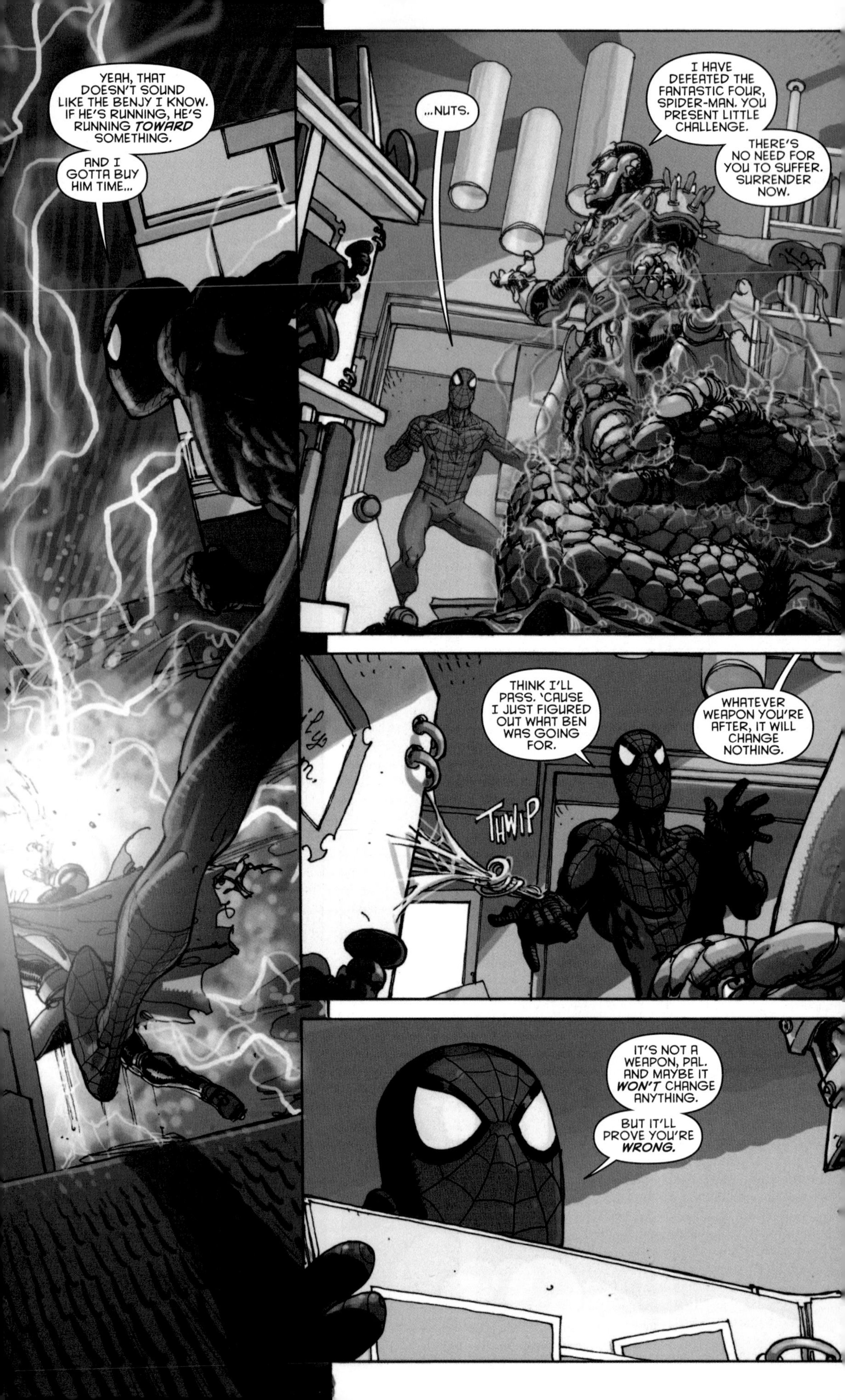
YEAH, THAT DOESN'T SOUND LIKE THE BENJY I KNOW. IF HE'S RUNNING, HE'S RUNNING *TOWARD* SOMETHING.
AND I GOTTA BUY HIM TIME...
...NUTS.
I HAVE DEFEATED THE FANTASTIC FOUR, SPIDER-MAN. YOU PRESENT LITTLE CHALLENGE.
THERE'S NO NEED FOR YOU TO SUFFER. SURRENDER NOW.
THINK I'LL PASS. 'CAUSE I JUST FIGURED OUT WHAT BEN WAS GOING FOR.
WHATEVER WEAPON YOU'RE AFTER, IT WILL CHANGE NOTHING.
THWIP
IT'S NOT A WEAPON, PAL. AND MAYBE IT *WON'T* CHANGE ANYTHING.
BUT IT'LL PROVE YOU'RE *WRONG.*

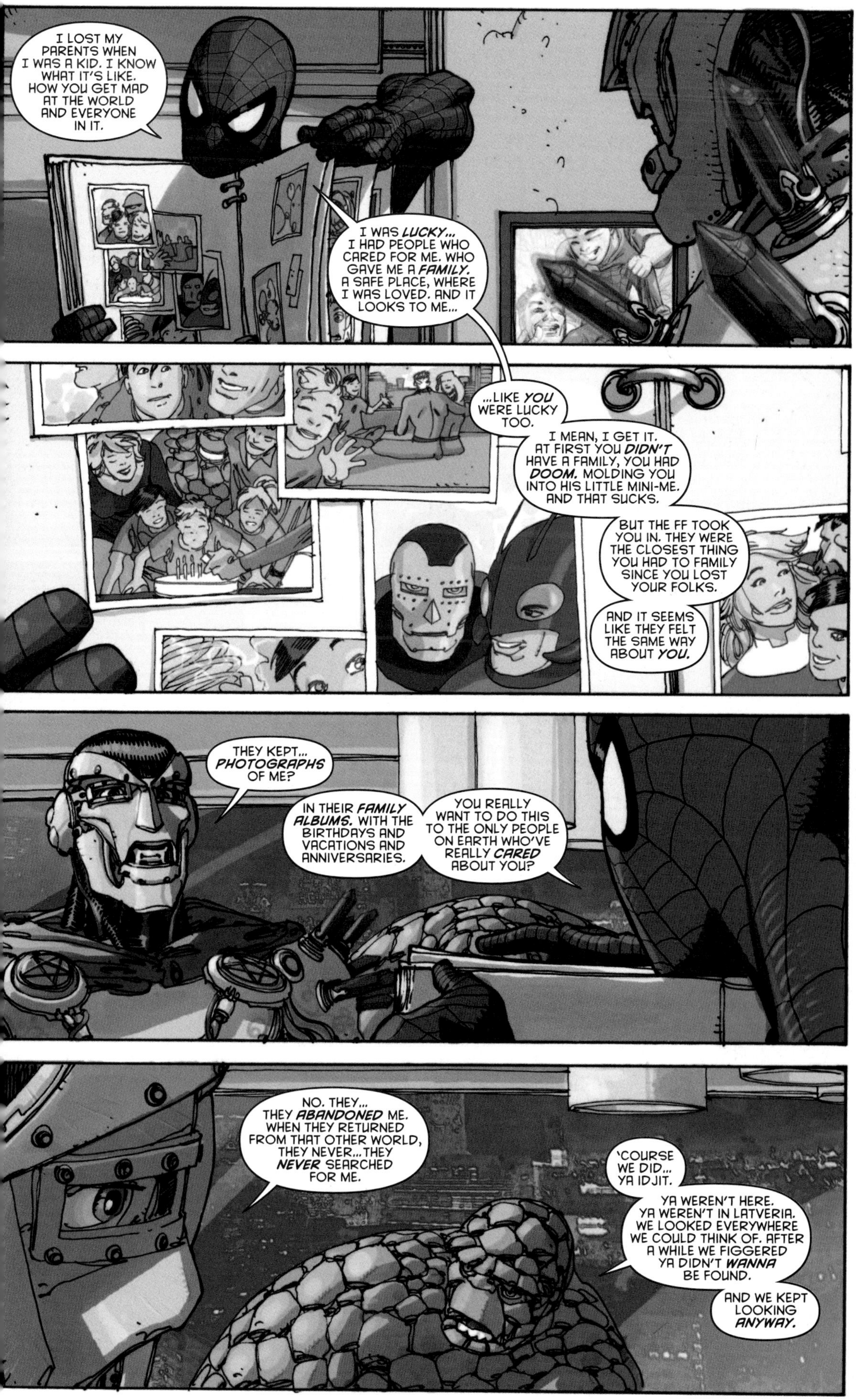
I LOST MY PARENTS WHEN I WAS A KID. I KNOW WHAT IT'S LIKE. HOW YOU GET MAD AT THE WORLD AND EVERYONE IN IT.
I WAS LUCKY... I HAD PEOPLE WHO CARED FOR ME. WHO GAVE ME A FAMILY. A SAFE PLACE, WHERE I WAS LOVED. AND IT LOOKS TO ME...
...LIKE YOU WERE LUCKY TOO.
I MEAN, I GET IT. AT FIRST YOU DIDN'T HAVE A FAMILY, YOU HAD DOOM. MOLDING YOU INTO HIS LITTLE MINI-ME. AND THAT SUCKS.
BUT THE FF TOOK YOU IN. THEY WERE THE CLOSEST THING YOU HAD TO FAMILY SINCE YOU LOST YOUR FOLKS.
AND IT SEEMS LIKE THEY FELT THE SAME WAY ABOUT YOU.
THEY KEPT... PHOTOGRAPHS OF ME?
IN THEIR FAMILY ALBUMS. WITH THE BIRTHDAYS AND VACATIONS AND ANNIVERSARIES.
YOU REALLY WANT TO DO THIS TO THE ONLY PEOPLE ON EARTH WHO'VE REALLY CARED ABOUT YOU?
NO. THEY... THEY ABANDONED ME. WHEN THEY RETURNED FROM THAT OTHER WORLD, THEY NEVER... THEY NEVER SEARCHED FOR ME.
'COURSE WE DID... YA IDJIT.
YA WEREN'T HERE. YA WEREN'T IN LATVERIA. WE LOOKED EVERYWHERE WE COULD THINK OF. AFTER A WHILE WE FIGGERED YA DIDN'T WANNA BE FOUND.
AND WE KEPT LOOKING ANYWAY.

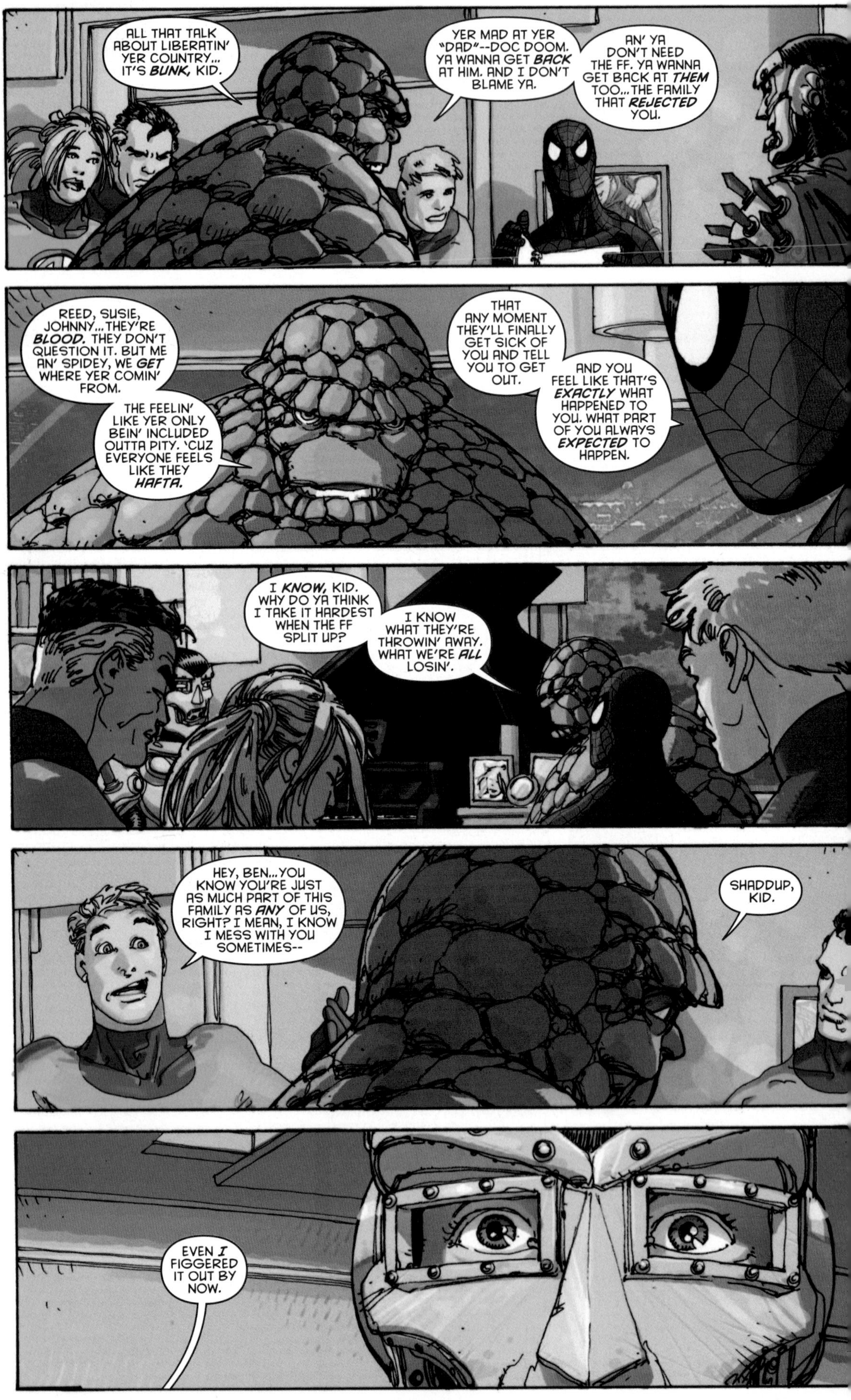
ALL THAT TALK ABOUT LIBERATIN' YER COUNTRY... IT'S BUNK, KID.
YER MAD AT YER "DAD"--DOC DOOM. YA WANNA GET BACK AT HIM. AND I DON'T BLAME YA.
AN' YA DON'T NEED THE FF. YA WANNA GET BACK AT THEM TOO...THE FAMILY THAT REJECTED YOU.
REED, SUSIE, JOHNNY...THEY'RE BLOOD. THEY DON'T QUESTION IT. BUT ME AN' SPIDEY, WE GET WHERE YER COMIN' FROM.
THE FEELIN' LIKE YER ONLY BEIN' INCLUDED OUTTA PITY. 'CUZ EVERYONE FEELS LIKE THEY HAFTA.
THAT ANY MOMENT THEY'LL FINALLY GET SICK OF YOU AND TELL YOU TO GET OUT.
AND YOU FEEL LIKE THAT'S EXACTLY WHAT HAPPENED TO YOU. WHAT PART OF YOU ALWAYS EXPECTED TO HAPPEN.
I KNOW, KID. WHY DO YA THINK I TAKE IT HARDEST WHEN THE FF SPLIT UP?
I KNOW WHAT THEY'RE THROWIN' AWAY. WHAT WE'RE ALL LOSIN'.
HEY, BEN...YOU KNOW YOU'RE JUST AS MUCH PART OF THIS FAMILY AS ANY OF US, RIGHT? I MEAN, I KNOW I MESS WITH YOU SOMETIMES--
SHADDUP, KID.
EVEN I FIGGERED IT OUT BY NOW.

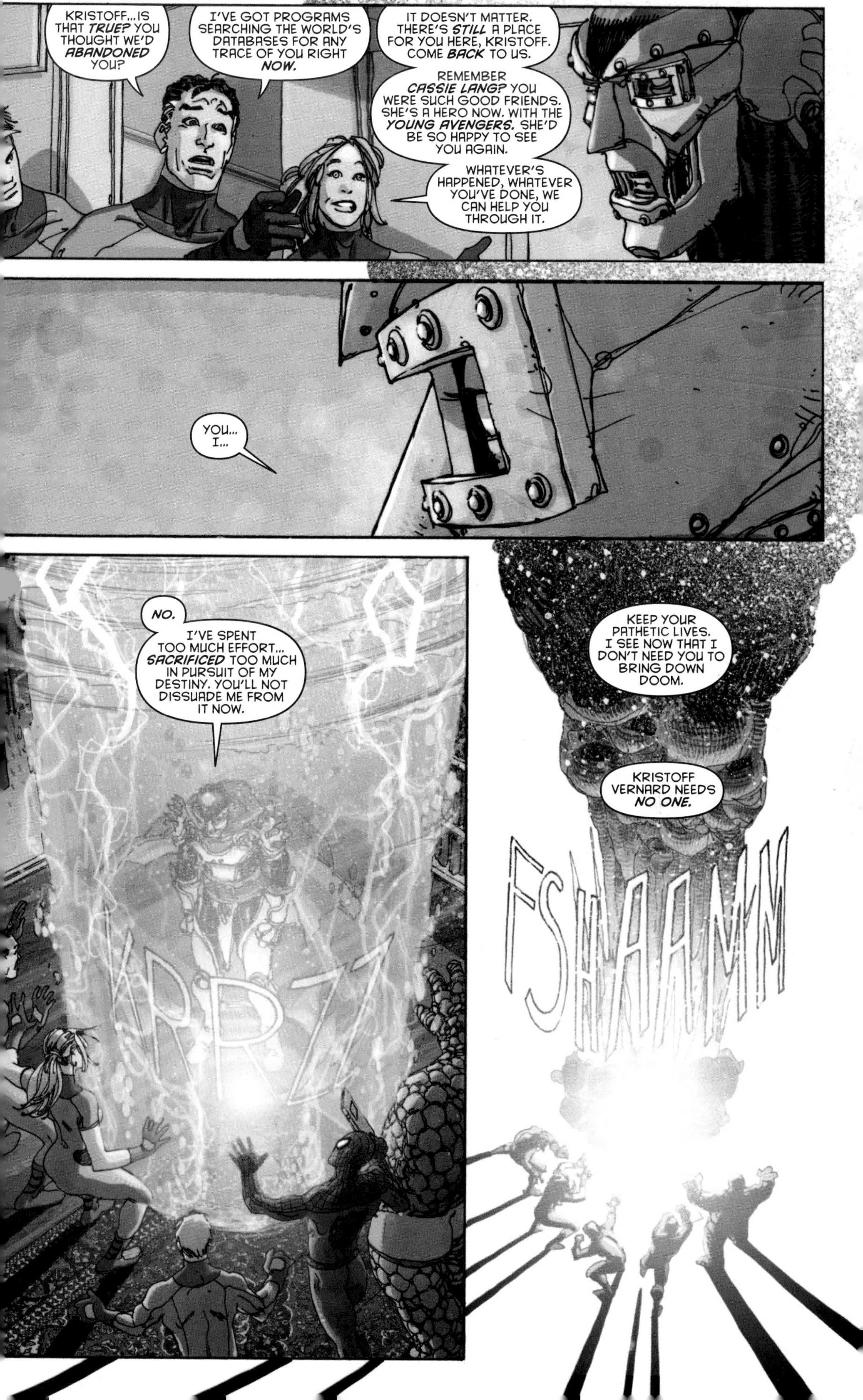
KRISTOFF...IS THAT TRUE? YOU THOUGHT WE'D ABANDONED YOU?
I'VE GOT PROGRAMS SEARCHING THE WORLD'S DATABASES FOR ANY TRACE OF YOU RIGHT NOW.
IT DOESN'T MATTER. THERE'S STILL A PLACE FOR YOU HERE, KRISTOFF. COME BACK TO US.
REMEMBER CASSIE LANG? YOU WERE SUCH GOOD FRIENDS. SHE'S A HERO NOW. WITH THE YOUNG AVENGERS. SHE'D BE SO HAPPY TO SEE YOU AGAIN.
WHATEVER'S HAPPENED, WHATEVER YOU'VE DONE, WE CAN HELP YOU THROUGH IT.
YOU... I...
NO.
I'VE SPENT TOO MUCH EFFORT... SACRIFICED TOO MUCH IN PURSUIT OF MY DESTINY. YOU'LL NOT DISSUADE ME FROM IT NOW.
KRRZZ
KEEP YOUR PATHETIC LIVES. I SEE NOW THAT I DON'T NEED YOU TO BRING DOWN DOOM.
KRISTOFF VERNARD NEEDS NO ONE.
FSHAAMM

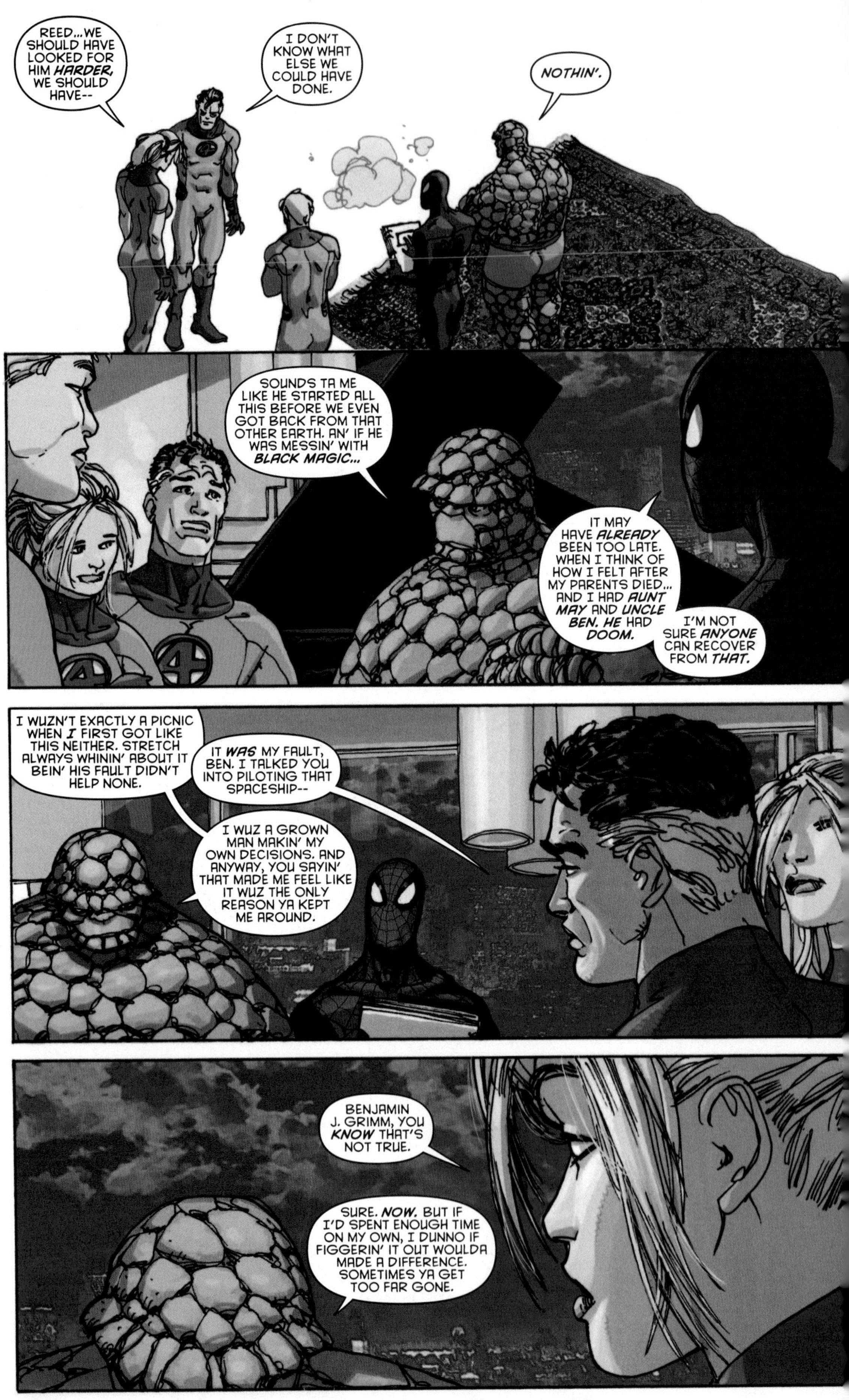
REED...WE SHOULD HAVE LOOKED FOR HIM HARDER, WE SHOULD HAVE--
I DON'T KNOW WHAT ELSE WE COULD HAVE DONE.
NOTHIN'.
SOUNDS TA ME LIKE HE STARTED ALL THIS BEFORE WE EVEN GOT BACK FROM THAT OTHER EARTH. AN' IF HE WAS MESSIN' WITH BLACK MAGIC...
IT MAY HAVE ALREADY BEEN TOO LATE. WHEN I THINK OF HOW I FELT AFTER MY PARENTS DIED... AND I HAD AUNT MAY AND UNCLE BEN. HE HAD DOOM.
I'M NOT SURE ANYONE CAN RECOVER FROM THAT.
I WUZN'T EXACTLY A PICNIC WHEN I FIRST GOT LIKE THIS NEITHER. STRETCH ALWAYS WHININ' ABOUT IT BEIN' HIS FAULT DIDN'T HELP NONE.
IT WAS MY FAULT, BEN. I TALKED YOU INTO PILOTING THAT SPACESHIP--
I WUZ A GROWN MAN MAKIN' MY OWN DECISIONS. AND ANYWAY, YOU SAYIN' THAT MADE ME FEEL LIKE IT WUZ THE ONLY REASON YA KEPT ME AROUND.
BENJAMIN J. GRIMM, YOU KNOW THAT'S NOT TRUE.
SURE. NOW. BUT IF I'D SPENT ENOUGH TIME ON MY OWN, I DUNNO IF FIGGERIN' IT OUT WOULDA MADE A DIFFERENCE. SOMETIMES YA GET TOO FAR GONE.

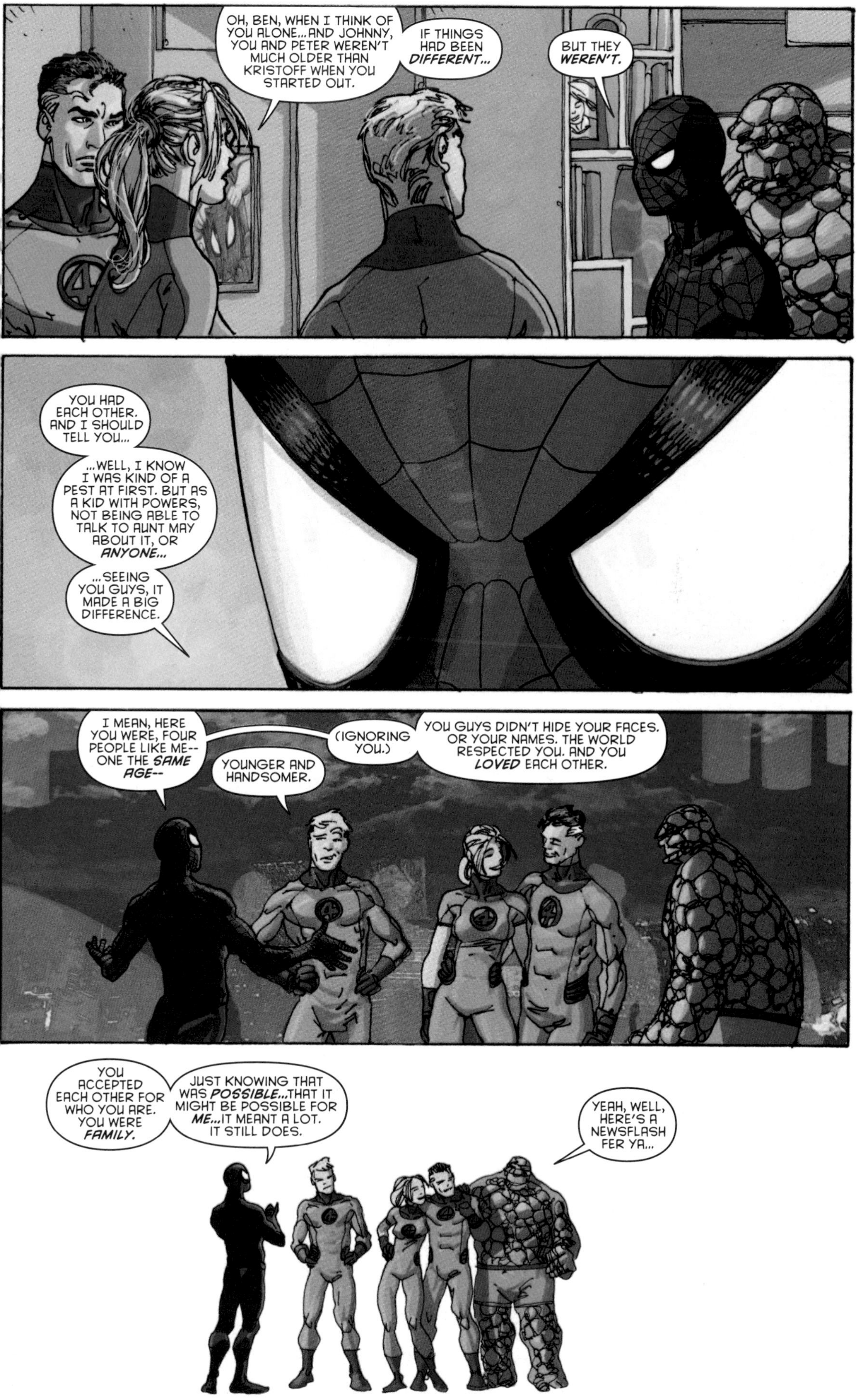
OH, BEN, WHEN I THINK OF YOU ALONE...AND JOHNNY, YOU AND PETER WEREN'T MUCH OLDER THAN KRISTOFF WHEN YOU STARTED OUT.
IF THINGS HAD BEEN *DIFFERENT...*
BUT THEY *WEREN'T.*
YOU HAD EACH OTHER. AND I SHOULD TELL YOU...
...WELL, I KNOW I WAS KIND OF A PEST AT FIRST. BUT AS A KID WITH POWERS, NOT BEING ABLE TO TALK TO AUNT MAY ABOUT IT, OR *ANYONE...*
...SEEING YOU GUYS, IT MADE A BIG DIFFERENCE.
I MEAN, HERE YOU WERE, FOUR PEOPLE LIKE ME--ONE THE *SAME AGE--*
YOUNGER AND HANDSOMER.
(IGNORING YOU.)
YOU GUYS DIDN'T HIDE YOUR FACES. OR YOUR NAMES. THE WORLD RESPECTED YOU. AND YOU *LOVED* EACH OTHER.
YOU ACCEPTED EACH OTHER FOR WHO YOU ARE. YOU WERE *FAMILY.*
JUST KNOWING THAT WAS *POSSIBLE...*THAT IT MIGHT BE POSSIBLE FOR *ME...*IT MEANT A LOT. IT STILL DOES.
YEAH, WELL, HERE'S A NEWSFLASH FER YA...

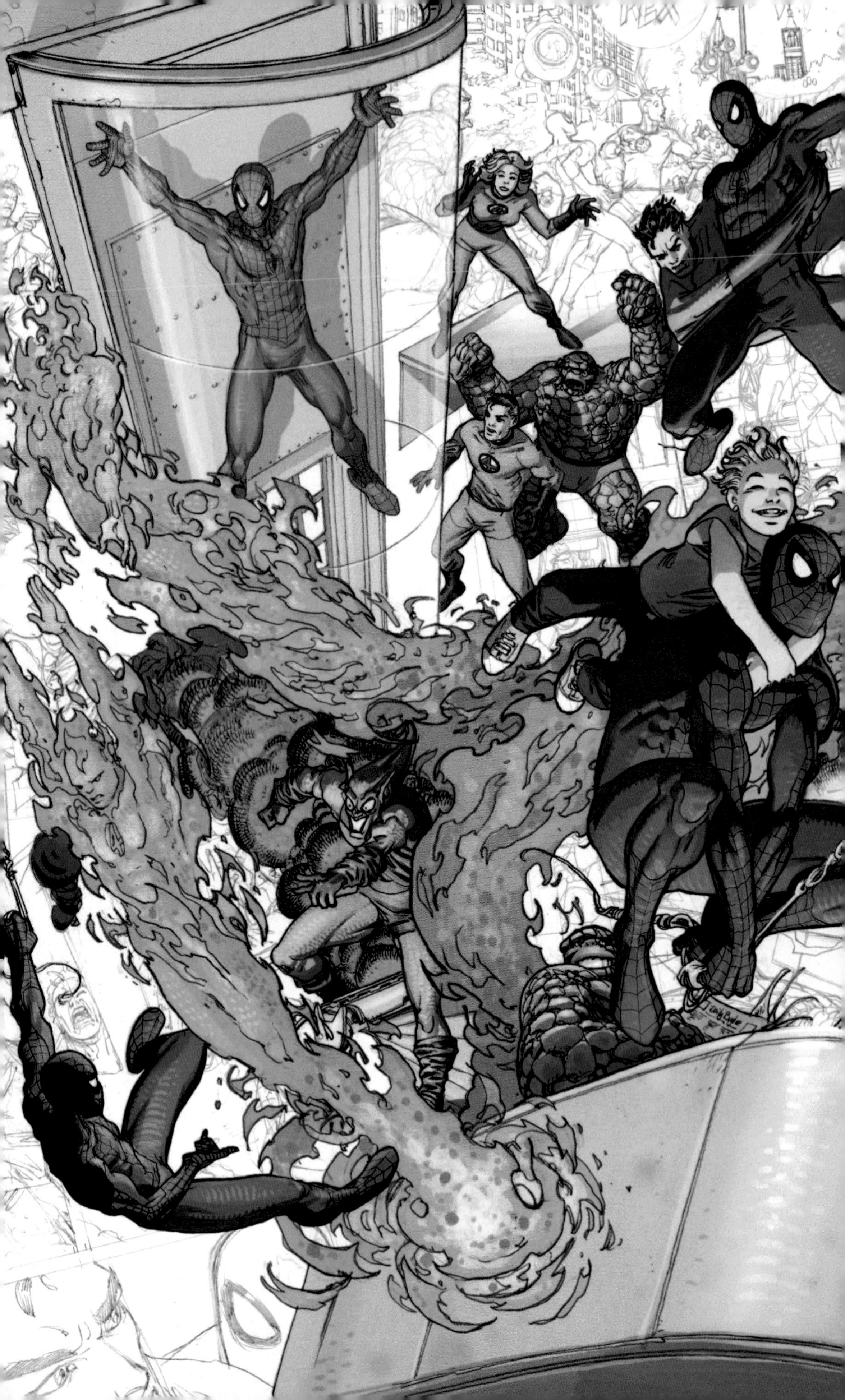

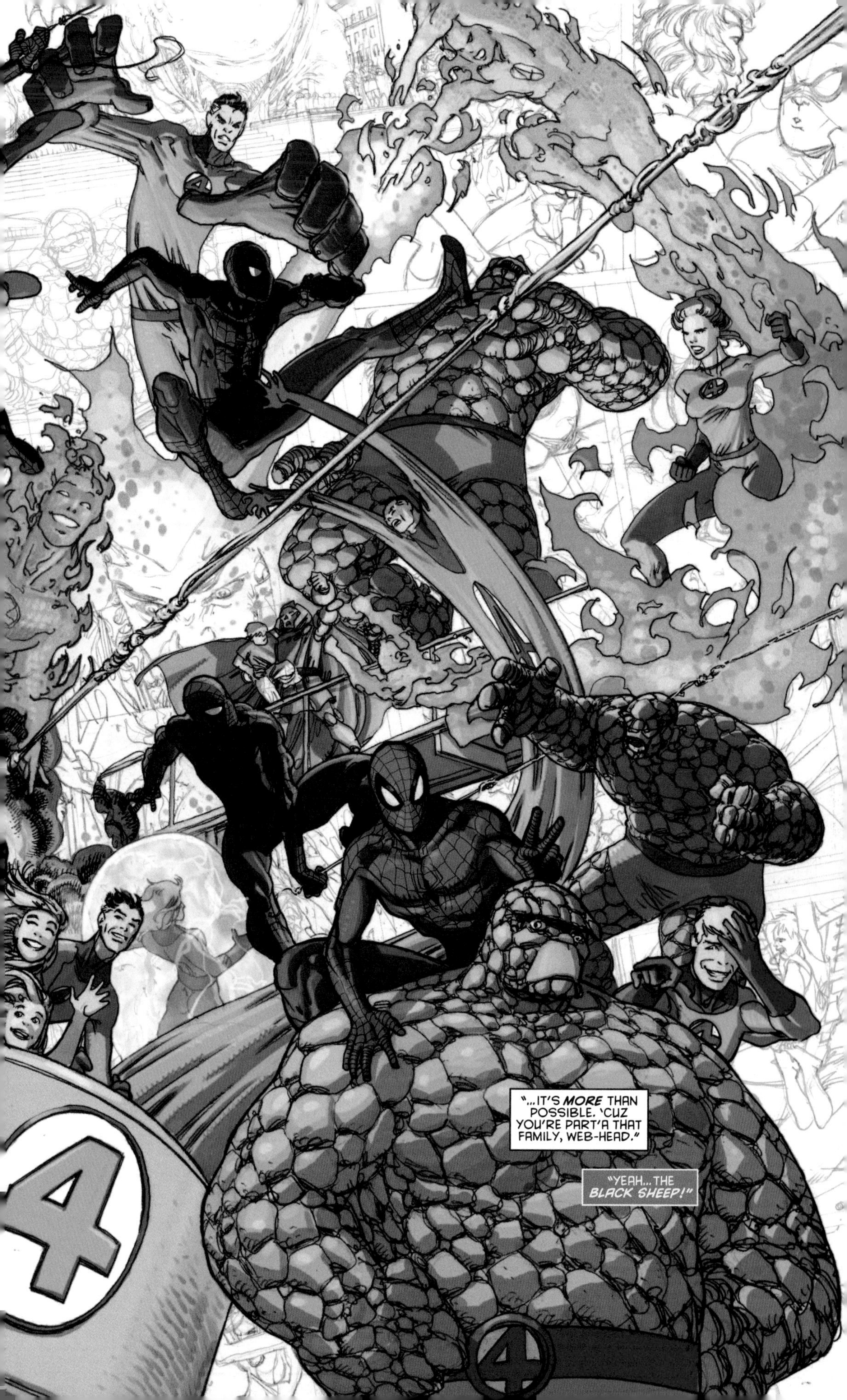
"...IT'S MORE THAN POSSIBLE. 'CUZ YOU'RE PART'A THAT FAMILY, WEB-HEAD."
"YEAH... THE BLACK SHEEP!"

BEN'S RIGHT, PETER. I KNOW YOU HAVE YOUR AUNT, BUT AS YOU SAID, SHE DOESN'T KNOW ABOUT...*THIS* SIDE OF YOUR LIFE.

AND I ENJOY HAVING SOMEONE TO TALK TO ABOUT MY EXPERIMENTS WHOSE EYES DON'T GLAZE OVER.

JOHNNY!

WHAT? IT'S HOW I EXPRESS THE LOVE!

PLUS THE KIDS ADORE YOU. AND WE'RE PRETTY FOND OF YOU OURSELVES.

THAT MEANS A LOT TO ME, SUE. I...I...

...I THINK I'VE GOT SOME WEBBING IN MY EYE...

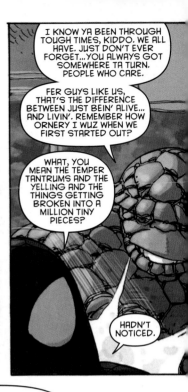

I KNOW YA BEEN THROUGH TOUGH TIMES, KIDDO. WE ALL HAVE. JUST DON'T EVER FORGET...YOU ALWAYS GOT SOMEWHERE TA TURN. PEOPLE WHO CARE.

FER GUYS LIKE US, THAT'S THE DIFFERENCE BETWEEN JUST BEIN' ALIVE... AND LIVIN'. REMEMBER HOW ORNERY I WUZ WHEN WE FIRST STARTED OUT?

WHAT, YOU MEAN THE TEMPER TANTRUMS AND THE YELLING AND THE THINGS GETTING BROKEN INTO A MILLION TINY PIECES?

HADN'T NOTICED.

YEAH, WE CAN LAUGH ABOUT IT NOW. BUT IF IT WUZN'T FER THESE FOLKS HERE...I DON'T KNOW WHERE I'D BE TODAY. I KNOW IT WOULDN'T BE A GOOD PLACE. NOT FER ME...AN' NOT FER ANYONE ELSE.

SO WHATEVER HAPPENS, PETE... WHATEVER LIFE HITS YA WITH...REMEMBER ONE THING. NO MATTER WHAT, YA GOT US. AN' NOBODY CAN EVER TAKE THAT AWAY.

"EXCEPT YOU."

END

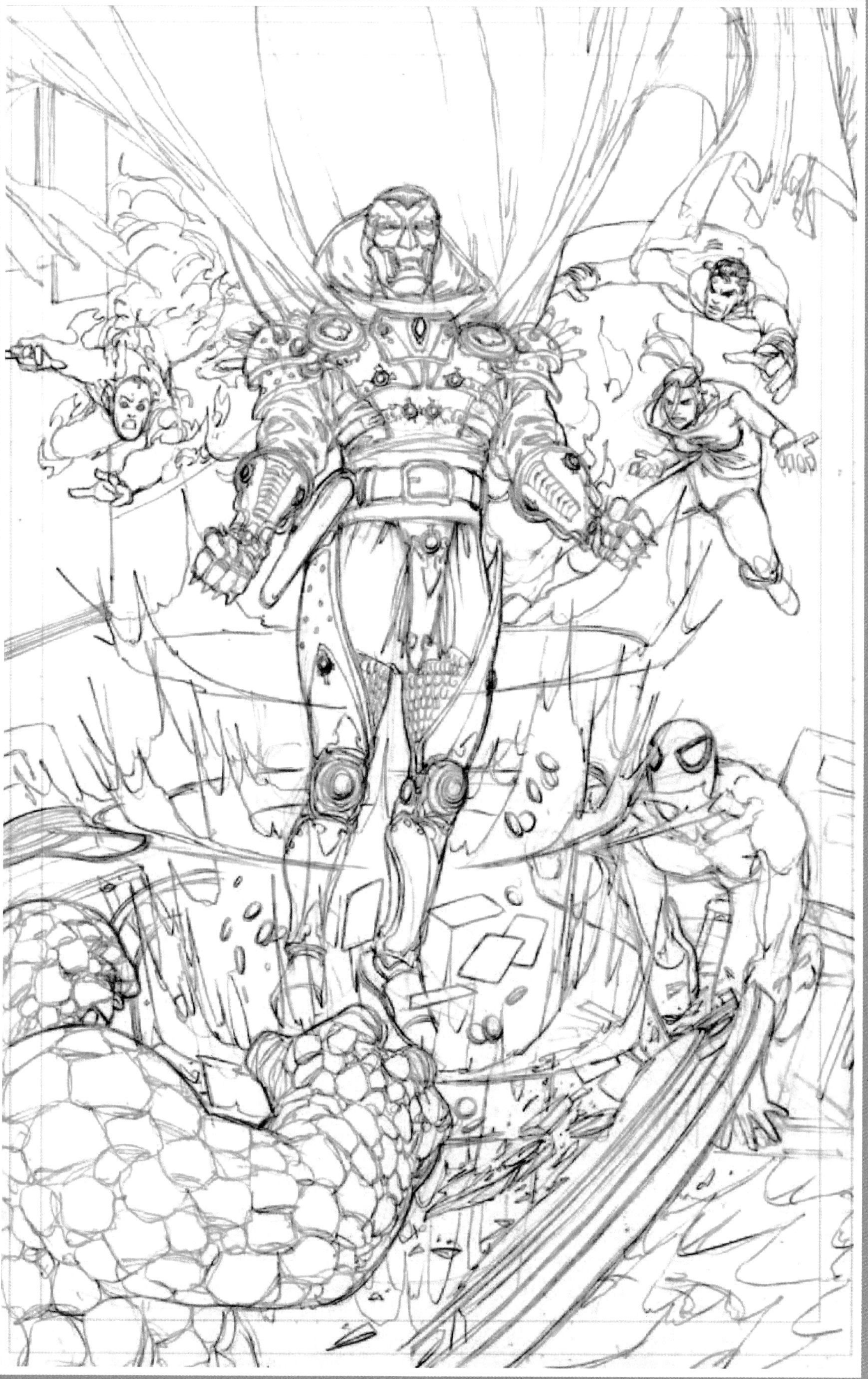

ISSUE #4, PAGE 4 UNUSED PENCILS

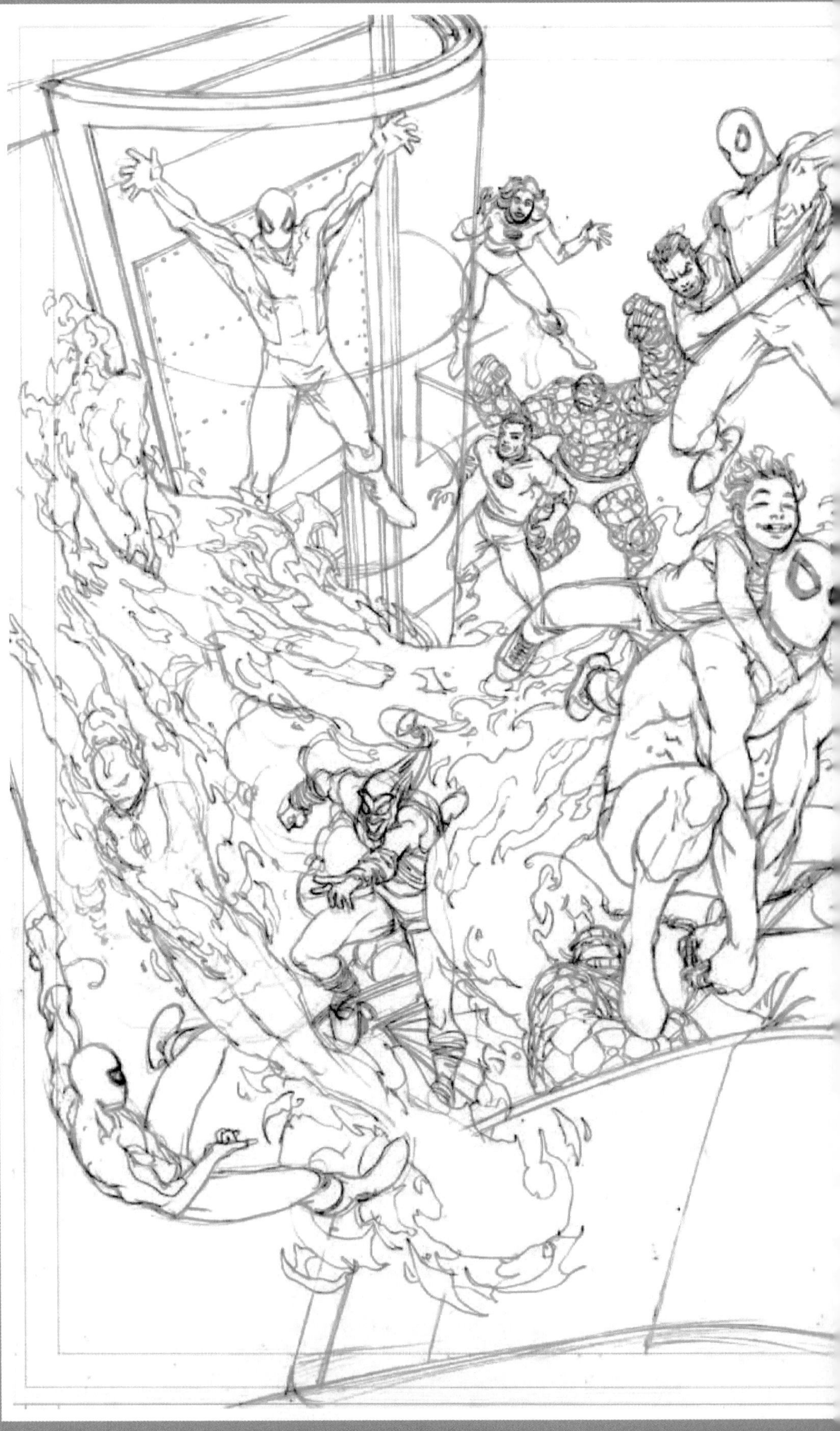

ISSUE #4, PAGES 20-21 PENCILS

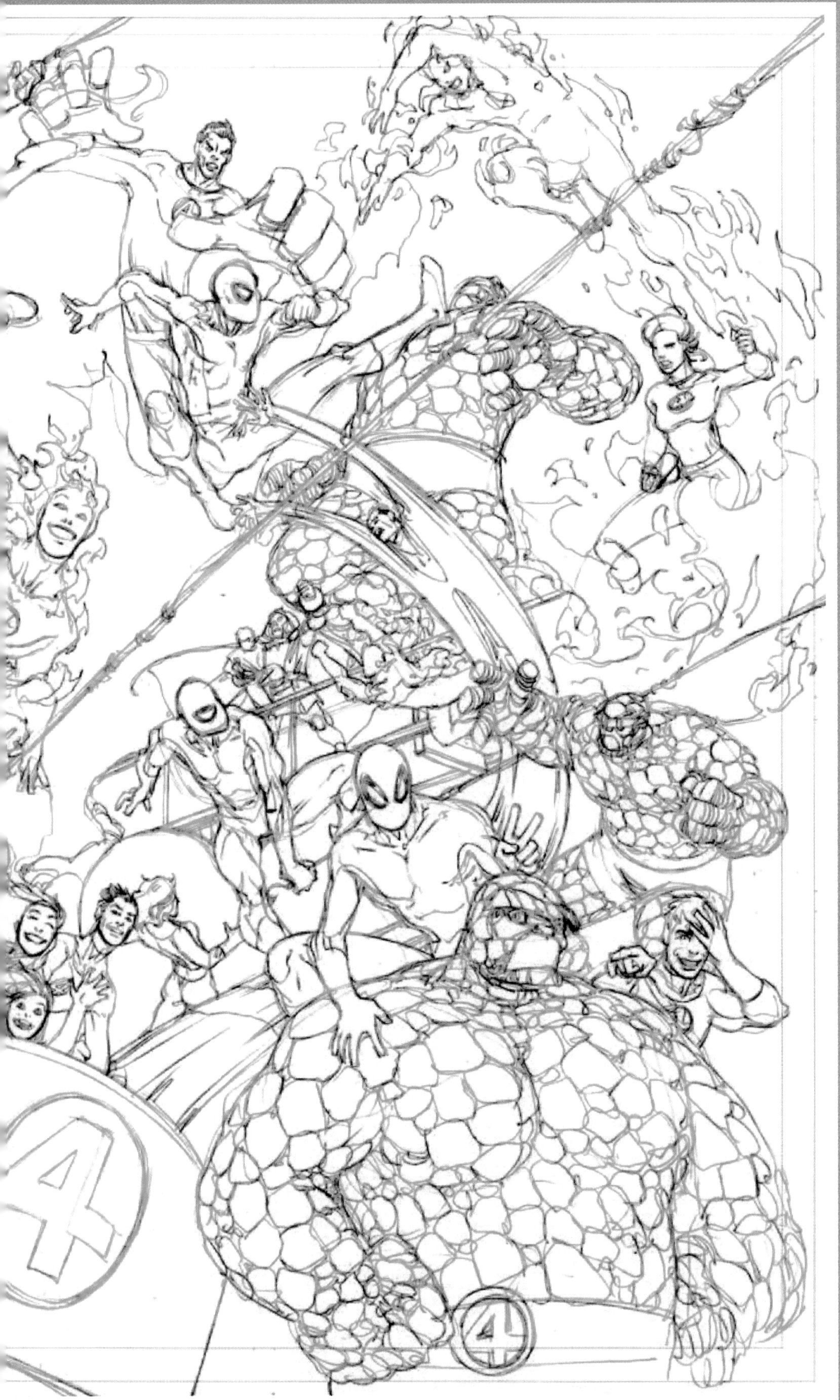

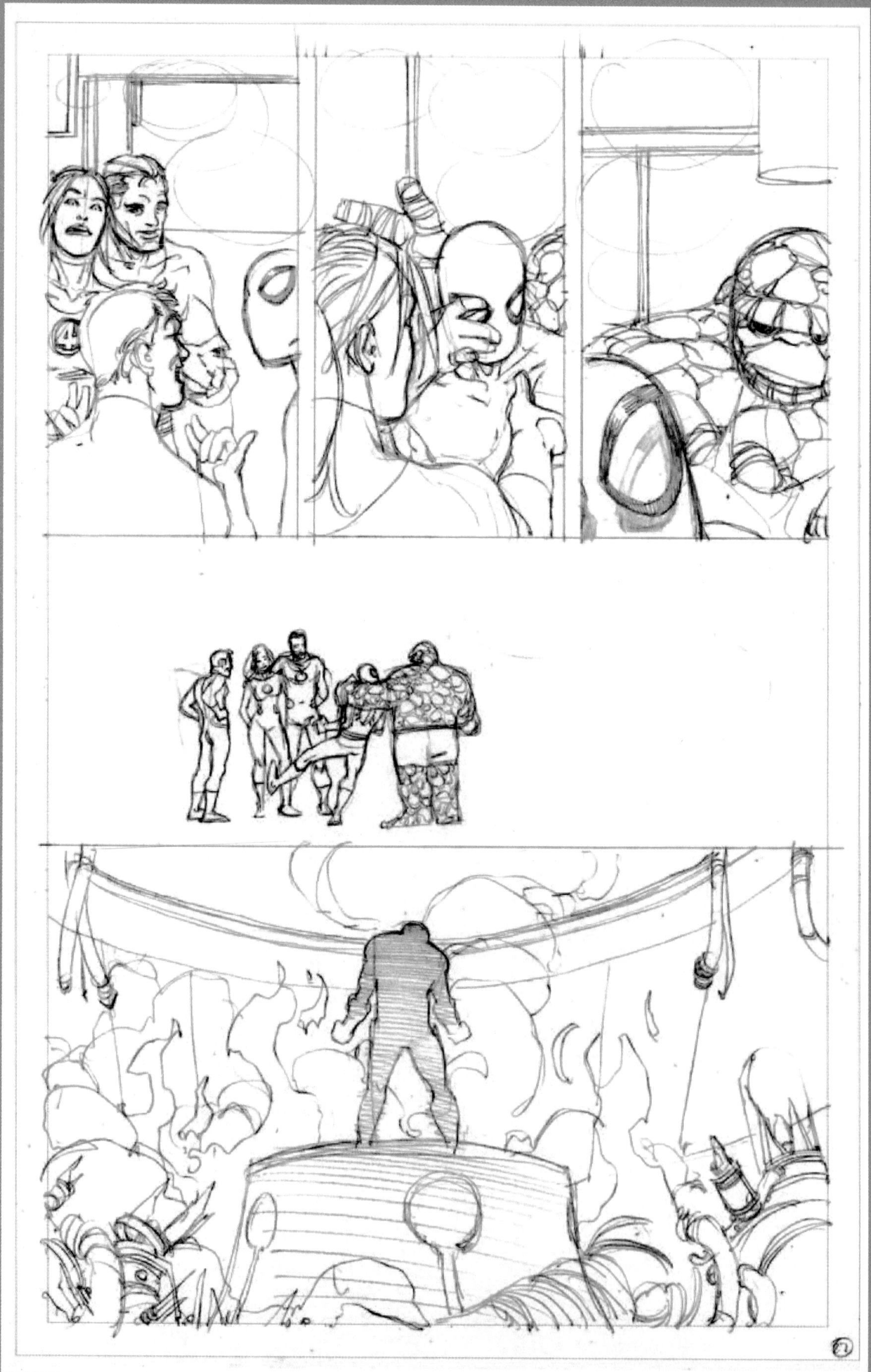

ISSUE #4, PAGE 22 PENCILS

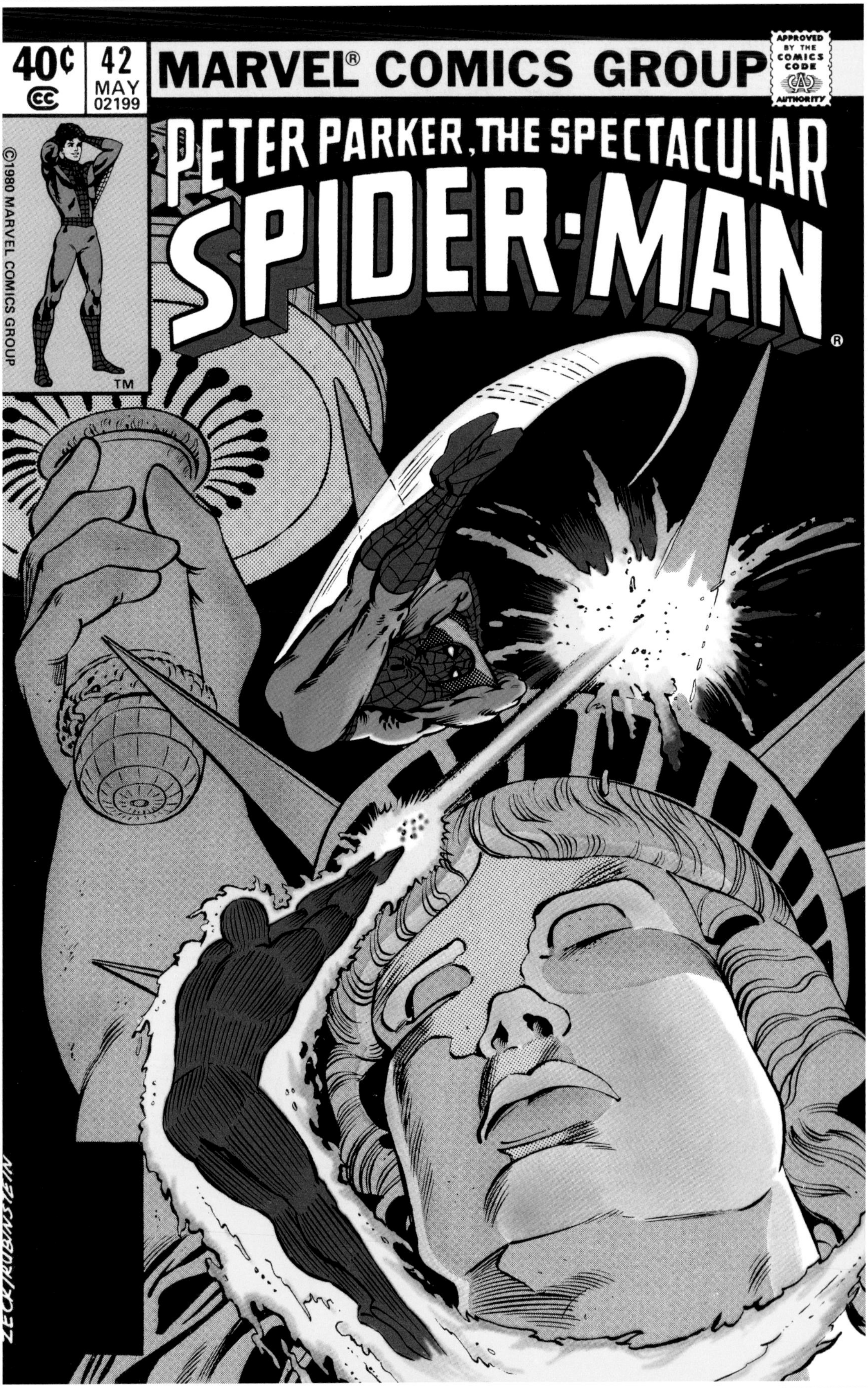
40¢
CC
42
MAY
02199
MARVEL® COMICS GROUP
APPROVED BY THE COMICS CODE AUTHORITY
PETER PARKER, THE SPECTACULAR
SPIDER-MAN®
©1980 MARVEL COMICS GROUP
TM
ZECK/RUBINSTEIN

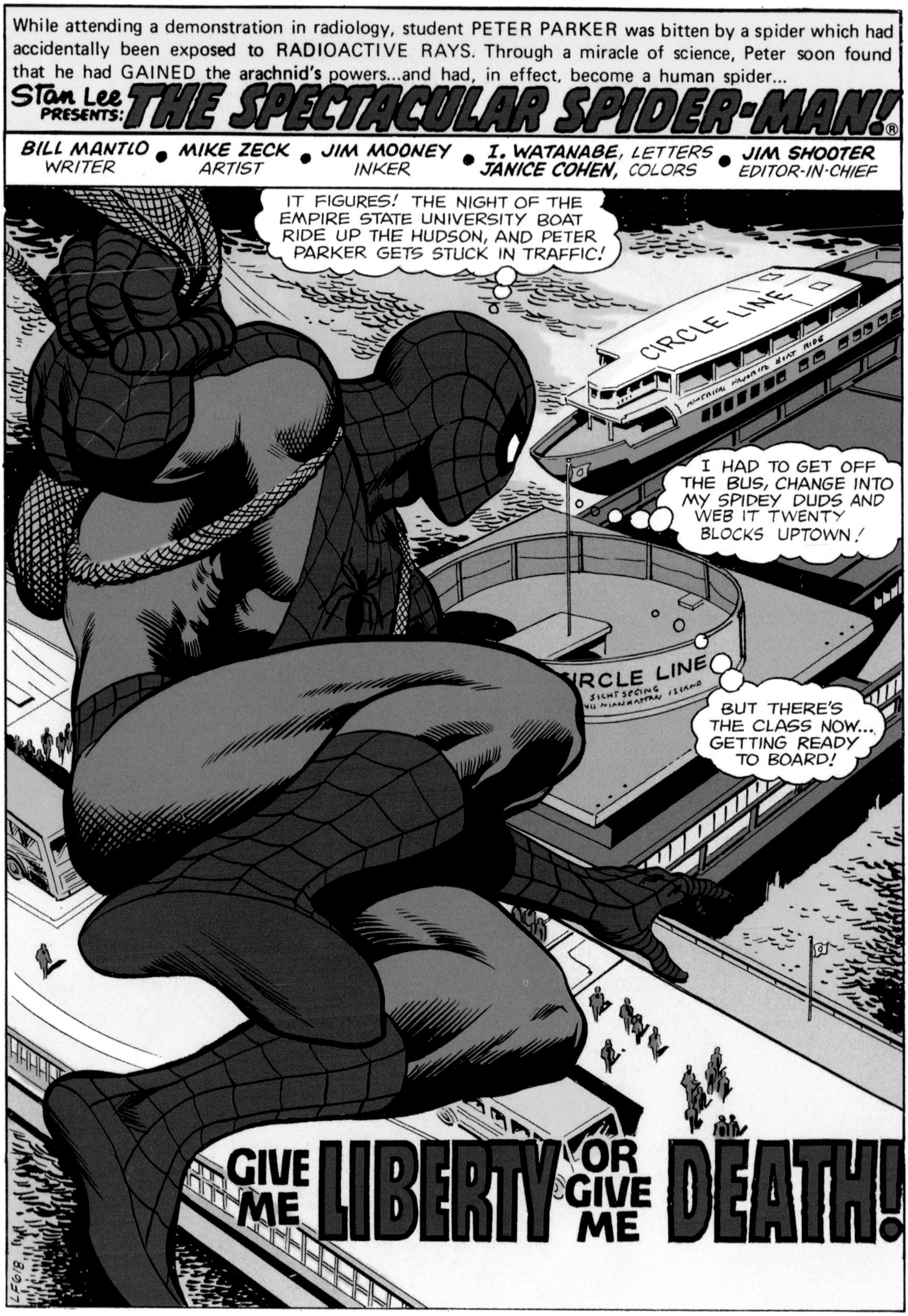
While attending a demonstration in radiology, student PETER PARKER was bitten by a spider which had accidentally been exposed to RADIOACTIVE RAYS. Through a miracle of science, Peter soon found that he had GAINED the arachnid's powers...and had, in effect, become a human spider...
STAN LEE PRESENTS: THE SPECTACULAR SPIDER-MAN!®
BILL MANTLO WRITER • MIKE ZECK ARTIST • JIM MOONEY INKER • I. WATANABE, LETTERS JANICE COHEN, COLORS • JIM SHOOTER EDITOR-IN-CHIEF
IT FIGURES! THE NIGHT OF THE EMPIRE STATE UNIVERSITY BOAT RIDE UP THE HUDSON, AND PETER PARKER GETS STUCK IN TRAFFIC!
CIRCLE LINE
I HAD TO GET OFF THE BUS, CHANGE INTO MY SPIDEY DUDS AND WEB IT TWENTY BLOCKS UPTOWN!
BUT THERE'S THE CLASS NOW... GETTING READY TO BOARD!
GIVE ME LIBERTY OR GIVE ME DEATH!

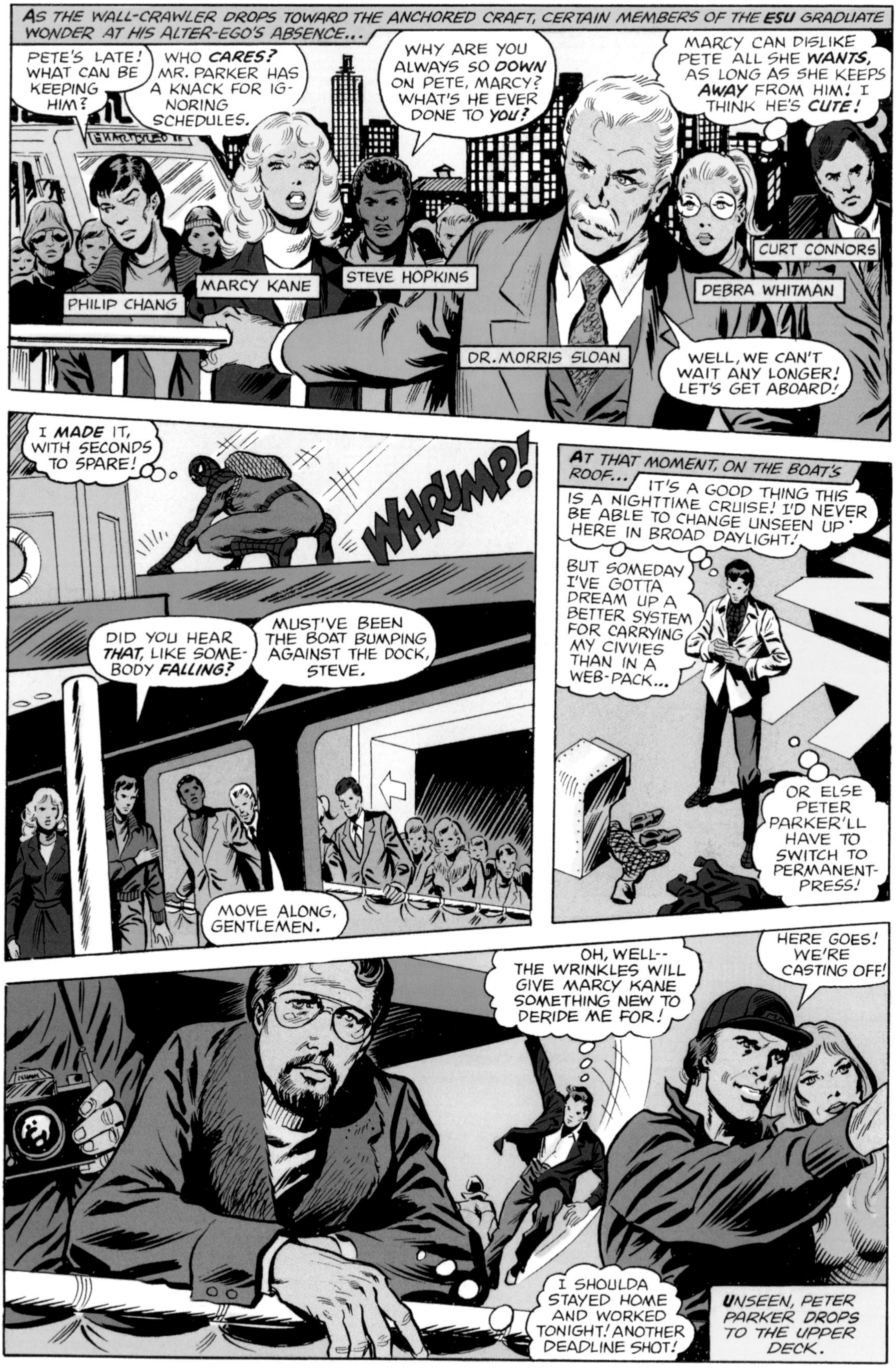
AS THE WALL-CRAWLER DROPS TOWARD THE ANCHORED CRAFT, CERTAIN MEMBERS OF THE ESU GRADUATE WONDER AT HIS ALTER-EGO'S ABSENCE...
PETE'S LATE! WHAT CAN BE KEEPING HIM?
WHO CARES? MR. PARKER HAS A KNACK FOR IG-NORING SCHEDULES.
WHY ARE YOU ALWAYS SO DOWN ON PETE, MARCY? WHAT'S HE EVER DONE TO YOU?
MARCY CAN DISLIKE PETE ALL SHE WANTS, AS LONG AS SHE KEEPS AWAY FROM HIM! I THINK HE'S CUTE!
PHILIP CHANG
MARCY KANE
STEVE HOPKINS
DR. MORRIS SLOAN
DEBRA WHITMAN
CURT CONNORS
WELL, WE CAN'T WAIT ANY LONGER! LET'S GET ABOARD!
I MADE IT, WITH SECONDS TO SPARE!
WHRUMP!
DID YOU HEAR THAT, LIKE SOME-BODY FALLING?
MUST'VE BEEN THE BOAT BUMPING AGAINST THE DOCK, STEVE.
MOVE ALONG, GENTLEMEN.
AT THAT MOMENT, ON THE BOAT'S ROOF...
IT'S A GOOD THING THIS IS A NIGHTTIME CRUISE! I'D NEVER BE ABLE TO CHANGE UNSEEN UP HERE IN BROAD DAYLIGHT!
BUT SOMEDAY I'VE GOTTA DREAM UP A BETTER SYSTEM FOR CARRYING MY CIVVIES THAN IN A WEB-PACK...
OR ELSE PETER PARKER'LL HAVE TO SWITCH TO PERMANENT-PRESS!
OH, WELL-- THE WRINKLES WILL GIVE MARCY KANE SOMETHING NEW TO DERIDE ME FOR!
HERE GOES! WE'RE CASTING OFF!
I SHOULDA STAYED HOME AND WORKED TONIGHT! ANOTHER DEADLINE SHOT!
UNSEEN, PETER PARKER DROPS TO THE UPPER DECK.

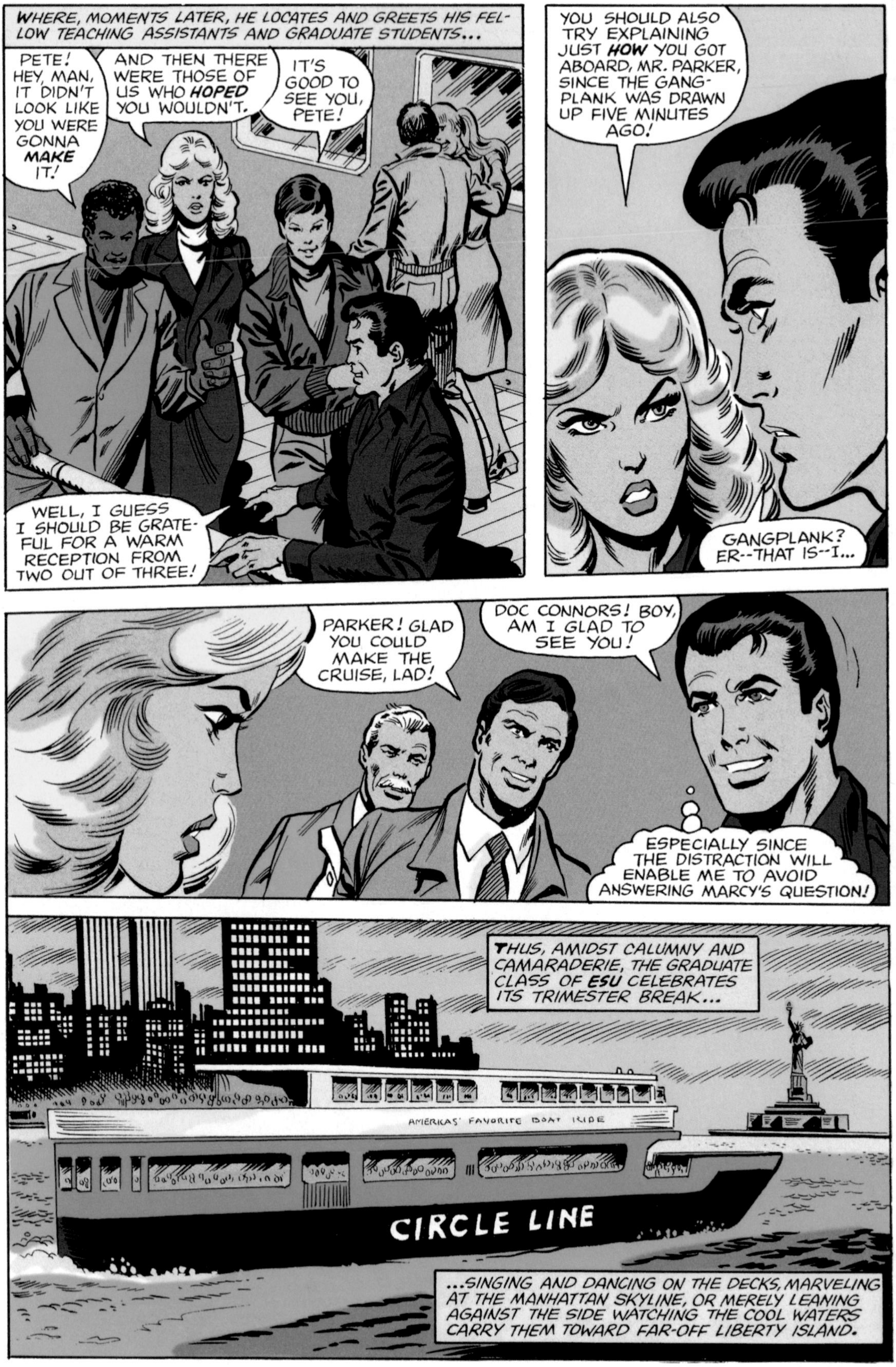
WHERE, MOMENTS LATER, HE LOCATES AND GREETS HIS FELLOW TEACHING ASSISTANTS AND GRADUATE STUDENTS...
PETE! HEY, MAN, IT DIDN'T LOOK LIKE YOU WERE GONNA MAKE IT!
AND THEN THERE WERE THOSE OF US WHO HOPED YOU WOULDN'T.
IT'S GOOD TO SEE YOU, PETE!
WELL, I GUESS I SHOULD BE GRATEFUL FOR A WARM RECEPTION FROM TWO OUT OF THREE!
YOU SHOULD ALSO TRY EXPLAINING JUST HOW YOU GOT ABOARD, MR. PARKER, SINCE THE GANGPLANK WAS DRAWN UP FIVE MINUTES AGO!
GANGPLANK? ER--THAT IS--I...
PARKER! GLAD YOU COULD MAKE THE CRUISE, LAD!
DOC CONNORS! BOY, AM I GLAD TO SEE YOU!
ESPECIALLY SINCE THE DISTRACTION WILL ENABLE ME TO AVOID ANSWERING MARCY'S QUESTION!
THUS, AMIDST CALUMNY AND CAMARADERIE, THE GRADUATE CLASS OF ESU CELEBRATES ITS TRIMESTER BREAK...
AMERICAS' FAVORITE BOAT RIDE
CIRCLE LINE
...SINGING AND DANCING ON THE DECKS, MARVELING AT THE MANHATTAN SKYLINE, OR MERELY LEANING AGAINST THE SIDE WATCHING THE COOL WATERS CARRY THEM TOWARD FAR-OFF LIBERTY ISLAND.

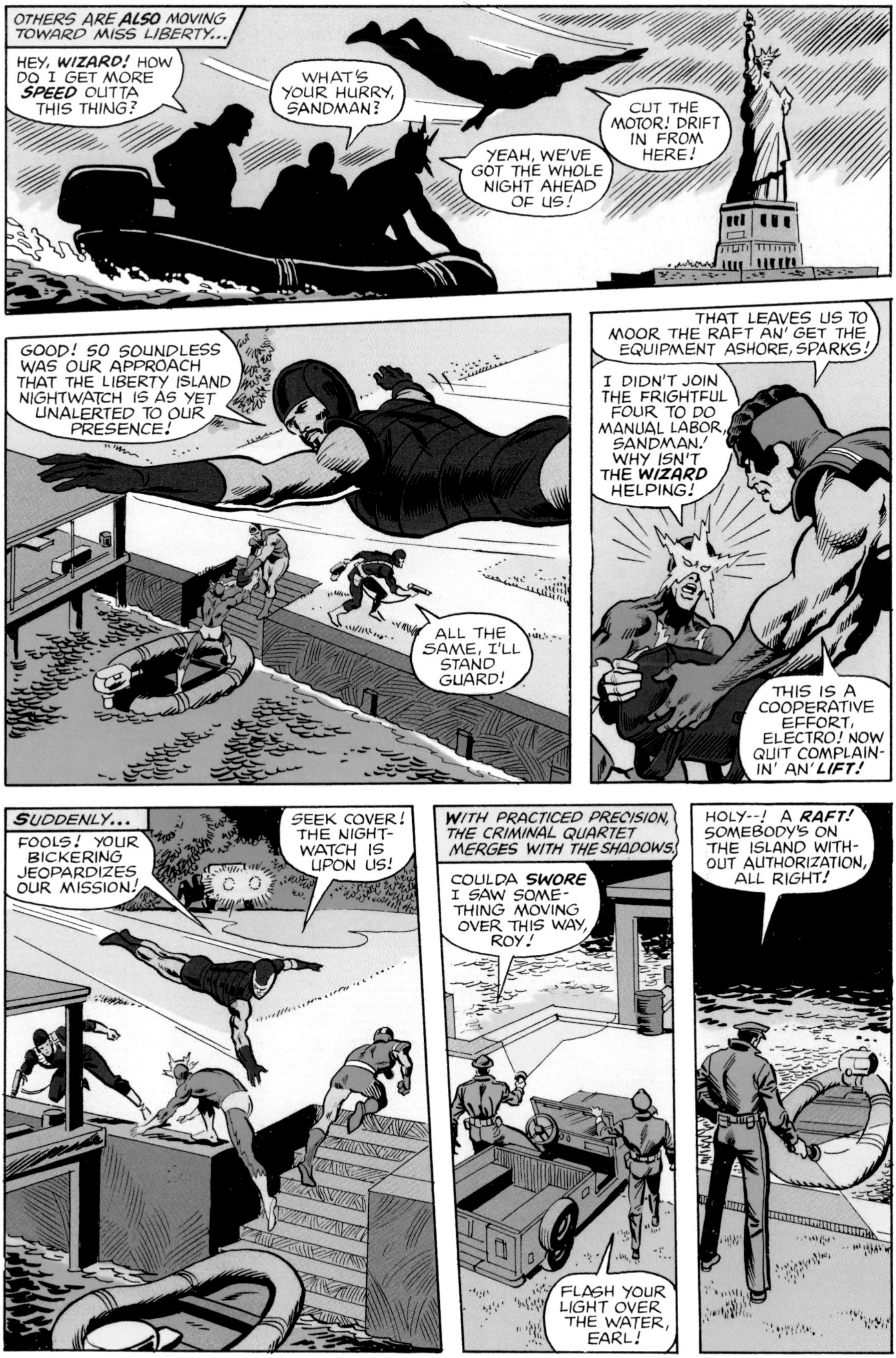

OTHERS ARE ALSO MOVING TOWARD MISS LIBERTY...
HEY, WIZARD! HOW DO I GET MORE SPEED OUTTA THIS THING?
WHAT'S YOUR HURRY, SANDMAN?
YEAH, WE'VE GOT THE WHOLE NIGHT AHEAD OF US!
CUT THE MOTOR! DRIFT IN FROM HERE!
GOOD! SO SOUNDLESS WAS OUR APPROACH THAT THE LIBERTY ISLAND NIGHTWATCH IS AS YET UNALERTED TO OUR PRESENCE!
ALL THE SAME, I'LL STAND GUARD!
THAT LEAVES US TO MOOR THE RAFT AN' GET THE EQUIPMENT ASHORE, SPARKS!
I DIDN'T JOIN THE FRIGHTFUL FOUR TO DO MANUAL LABOR, SANDMAN! WHY ISN'T THE WIZARD HELPING!
THIS IS A COOPERATIVE EFFORT, ELECTRO! NOW QUIT COMPLAIN-IN' AN' LIFT!
SUDDENLY...
FOOLS! YOUR BICKERING JEOPARDIZES OUR MISSION!
SEEK COVER! THE NIGHT-WATCH IS UPON US!
WITH PRACTICED PRECISION, THE CRIMINAL QUARTET MERGES WITH THE SHADOWS.
COULDA SWORE I SAW SOME-THING MOVING OVER THIS WAY, ROY!
FLASH YOUR LIGHT OVER THE WATER, EARL!
HOLY--! A RAFT! SOMEBODY'S ON THE ISLAND WITH-OUT AUTHORIZATION, ALL RIGHT!

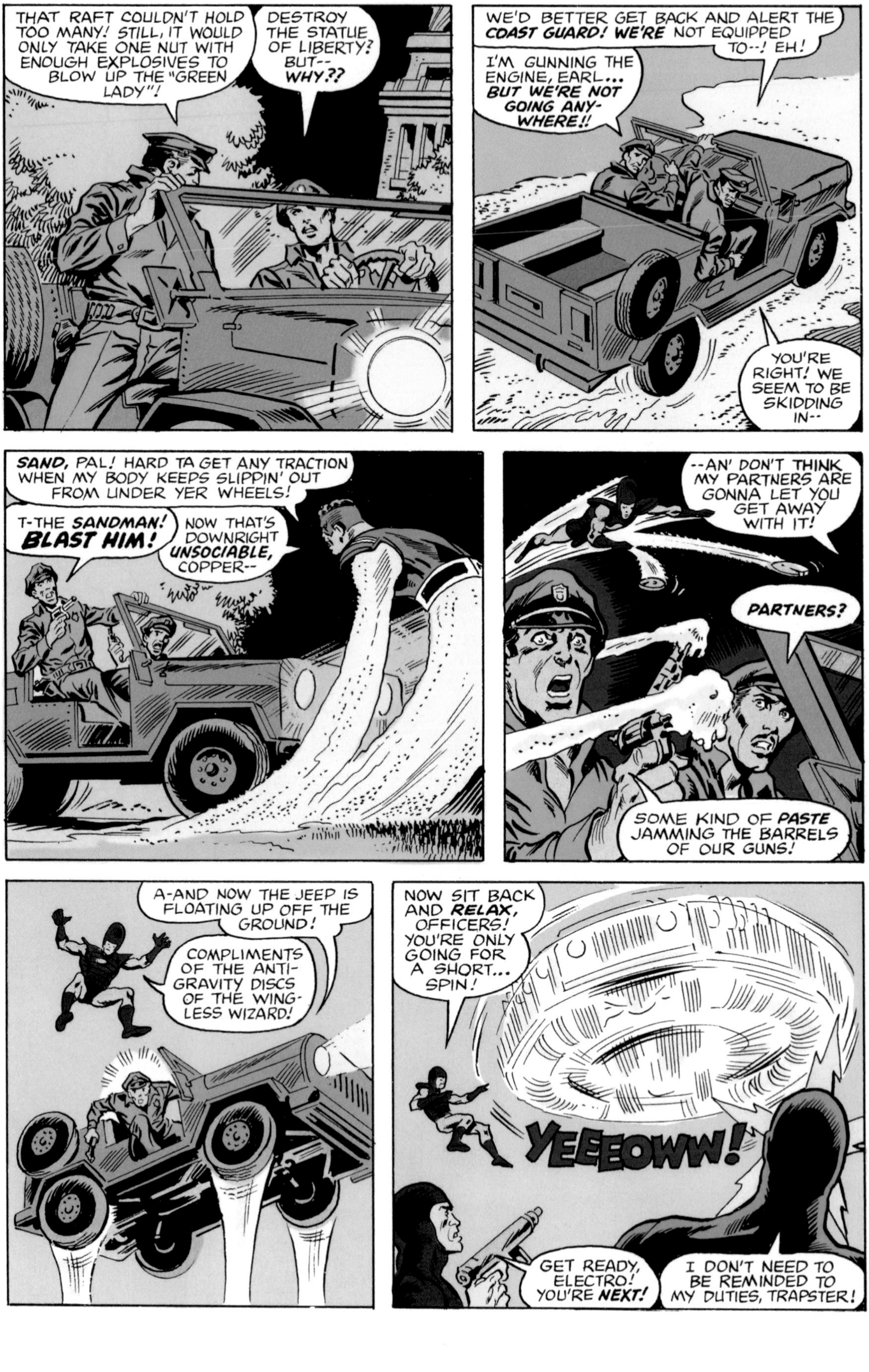
THAT RAFT COULDN'T HOLD TOO MANY! STILL, IT WOULD ONLY TAKE ONE NUT WITH ENOUGH EXPLOSIVES TO BLOW UP THE "GREEN LADY"!
DESTROY THE STATUE OF LIBERTY? BUT-- WHY??
WE'D BETTER GET BACK AND ALERT THE COAST GUARD! WE'RE NOT EQUIPPED TO--! EH!
I'M GUNNING THE ENGINE, EARL... BUT WE'RE NOT GOING ANYWHERE!!
YOU'RE RIGHT! WE SEEM TO BE SKIDDING IN--
SAND, PAL! HARD TA GET ANY TRACTION WHEN MY BODY KEEPS SLIPPIN' OUT FROM UNDER YER WHEELS!
T-THE SANDMAN! BLAST HIM!
NOW THAT'S DOWNRIGHT UNSOCIABLE, COPPER--
--AN' DON'T THINK MY PARTNERS ARE GONNA LET YOU GET AWAY WITH IT!
PARTNERS?
SOME KIND OF PASTE JAMMING THE BARRELS OF OUR GUNS!
A-AND NOW THE JEEP IS FLOATING UP OFF THE GROUND!
COMPLIMENTS OF THE ANTI-GRAVITY DISCS OF THE WINGLESS WIZARD!
NOW SIT BACK AND RELAX, OFFICERS! YOU'RE ONLY GOING FOR A SHORT... SPIN!
YEEEOWW!
GET READY, ELECTRO! YOU'RE NEXT!
I DON'T NEED TO BE REMINDED TO MY DUTIES, TRAPSTER!

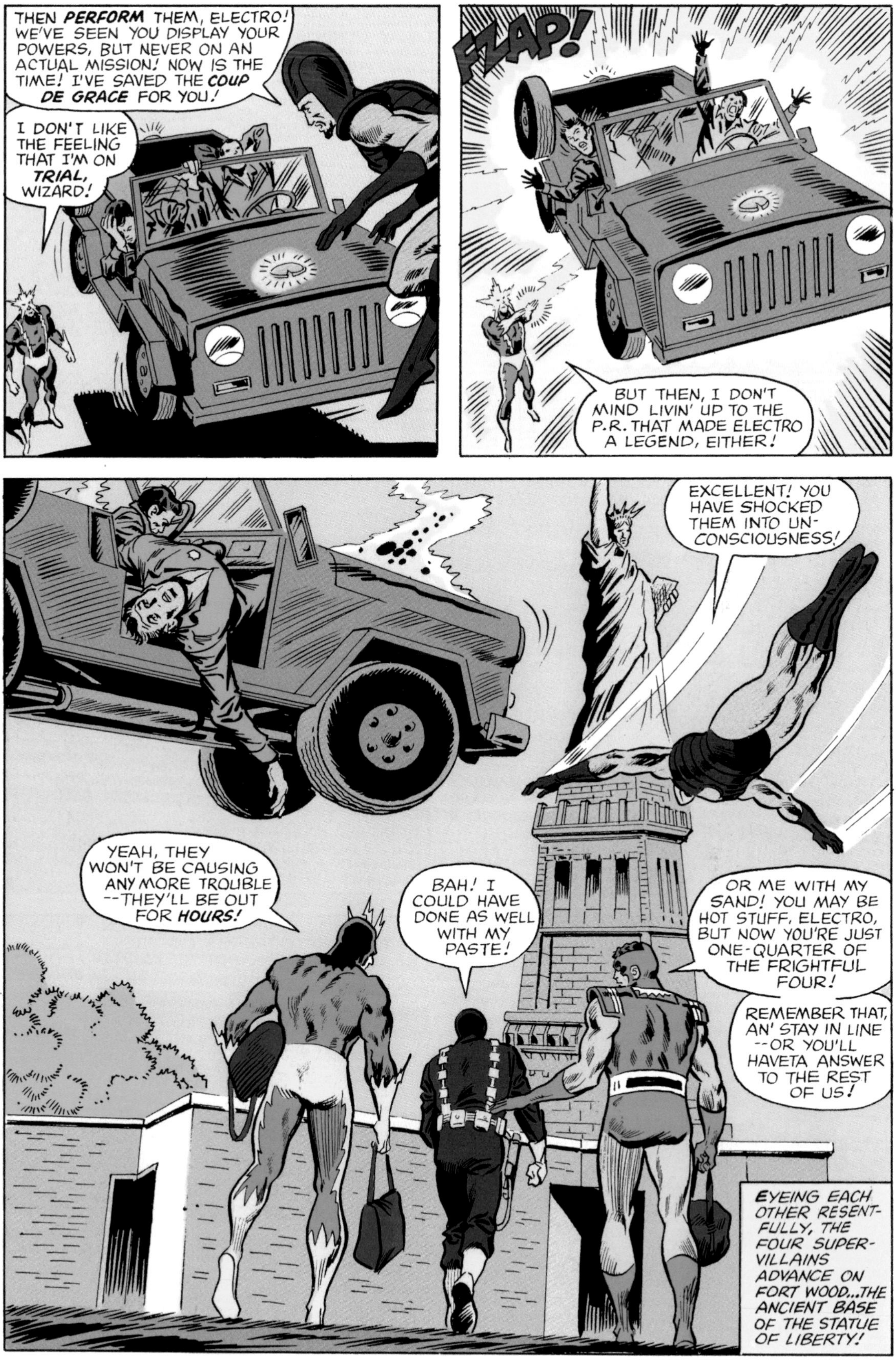
THEN PERFORM THEM, ELECTRO! WE'VE SEEN YOU DISPLAY YOUR POWERS, BUT NEVER ON AN ACTUAL MISSION! NOW IS THE TIME! I'VE SAVED THE COUP DE GRACE FOR YOU!
I DON'T LIKE THE FEELING THAT I'M ON TRIAL, WIZARD!
FZAP!
BUT THEN, I DON'T MIND LIVIN' UP TO THE P.R. THAT MADE ELECTRO A LEGEND, EITHER!
EXCELLENT! YOU HAVE SHOCKED THEM INTO UN-CONSCIOUSNESS!
YEAH, THEY WON'T BE CAUSING ANY MORE TROUBLE --THEY'LL BE OUT FOR HOURS!
BAH! I COULD HAVE DONE AS WELL WITH MY PASTE!
OR ME WITH MY SAND! YOU MAY BE HOT STUFF, ELECTRO, BUT NOW YOU'RE JUST ONE-QUARTER OF THE FRIGHTFUL FOUR!
REMEMBER THAT, AN' STAY IN LINE --OR YOU'LL HAVETA ANSWER TO THE REST OF US!
EYEING EACH OTHER RESENT-FULLY, THE FOUR SUPER-VILLAINS ADVANCE ON FORT WOOD...THE ANCIENT BASE OF THE STATUE OF LIBERTY!

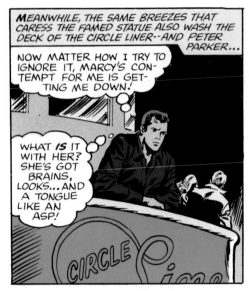

MEANWHILE, THE SAME BREEZES THAT CARESS THE FAMED STATUE ALSO WASH THE DECK OF THE CIRCLE LINER--AND PETER PARKER...

NOW MATTER HOW I TRY TO IGNORE IT, MARCY'S CONTEMPT FOR ME IS GETTING ME DOWN!

WHAT *IS* IT WITH HER? SHE'S GOT BRAINS, LOOKS...AND A TONGUE LIKE AN ASP!

I DON'T EVEN KNOW WHY I PAY ATTENTION TO HER. MAYBE I'M ATTRACTED TO HER? AM I *THAT* LONELY SINCE MARY JANE AND I BROKE UP?

PETE?

OH, HI DEBRA. I DIDN'T HEAR YOU COME UP.

NO, YOU LOST IN THOUGHT. WRESTLING WITH THE GREAT RIDDLES OF SCIENCE?

DON'T KID YOURSELF, DEB. I WASN'T SOLVING ANY GREAT PROBLEMS PLAGUING THE ADVANCE OF BIOCHEMISTRY.

I'M LUCKY IF I CAN SOLVE MY OWN PERSONAL PROBLEMS HALF THE TIME!

STILL, I'VE *WATCHED* YOU, PETE! YOU'RE A BRILLIANT STUDENT! A GREAT TEACHING ASSISTANT.

YOU'VE SO MUCH TO LOOK FORWARD TO FOR THE REST OF YOUR LIFE. AND ME, I'M ONLY DR. SLOAN'S *SECRETARY.* MAYBE IF I'M LUCKY I'LL GO FROM A TYPING POOL TO A SUBURBAN SWIMMING POOL COMPLETE WITH A HUSBAND AND 2.5 KIDS.

HEY, DEB--COME ON! YOU'VE GOT MORE ON THE BALL THAN *THAT!* THERE'S DIFFERENT TYPES OF SMART--YOU'VE GOT THE *COMMON SENSE* KIND! YOU'RE RATING YOURSELF TOO *LOW,* LADY!

I--I WISH I COULD *BELIEVE* THAT, PETE.

AND SOMEHOW, WHEN YOU SAY IT, I ALMOST *DO.*

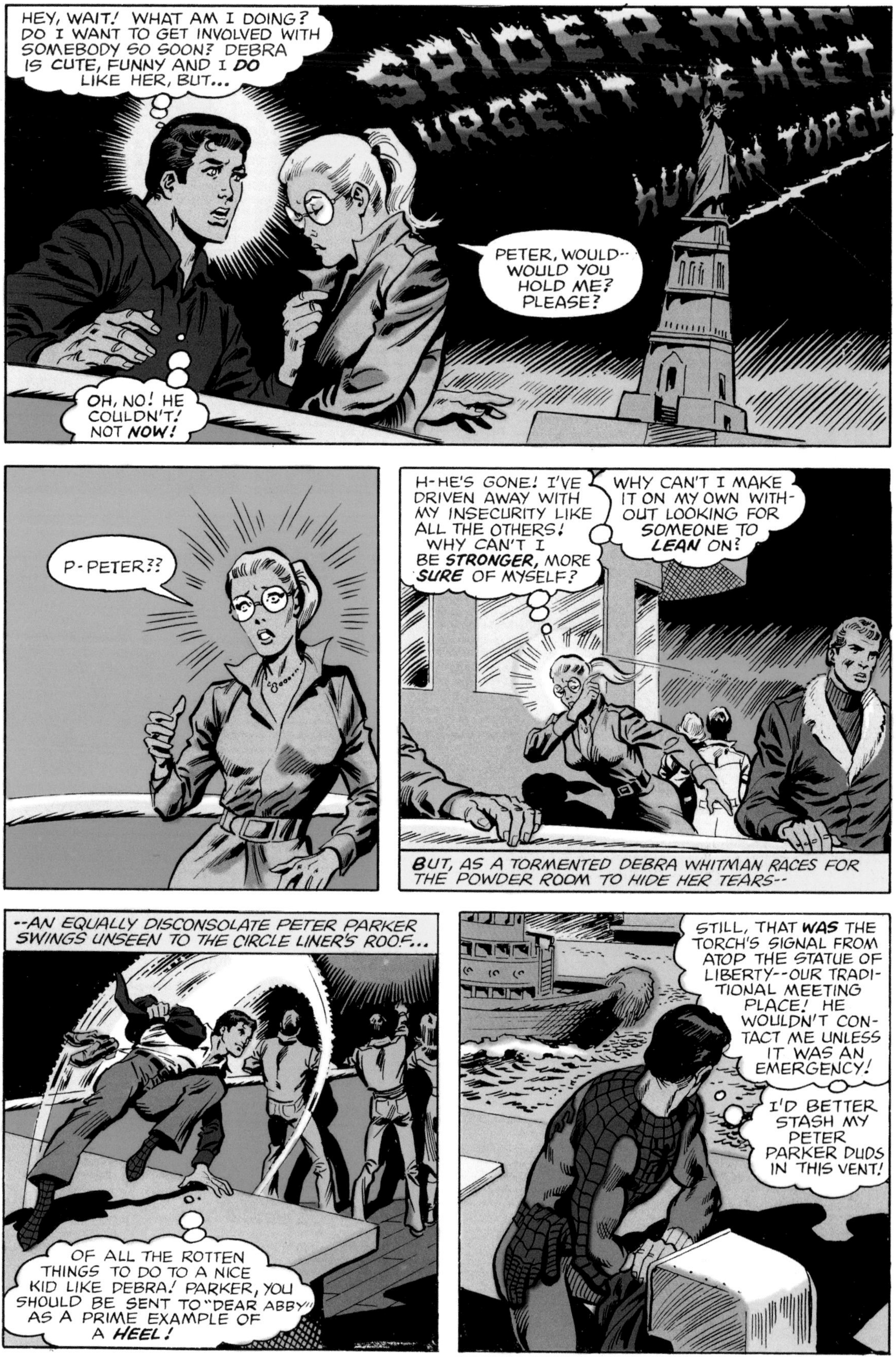

HEY, WAIT! WHAT AM I DOING? DO I WANT TO GET INVOLVED WITH SOMEBODY SO SOON? DEBRA IS CUTE, FUNNY AND I DO LIKE HER, BUT...
PETER, WOULD-- WOULD YOU HOLD ME? PLEASE?
OH, NO! HE COULDN'T! NOT NOW!
P-PETER??
H-HE'S GONE! I'VE DRIVEN AWAY WITH MY INSECURITY LIKE ALL THE OTHERS! WHY CAN'T I BE STRONGER, MORE SURE OF MYSELF?
WHY CAN'T I MAKE IT ON MY OWN WITHOUT LOOKING FOR SOMEONE TO LEAN ON?
BUT, AS A TORMENTED DEBRA WHITMAN RACES FOR THE POWDER ROOM TO HIDE HER TEARS--
--AN EQUALLY DISCONSOLATE PETER PARKER SWINGS UNSEEN TO THE CIRCLE LINER'S ROOF...
OF ALL THE ROTTEN THINGS TO DO TO A NICE KID LIKE DEBRA! PARKER, YOU SHOULD BE SENT TO "DEAR ABBY" AS A PRIME EXAMPLE OF A HEEL!
STILL, THAT WAS THE TORCH'S SIGNAL FROM ATOP THE STATUE OF LIBERTY--OUR TRADITIONAL MEETING PLACE! HE WOULDN'T CONTACT ME UNLESS IT WAS AN EMERGENCY!
I'D BETTER STASH MY PETER PARKER DUDS IN THIS VENT!

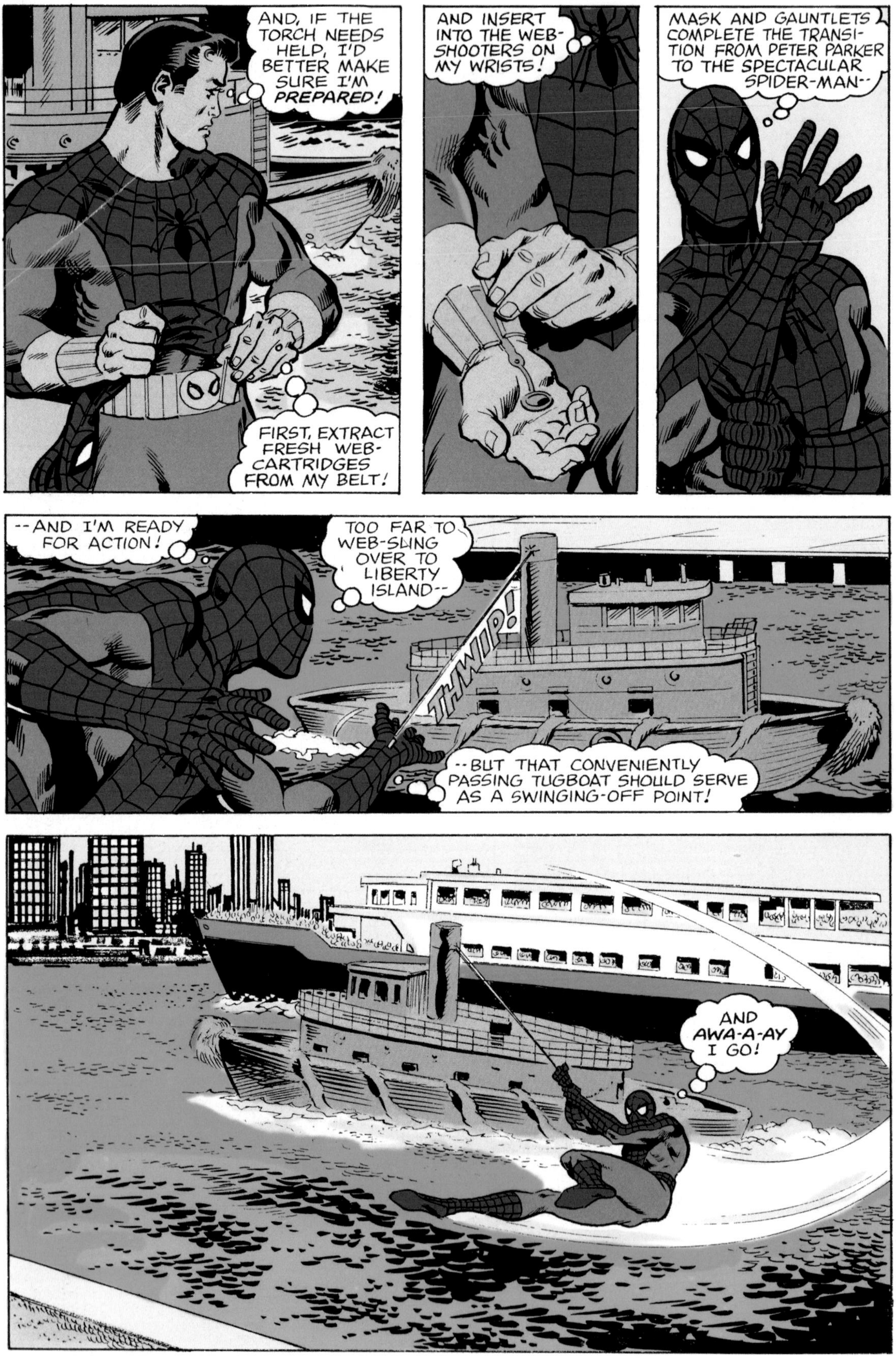
AND, IF THE TORCH NEEDS HELP, I'D BETTER MAKE SURE I'M *PREPARED!*
FIRST, EXTRACT FRESH WEB-CARTRIDGES FROM MY BELT!
AND INSERT INTO THE WEB-SHOOTERS ON MY WRISTS!
MASK AND GAUNTLETS COMPLETE THE TRANSITION FROM PETER PARKER TO THE SPECTACULAR SPIDER-MAN--
--AND I'M READY FOR ACTION!
TOO FAR TO WEB-SLING OVER TO LIBERTY ISLAND--
THWIP!
--BUT THAT CONVENIENTLY PASSING TUGBOAT SHOULD SERVE AS A SWINGING-OFF POINT!
AND AWA-A-AY I GO!

WHOOPS! UNDERESTIMATED THE DISTANCE TO SHORE! WEB-LINE'S TOO *SHORT!* I'M GONNA DROP...

...INTO THE DRINK!

SPLASH!

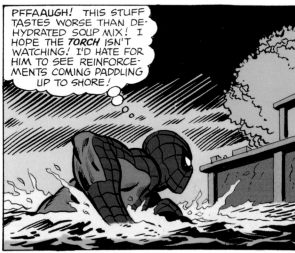

PFFAAUGH! THIS STUFF TASTES WORSE THAN DE-HYDRATED SOUP MIX! I HOPE THE *TORCH* ISN'T WATCHING! I'D HATE FOR HIM TO SEE REINFORCE-MENTS COMING PADDLING UP TO SHORE!

SCALING THE SEAWALL, SPIDER-MAN IS STOPPED SHORT BY THE SIGHT OF...

A FLOATING JEEP AND TWO KAYOED COPS? *WEIRD!*

BUT THOSE TWO OFFICERS DON'T SEEM TO BE IN ANY IMMEDIATE DANGER!

I'LL LET THEM SLEEP IT OFF WHILE I LOCATE THE TORCH!

WHO, UNLESS SOMETHING'S HAPPENED TO HIM SINCE HE BLAZED HIS MESSAGE ACROSS THE SKY, SHOULD BE WAITING FOR ME AT OUR USUAL MEETING-PLACE...

ATOP LADY LIBERTY'S TORCH!

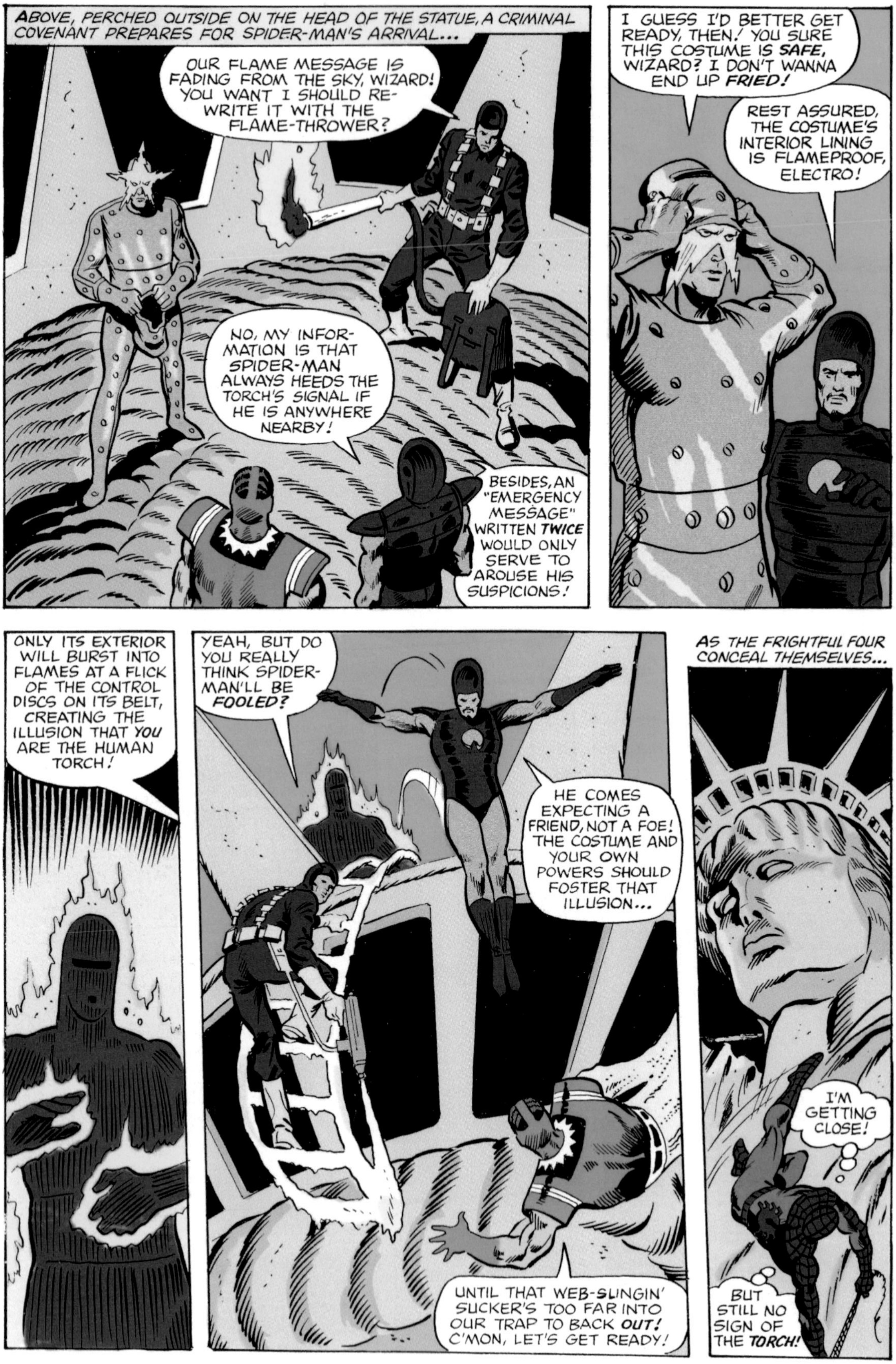
ABOVE, PERCHED OUTSIDE ON THE HEAD OF THE STATUE, A CRIMINAL COVENANT PREPARES FOR SPIDER-MAN'S ARRIVAL...
OUR FLAME MESSAGE IS FADING FROM THE SKY, WIZARD! YOU WANT I SHOULD RE-WRITE IT WITH THE FLAME-THROWER?
NO, MY INFORMATION IS THAT SPIDER-MAN ALWAYS HEEDS THE TORCH'S SIGNAL IF HE IS ANYWHERE NEARBY!
BESIDES, AN "EMERGENCY MESSAGE" WRITTEN TWICE WOULD ONLY SERVE TO AROUSE HIS SUSPICIONS!
I GUESS I'D BETTER GET READY, THEN! YOU SURE THIS COSTUME IS SAFE, WIZARD? I DON'T WANNA END UP FRIED!
REST ASSURED, THE COSTUME'S INTERIOR LINING IS FLAMEPROOF, ELECTRO!
ONLY ITS EXTERIOR WILL BURST INTO FLAMES AT A FLICK OF THE CONTROL DISCS ON ITS BELT, CREATING THE ILLUSION THAT YOU ARE THE HUMAN TORCH!
YEAH, BUT DO YOU REALLY THINK SPIDER-MAN'LL BE FOOLED?
HE COMES EXPECTING A FRIEND, NOT A FOE! THE COSTUME AND YOUR OWN POWERS SHOULD FOSTER THAT ILLUSION...
UNTIL THAT WEB-SLINGIN' SUCKER'S TOO FAR INTO OUR TRAP TO BACK OUT! C'MON, LET'S GET READY!
AS THE FRIGHTFUL FOUR CONCEAL THEMSELVES...
I'M GETTING CLOSE!
BUT STILL NO SIGN OF THE TORCH!

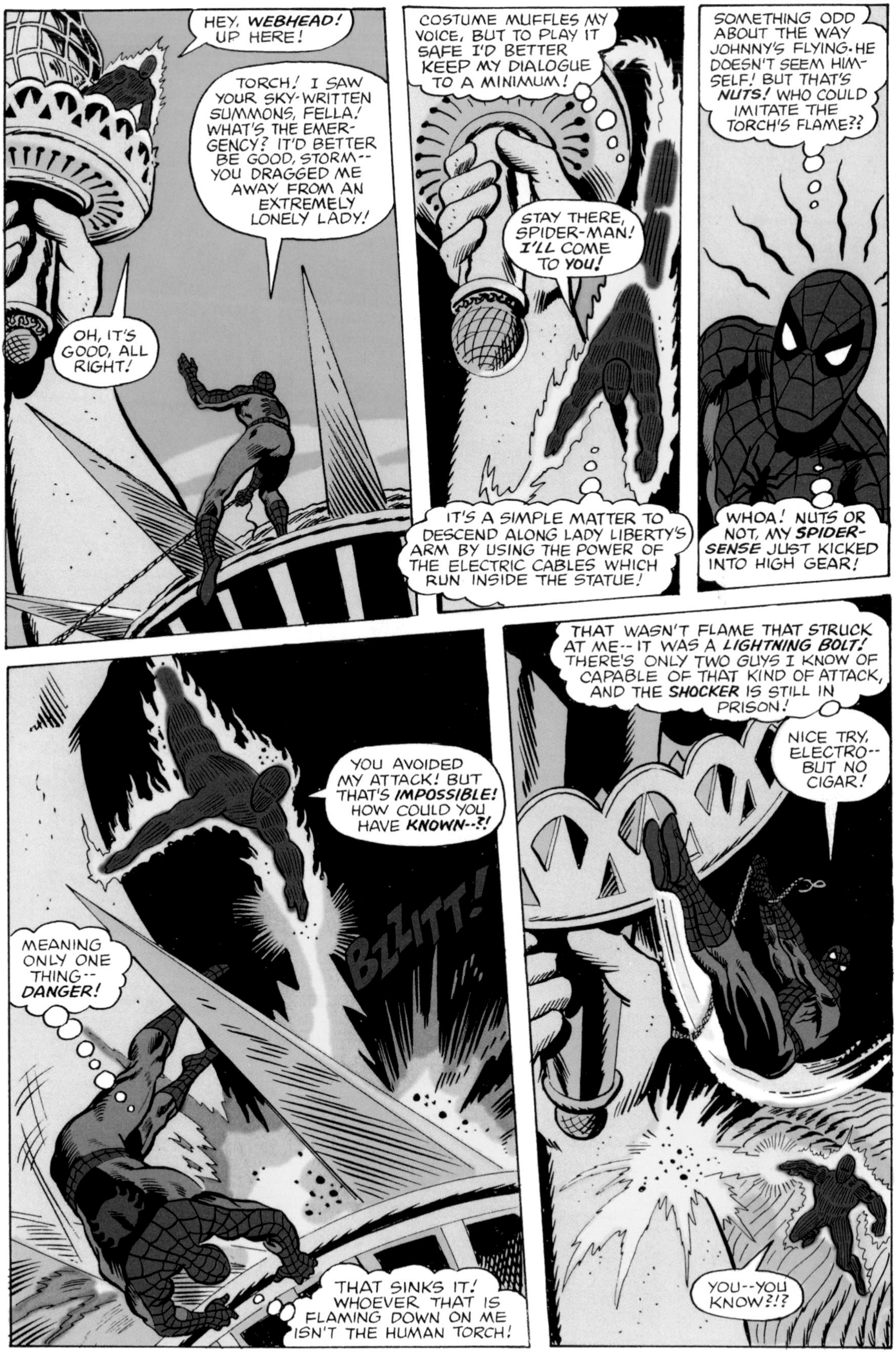
HEY, WEBHEAD! UP HERE!
TORCH! I SAW YOUR SKY-WRITTEN SUMMONS, FELLA! WHAT'S THE EMERGENCY? IT'D BETTER BE GOOD, STORM-- YOU DRAGGED ME AWAY FROM AN EXTREMELY LONELY LADY!
OH, IT'S GOOD, ALL RIGHT!
COSTUME MUFFLES MY VOICE, BUT TO PLAY IT SAFE I'D BETTER KEEP MY DIALOGUE TO A MINIMUM!
STAY THERE, SPIDER-MAN! I'LL COME TO YOU!
IT'S A SIMPLE MATTER TO DESCEND ALONG LADY LIBERTY'S ARM BY USING THE POWER OF THE ELECTRIC CABLES WHICH RUN INSIDE THE STATUE!
SOMETHING ODD ABOUT THE WAY JOHNNY'S FLYING. HE DOESN'T SEEM HIMSELF! BUT THAT'S NUTS! WHO COULD IMITATE THE TORCH'S FLAME??
WHOA! NUTS OR NOT, MY SPIDER-SENSE JUST KICKED INTO HIGH GEAR!
YOU AVOIDED MY ATTACK! BUT THAT'S IMPOSSIBLE! HOW COULD YOU HAVE KNOWN--?!
BZZITT!
MEANING ONLY ONE THING-- DANGER!
THAT SINKS IT! WHOEVER THAT IS FLAMING DOWN ON ME ISN'T THE HUMAN TORCH!
THAT WASN'T FLAME THAT STRUCK AT ME-- IT WAS A LIGHTNING BOLT! THERE'S ONLY TWO GUYS I KNOW OF CAPABLE OF THAT KIND OF ATTACK, AND THE SHOCKER IS STILL IN PRISON!
NICE TRY, ELECTRO-- BUT NO CIGAR!
YOU--YOU KNOW?!?

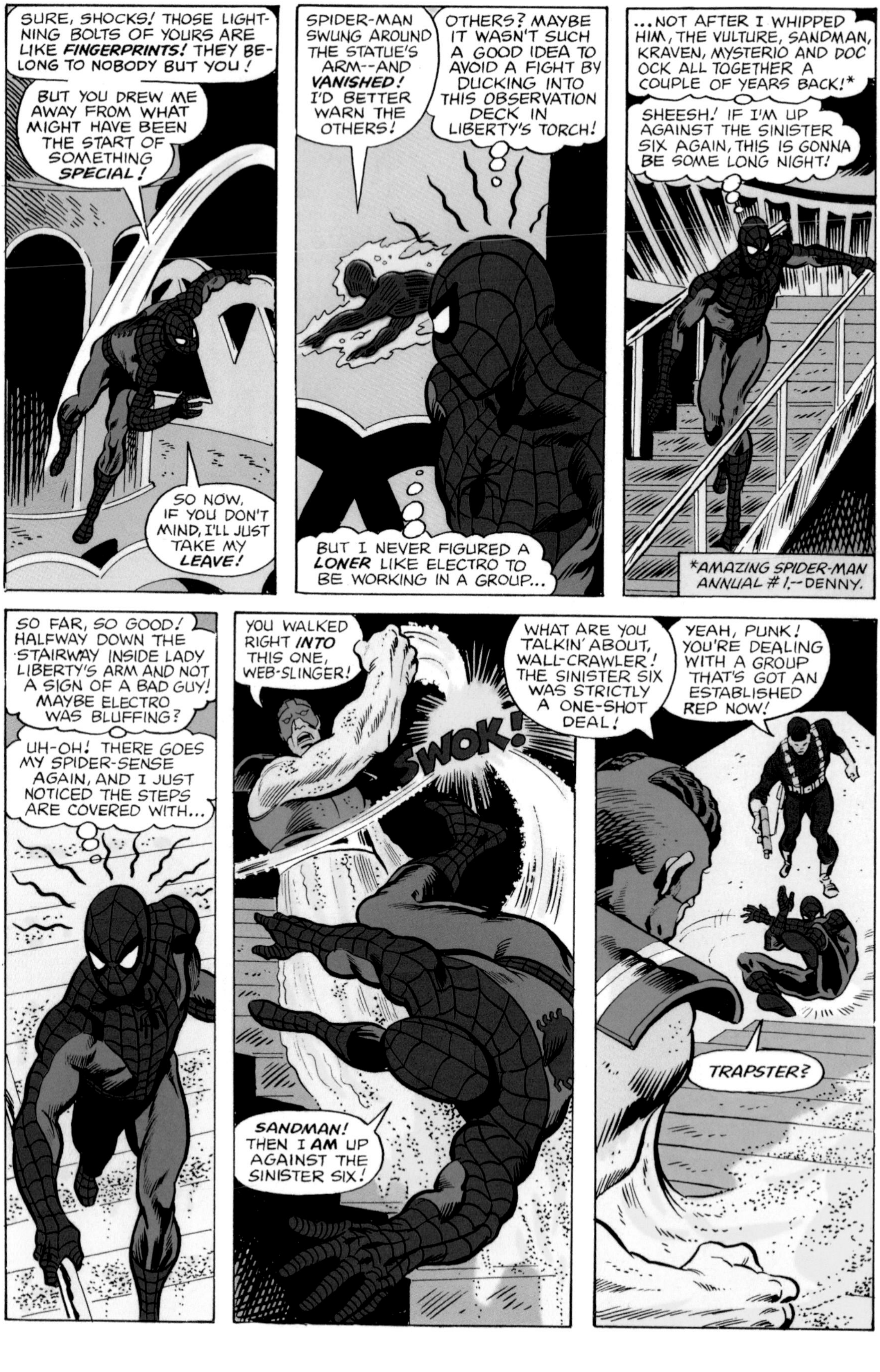
SURE, SHOCKS! THOSE LIGHTNING BOLTS OF YOURS ARE LIKE FINGERPRINTS! THEY BELONG TO NOBODY BUT YOU!
BUT YOU DREW ME AWAY FROM WHAT MIGHT HAVE BEEN THE START OF SOMETHING SPECIAL!
SO NOW, IF YOU DON'T MIND, I'LL JUST TAKE MY LEAVE!
SPIDER-MAN SWUNG AROUND THE STATUE'S ARM--AND VANISHED! I'D BETTER WARN THE OTHERS!
OTHERS? MAYBE IT WASN'T SUCH A GOOD IDEA TO AVOID A FIGHT BY DUCKING INTO THIS OBSERVATION DECK IN LIBERTY'S TORCH!
BUT I NEVER FIGURED A LONER LIKE ELECTRO TO BE WORKING IN A GROUP...
...NOT AFTER I WHIPPED HIM, THE VULTURE, SANDMAN, KRAVEN, MYSTERIO AND DOC OCK ALL TOGETHER A COUPLE OF YEARS BACK!*
SHEESH! IF I'M UP AGAINST THE SINISTER SIX AGAIN, THIS IS GONNA BE SOME LONG NIGHT!
*AMAZING SPIDER-MAN ANNUAL #1.--DENNY.
SO FAR, SO GOOD! HALFWAY DOWN THE STAIRWAY INSIDE LADY LIBERTY'S ARM AND NOT A SIGN OF A BAD GUY! MAYBE ELECTRO WAS BLUFFING?
UH-OH! THERE GOES MY SPIDER-SENSE AGAIN, AND I JUST NOTICED THE STEPS ARE COVERED WITH...
YOU WALKED RIGHT INTO THIS ONE, WEB-SLINGER!
SWOK!
SANDMAN! THEN I AM UP AGAINST THE SINISTER SIX!
WHAT ARE YOU TALKIN' ABOUT, WALL-CRAWLER! THE SINISTER SIX WAS STRICTLY A ONE-SHOT DEAL!
YEAH, PUNK! YOU'RE DEALING WITH A GROUP THAT'S GOT AN ESTABLISHED REP NOW!
TRAPSTER?

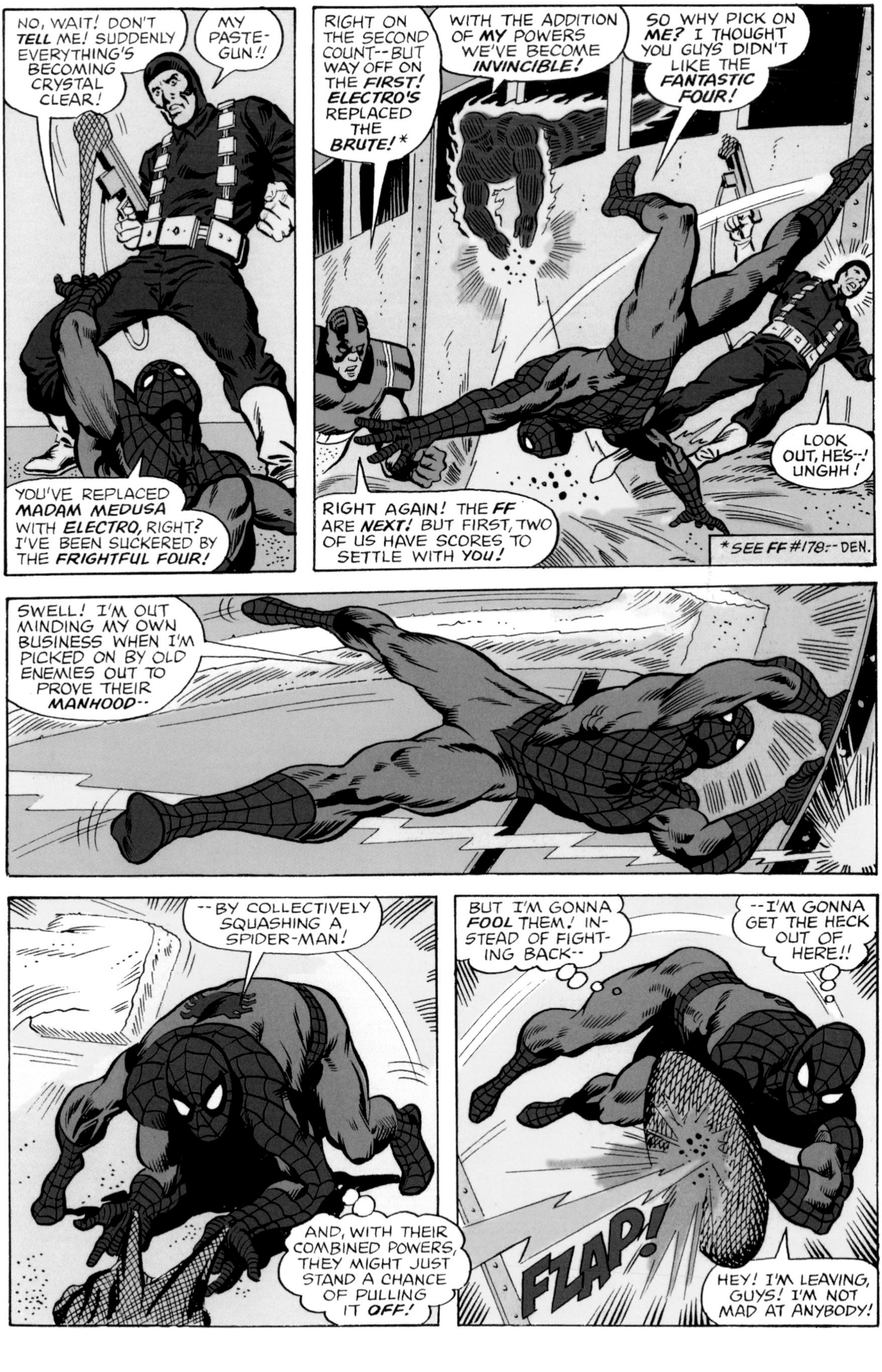
NO, WAIT! DON'T TELL ME! SUDDENLY EVERYTHING'S BECOMING CRYSTAL CLEAR!
MY PASTE-GUN!!
YOU'VE REPLACED MADAM MEDUSA WITH ELECTRO, RIGHT? I'VE BEEN SUCKERED BY THE FRIGHTFUL FOUR!
RIGHT ON THE SECOND COUNT--BUT WAY OFF ON THE FIRST! ELECTRO'S REPLACED THE BRUTE!*
WITH THE ADDITION OF MY POWERS WE'VE BECOME INVINCIBLE!
SO WHY PICK ON ME? I THOUGHT YOU GUYS DIDN'T LIKE THE FANTASTIC FOUR!
RIGHT AGAIN! THE FF ARE NEXT! BUT FIRST, TWO OF US HAVE SCORES TO SETTLE WITH YOU!
LOOK OUT, HE'S--! UNGHH!
*SEE FF #178.--DEN.
SWELL! I'M OUT MINDING MY OWN BUSINESS WHEN I'M PICKED ON BY OLD ENEMIES OUT TO PROVE THEIR MANHOOD--
--BY COLLECTIVELY SQUASHING A SPIDER-MAN!
AND, WITH THEIR COMBINED POWERS, THEY MIGHT JUST STAND A CHANCE OF PULLING IT OFF!
BUT I'M GONNA FOOL THEM! INSTEAD OF FIGHTING BACK--
--I'M GONNA GET THE HECK OUT OF HERE!!
FZAP!
HEY! I'M LEAVING, GUYS! I'M NOT MAD AT ANYBODY!

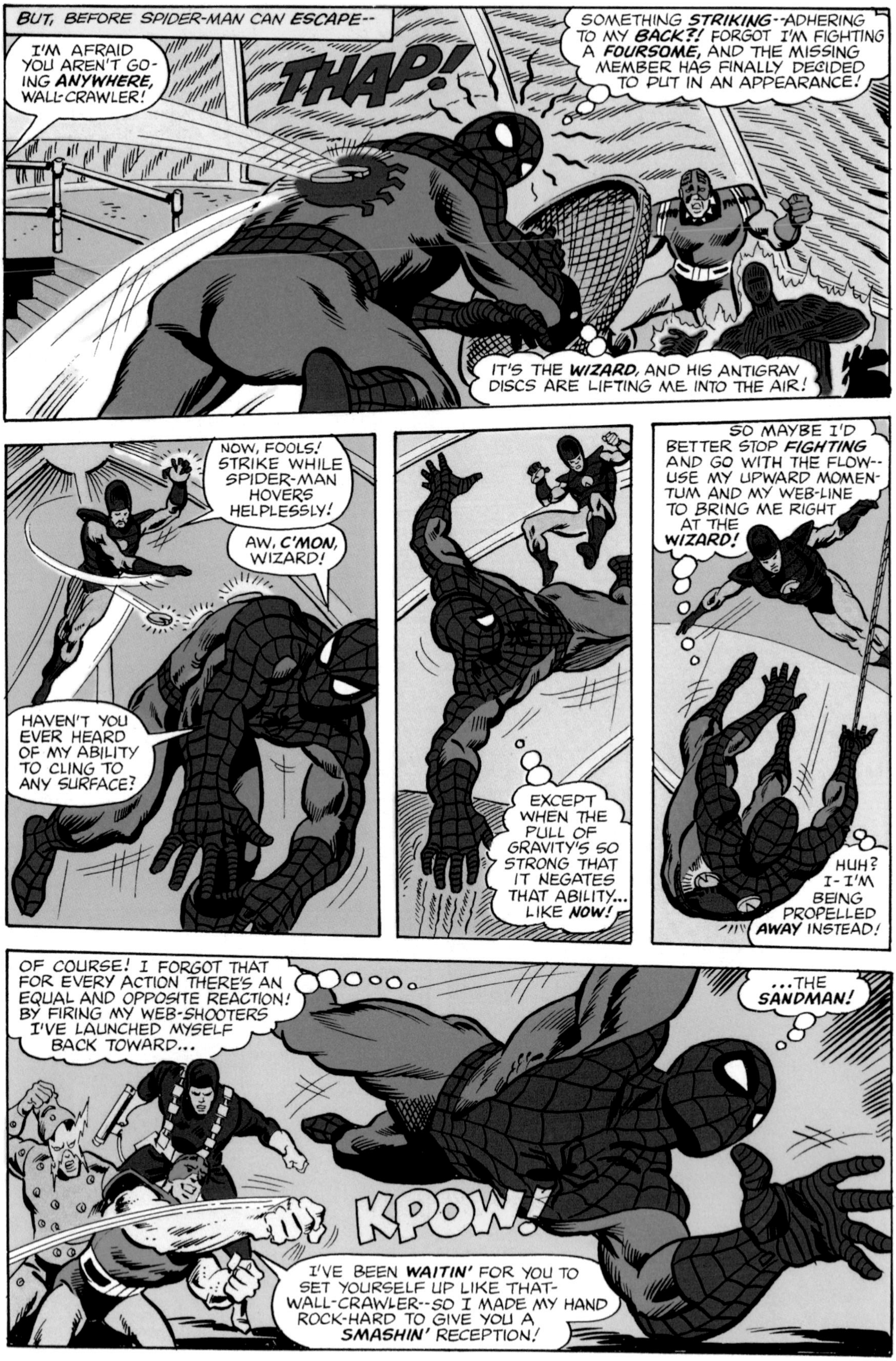
BUT, BEFORE SPIDER-MAN CAN ESCAPE--
I'M AFRAID YOU AREN'T GOING ANYWHERE, WALL-CRAWLER!
THAP!
SOMETHING STRIKING--ADHERING TO MY BACK?! FORGOT I'M FIGHTING A FOURSOME, AND THE MISSING MEMBER HAS FINALLY DECIDED TO PUT IN AN APPEARANCE!
IT'S THE WIZARD, AND HIS ANTIGRAV DISCS ARE LIFTING ME INTO THE AIR!
NOW, FOOLS! STRIKE WHILE SPIDER-MAN HOVERS HELPLESSLY!
AW, C'MON, WIZARD!
HAVEN'T YOU EVER HEARD OF MY ABILITY TO CLING TO ANY SURFACE?
EXCEPT WHEN THE PULL OF GRAVITY'S SO STRONG THAT IT NEGATES THAT ABILITY... LIKE NOW!
SO MAYBE I'D BETTER STOP FIGHTING AND GO WITH THE FLOW--USE MY UPWARD MOMENTUM AND MY WEB-LINE TO BRING ME RIGHT AT THE WIZARD!
HUH? I-I'M BEING PROPELLED AWAY INSTEAD!
OF COURSE! I FORGOT THAT FOR EVERY ACTION THERE'S AN EQUAL AND OPPOSITE REACTION! BY FIRING MY WEB-SHOOTERS I'VE LAUNCHED MYSELF BACK TOWARD...
...THE SANDMAN!
KPOW!
I'VE BEEN WAITIN' FOR YOU TO SET YOURSELF UP LIKE THAT-WALL-CRAWLER--SO I MADE MY HAND ROCK-HARD TO GIVE YOU A SMASHIN' RECEPTION!

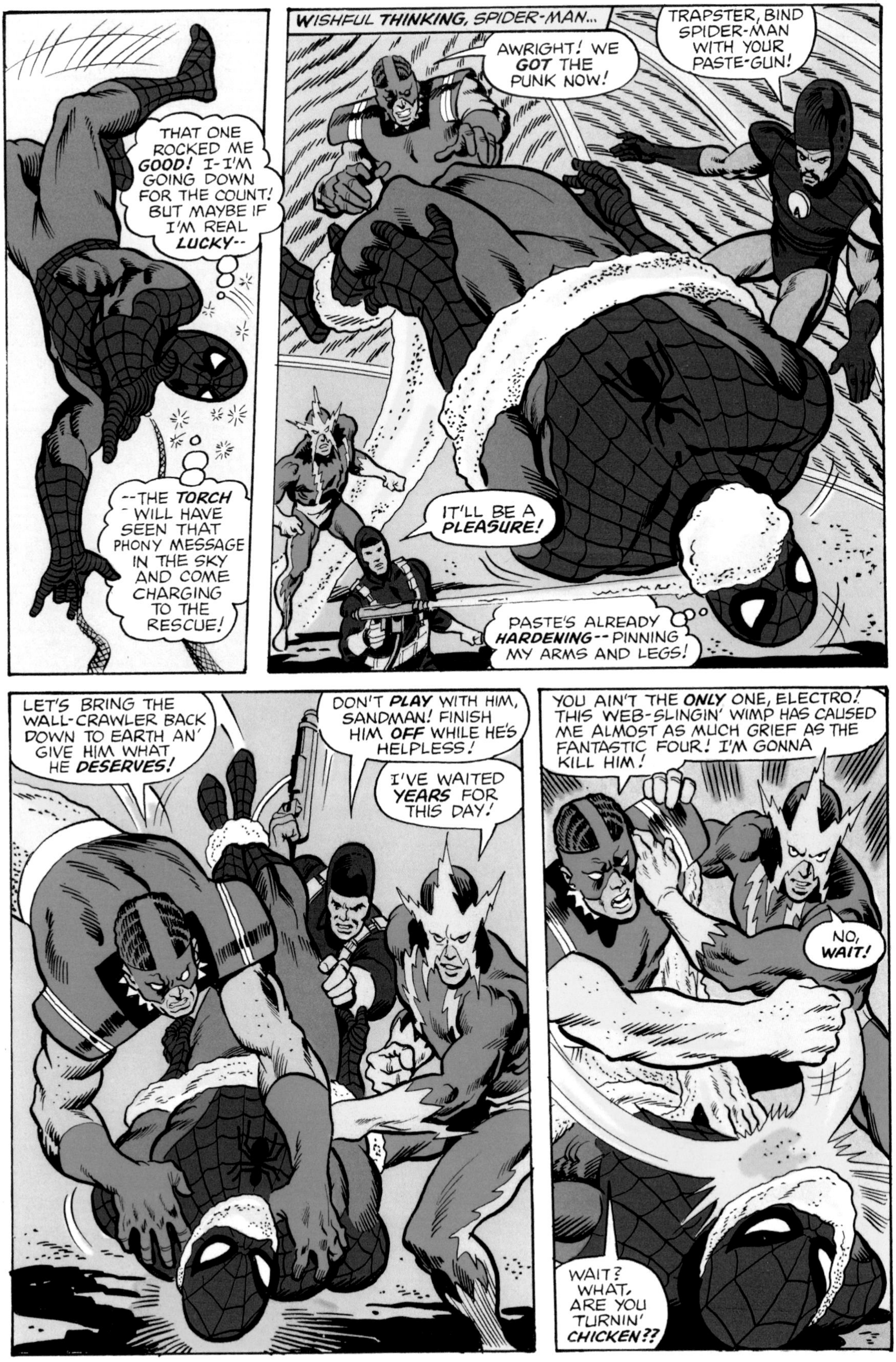
THAT ONE ROCKED ME GOOD! I-I'M GOING DOWN FOR THE COUNT! BUT MAYBE IF I'M REAL LUCKY--
--THE TORCH WILL HAVE SEEN THAT PHONY MESSAGE IN THE SKY AND COME CHARGING TO THE RESCUE!
WISHFUL THINKING, SPIDER-MAN...
AWRIGHT! WE GOT THE PUNK NOW!
TRAPSTER, BIND SPIDER-MAN WITH YOUR PASTE-GUN!
IT'LL BE A PLEASURE!
PASTE'S ALREADY HARDENING-- PINNING MY ARMS AND LEGS!
LET'S BRING THE WALL-CRAWLER BACK DOWN TO EARTH AN' GIVE HIM WHAT HE DESERVES!
DON'T PLAY WITH HIM, SANDMAN! FINISH HIM OFF WHILE HE'S HELPLESS!
I'VE WAITED YEARS FOR THIS DAY!
YOU AIN'T THE ONLY ONE, ELECTRO! THIS WEB-SLINGIN' WIMP HAS CAUSED ME ALMOST AS MUCH GRIEF AS THE FANTASTIC FOUR! I'M GONNA KILL HIM!
NO, WAIT!
WAIT? WHAT, ARE YOU TURNIN' CHICKEN??

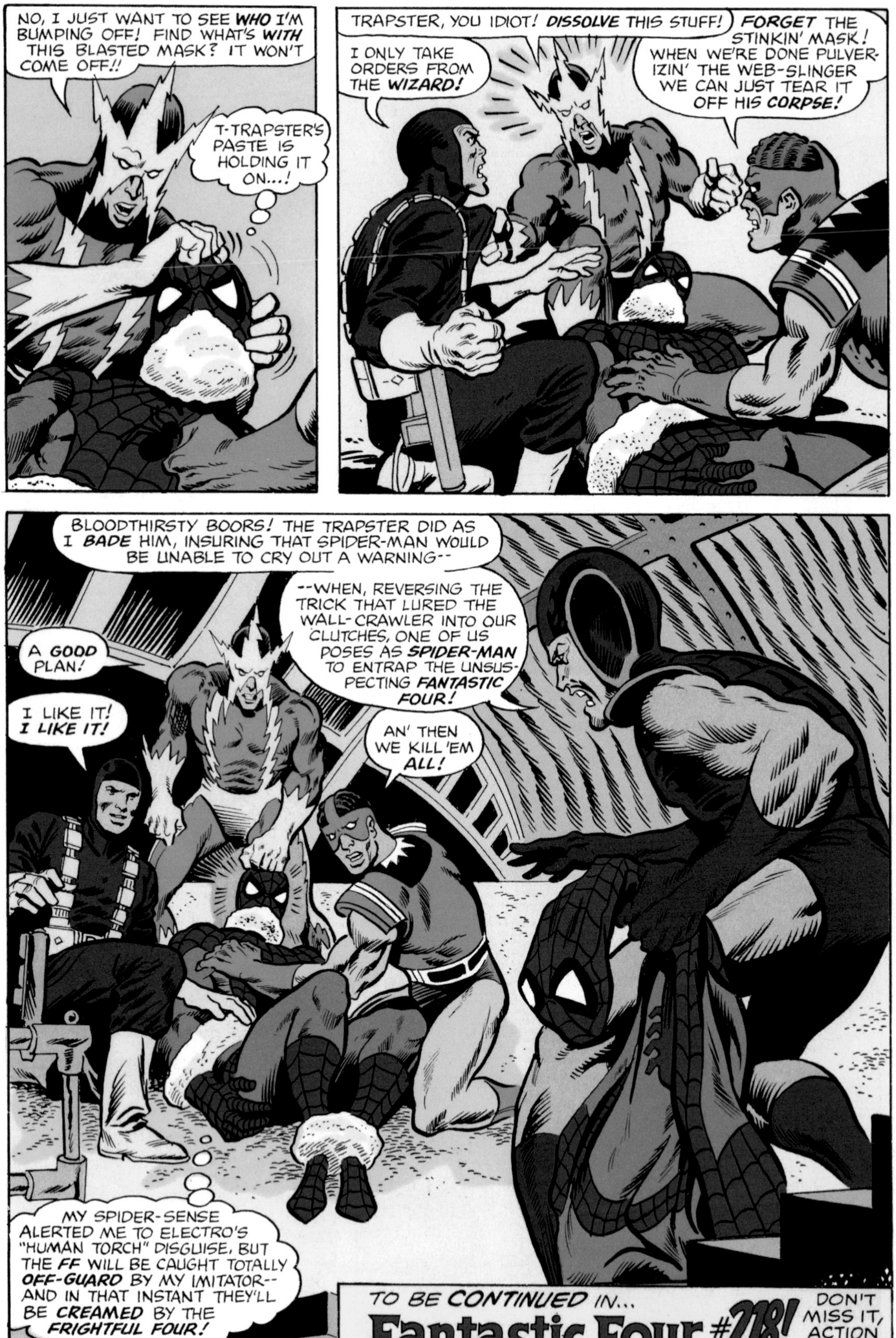
NO, I JUST WANT TO SEE WHO I'M BUMPING OFF! FIND WHAT'S WITH THIS BLASTED MASK? IT WON'T COME OFF!!
T-TRAPSTER'S PASTE IS HOLDING IT ON...!
TRAPSTER, YOU IDIOT! DISSOLVE THIS STUFF!
I ONLY TAKE ORDERS FROM THE WIZARD!
FORGET THE STINKIN' MASK! WHEN WE'RE DONE PULVERIZIN' THE WEB-SLINGER WE CAN JUST TEAR IT OFF HIS CORPSE!
BLOODTHIRSTY BOORS! THE TRAPSTER DID AS I BADE HIM, INSURING THAT SPIDER-MAN WOULD BE UNABLE TO CRY OUT A WARNING--
--WHEN, REVERSING THE TRICK THAT LURED THE WALL-CRAWLER INTO OUR CLUTCHES, ONE OF US POSES AS SPIDER-MAN TO ENTRAP THE UNSUSPECTING FANTASTIC FOUR!
A GOOD PLAN!
I LIKE IT! I LIKE IT!
AN' THEN WE KILL 'EM ALL!
MY SPIDER-SENSE ALERTED ME TO ELECTRO'S "HUMAN TORCH" DISGUISE, BUT THE FF WILL BE CAUGHT TOTALLY OFF-GUARD BY MY IMITATOR--AND IN THAT INSTANT THEY'LL BE CREAMED BY THE FRIGHTFUL FOUR!
BILL
TO BE CONTINUED IN...
Fantastic Four #218!
DON'T MISS IT, ACTION LOVERS!

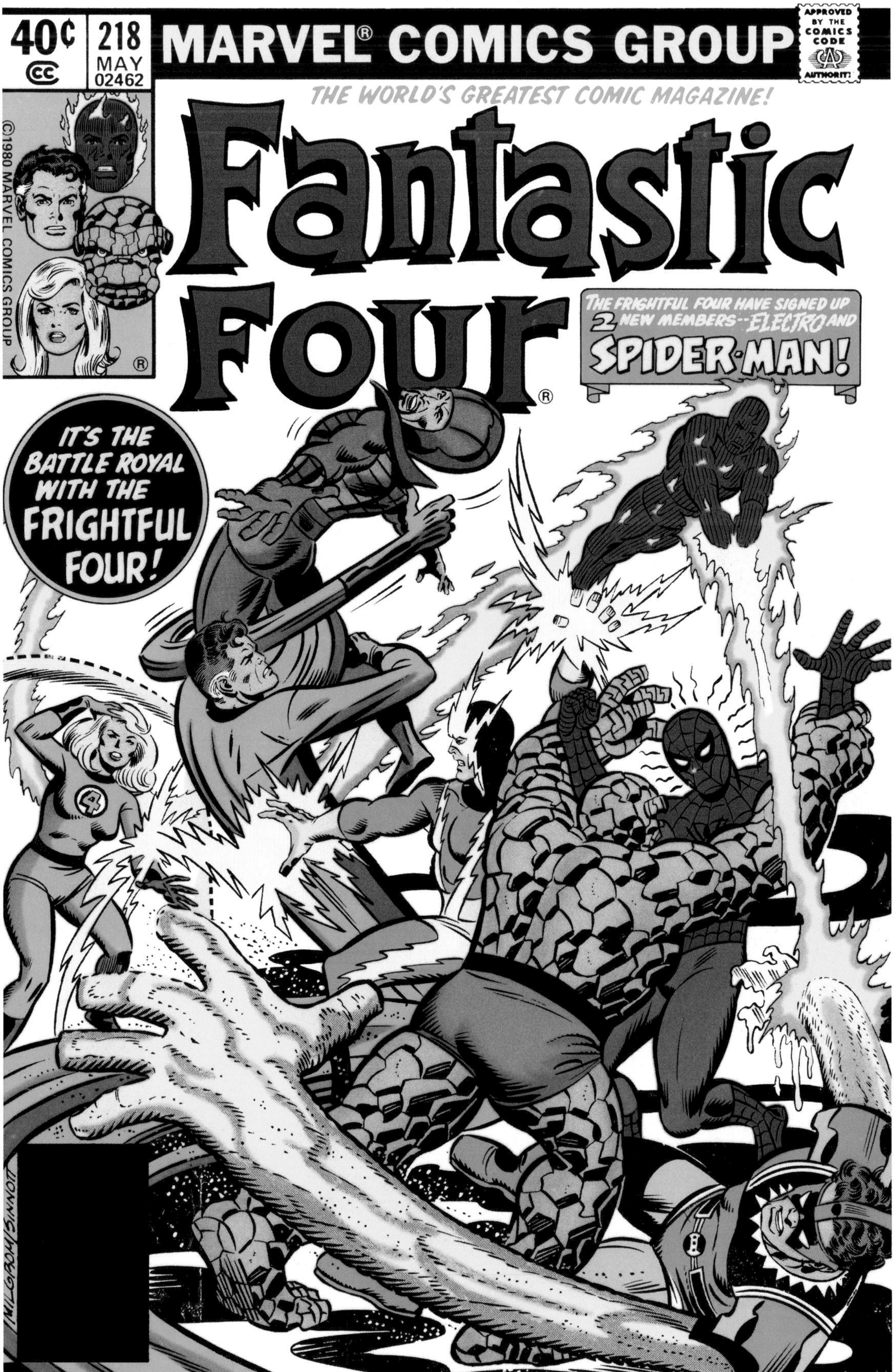
40¢
CC
218
MAY
02462
MARVEL® COMICS GROUP
APPROVED BY THE COMICS CODE AUTHORITY
THE WORLD'S GREATEST COMIC MAGAZINE!
Fantastic Four®
©1980 MARVEL COMICS GROUP
THE FRIGHTFUL FOUR HAVE SIGNED UP 2 NEW MEMBERS--ELECTRO AND SPIDER-MAN!
IT'S THE BATTLE ROYAL WITH THE FRIGHTFUL FOUR!

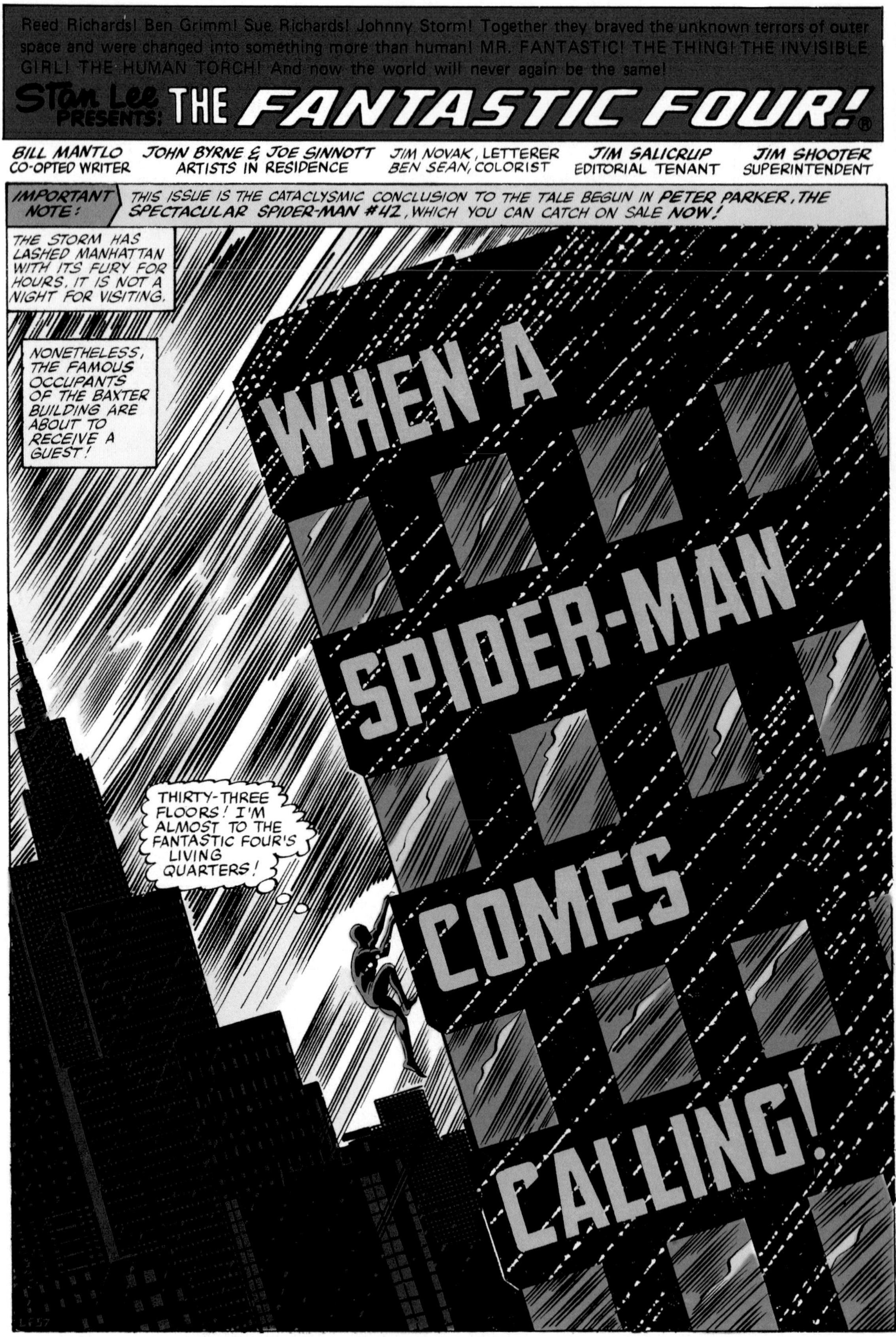
Reed Richards! Ben Grimm! Sue Richards! Johnny Storm! Together they braved the unknown terrors of outer space and were changed into something more than human! MR. FANTASTIC! THE THING! THE INVISIBLE GIRL! THE HUMAN TORCH! And now the world will never again be the same!
Stan Lee PRESENTS: THE FANTASTIC FOUR!®
BILL MANTLO CO-OPTED WRITER
JOHN BYRNE & JOE SINNOTT ARTISTS IN RESIDENCE
JIM NOVAK, LETTERER BEN SEAN, COLORIST
JIM SALICRUP EDITORIAL TENANT
JIM SHOOTER SUPERINTENDENT
IMPORTANT NOTE: THIS ISSUE IS THE CATACLYSMIC CONCLUSION TO THE TALE BEGUN IN PETER PARKER, THE SPECTACULAR SPIDER-MAN #42, WHICH YOU CAN CATCH ON SALE NOW!
THE STORM HAS LASHED MANHATTAN WITH ITS FURY FOR HOURS. IT IS NOT A NIGHT FOR VISITING.
NONETHELESS, THE FAMOUS OCCUPANTS OF THE BAXTER BUILDING ARE ABOUT TO RECEIVE A GUEST!
WHEN A SPIDER-MAN COMES CALLING!
THIRTY-THREE FLOORS! I'M ALMOST TO THE FANTASTIC FOUR'S LIVING QUARTERS!

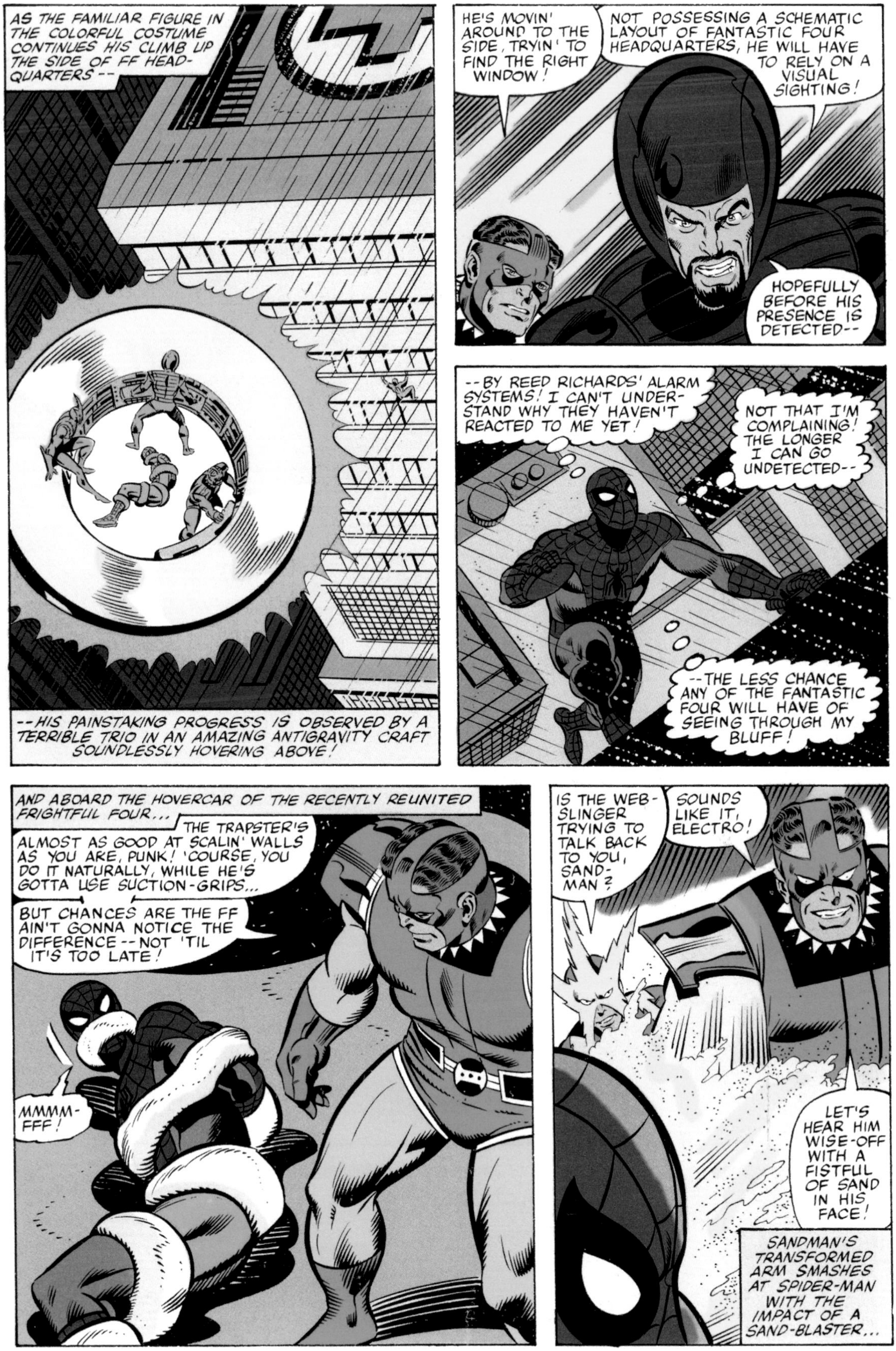

AS THE FAMILIAR FIGURE IN THE COLORFUL COSTUME CONTINUES HIS CLIMB UP THE SIDE OF FF HEAD-QUARTERS --
--HIS PAINSTAKING PROGRESS IS OBSERVED BY A TERRIBLE TRIO IN AN AMAZING ANTIGRAVITY CRAFT SOUNDLESSLY HOVERING ABOVE!
HE'S MOVIN' AROUND TO THE SIDE, TRYIN' TO FIND THE RIGHT WINDOW!
NOT POSSESSING A SCHEMATIC LAYOUT OF FANTASTIC FOUR HEADQUARTERS, HE WILL HAVE TO RELY ON A VISUAL SIGHTING!
HOPEFULLY BEFORE HIS PRESENCE IS DETECTED--
--BY REED RICHARDS' ALARM SYSTEMS! I CAN'T UNDER-STAND WHY THEY HAVEN'T REACTED TO ME YET!
NOT THAT I'M COMPLAINING! THE LONGER I CAN GO UNDETECTED--
--THE LESS CHANCE ANY OF THE FANTASTIC FOUR WILL HAVE OF SEEING THROUGH MY BLUFF!
AND ABOARD THE HOVERCAR OF THE RECENTLY REUNITED FRIGHTFUL FOUR...
THE TRAPSTER'S ALMOST AS GOOD AT SCALIN' WALLS AS YOU ARE, PUNK! 'COURSE, YOU DO IT NATURALLY, WHILE HE'S GOTTA USE SUCTION-GRIPS...
BUT CHANCES ARE THE FF AIN'T GONNA NOTICE THE DIFFERENCE --NOT 'TIL IT'S TOO LATE!
MMMM-FFF!
IS THE WEB-SLINGER TRYING TO TALK BACK TO YOU, SAND-MAN?
SOUNDS LIKE IT, ELECTRO!
LET'S HEAR HIM WISE-OFF WITH A FISTFUL OF SAND IN HIS FACE!
SANDMAN'S TRANSFORMED ARM SMASHES AT SPIDER-MAN WITH THE IMPACT OF A SAND-BLASTER...

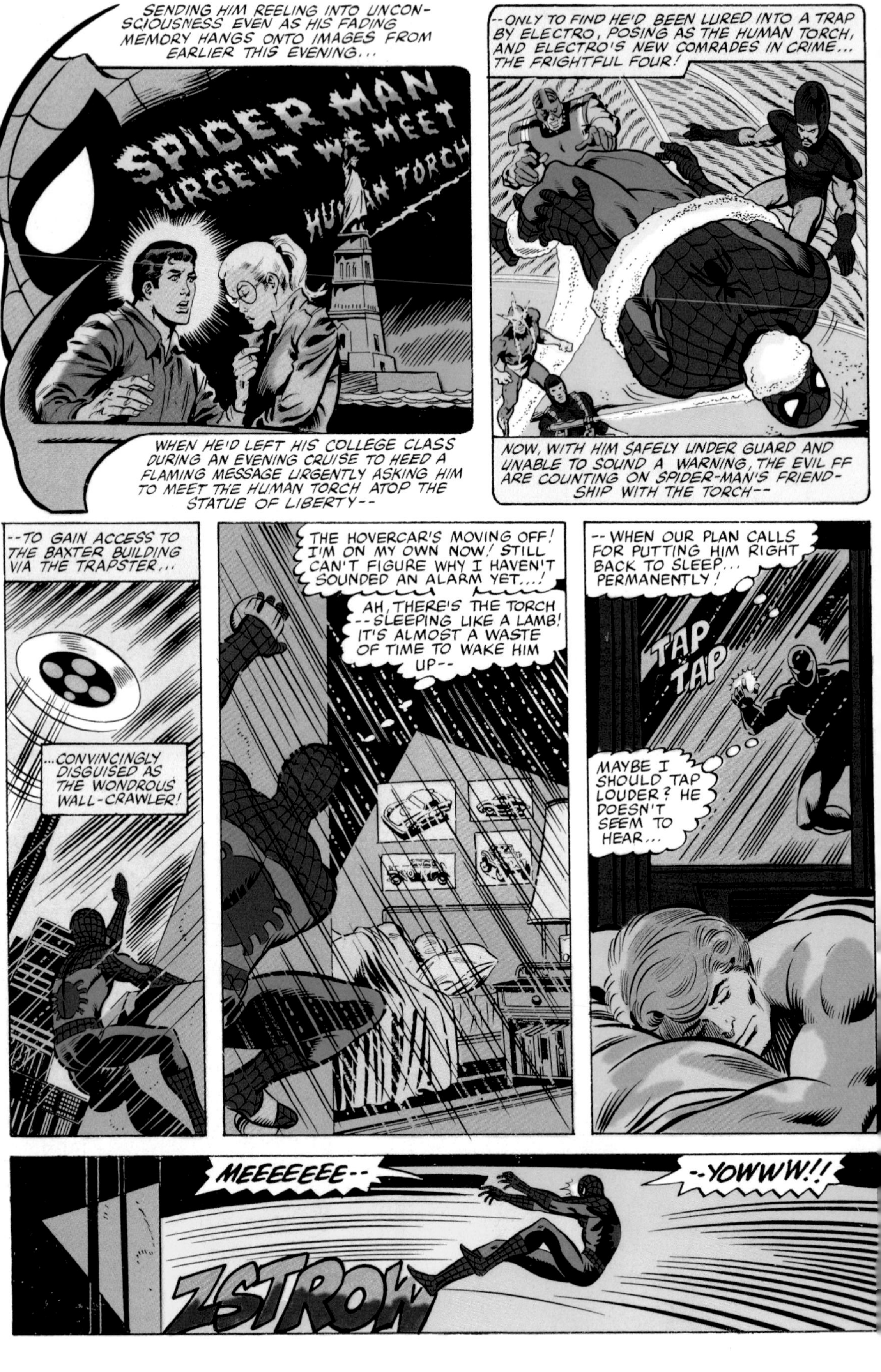
SENDING HIM REELING INTO UNCONSCIOUSNESS EVEN AS HIS FADING MEMORY HANGS ONTO IMAGES FROM EARLIER THIS EVENING...
SPIDER MAN URGENT WE MEET HUMAN TORCH
WHEN HE'D LEFT HIS COLLEGE CLASS DURING AN EVENING CRUISE TO HEED A FLAMING MESSAGE URGENTLY ASKING HIM TO MEET THE HUMAN TORCH ATOP THE STATUE OF LIBERTY--
--ONLY TO FIND HE'D BEEN LURED INTO A TRAP BY ELECTRO, POSING AS THE HUMAN TORCH, AND ELECTRO'S NEW COMRADES IN CRIME... THE FRIGHTFUL FOUR!
NOW, WITH HIM SAFELY UNDER GUARD AND UNABLE TO SOUND A WARNING, THE EVIL FF ARE COUNTING ON SPIDER-MAN'S FRIENDSHIP WITH THE TORCH--
--TO GAIN ACCESS TO THE BAXTER BUILDING VIA THE TRAPSTER...
...CONVINCINGLY DISGUISED AS THE WONDROUS WALL-CRAWLER!
THE HOVERCAR'S MOVING OFF! I'M ON MY OWN NOW! STILL CAN'T FIGURE WHY I HAVEN'T SOUNDED AN ALARM YET...!
AH, THERE'S THE TORCH --SLEEPING LIKE A LAMB! IT'S ALMOST A WASTE OF TIME TO WAKE HIM UP--
--WHEN OUR PLAN CALLS FOR PUTTING HIM RIGHT BACK TO SLEEP... PERMANENTLY!
TAP TAP
MAYBE I SHOULD TAP LOUDER? HE DOESN'T SEEM TO HEAR...
MEEEEEEE--
--YOWWW!!
ZSTROW

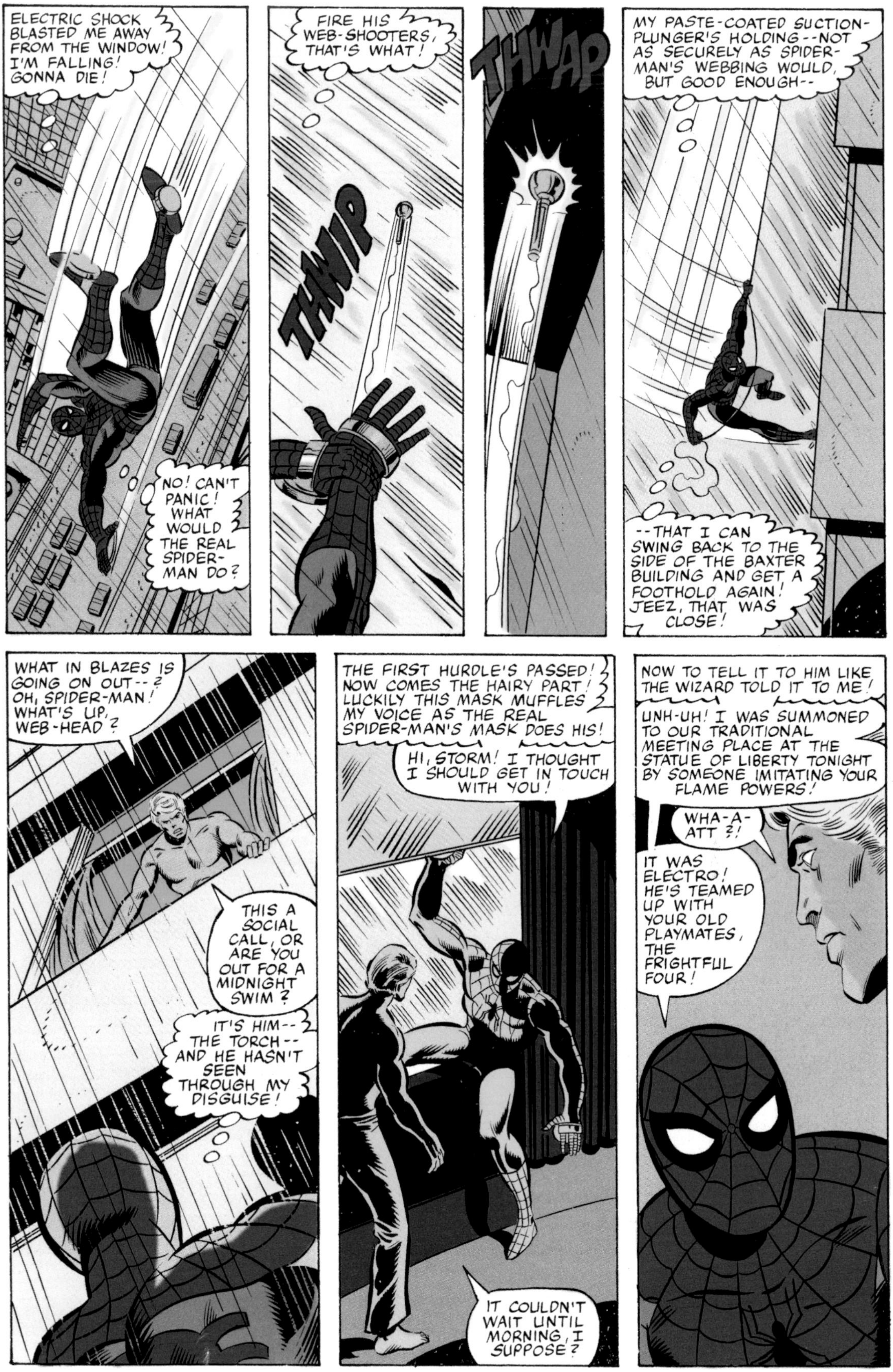
ELECTRIC SHOCK BLASTED ME AWAY FROM THE WINDOW! I'M FALLING! GONNA DIE!
NO! CAN'T PANIC! WHAT WOULD THE REAL SPIDER-MAN DO?
FIRE HIS WEB-SHOOTERS, THAT'S WHAT!
THWIP
THWAP
MY PASTE-COATED SUCTION-PLUNGER'S HOLDING--NOT AS SECURELY AS SPIDER-MAN'S WEBBING WOULD, BUT GOOD ENOUGH--
--THAT I CAN SWING BACK TO THE SIDE OF THE BAXTER BUILDING AND GET A FOOTHOLD AGAIN! JEEZ, THAT WAS CLOSE!
WHAT IN BLAZES IS GOING ON OUT--? OH, SPIDER-MAN! WHAT'S UP, WEB-HEAD?
THIS A SOCIAL CALL, OR ARE YOU OUT FOR A MIDNIGHT SWIM?
IT'S HIM--THE TORCH--AND HE HASN'T SEEN THROUGH MY DISGUISE!
THE FIRST HURDLE'S PASSED! NOW COMES THE HAIRY PART! LUCKILY THIS MASK MUFFLES MY VOICE AS THE REAL SPIDER-MAN'S MASK DOES HIS!
HI, STORM! I THOUGHT I SHOULD GET IN TOUCH WITH YOU!
IT COULDN'T WAIT UNTIL MORNING, I SUPPOSE?
NOW TO TELL IT TO HIM LIKE THE WIZARD TOLD IT TO ME!
UNH-UH! I WAS SUMMONED TO OUR TRADITIONAL MEETING PLACE AT THE STATUE OF LIBERTY TONIGHT BY SOMEONE IMITATING YOUR FLAME POWERS!
WHA-A-ATT?!
IT WAS ELECTRO! HE'S TEAMED UP WITH YOUR OLD PLAYMATES, THE FRIGHTFUL FOUR!

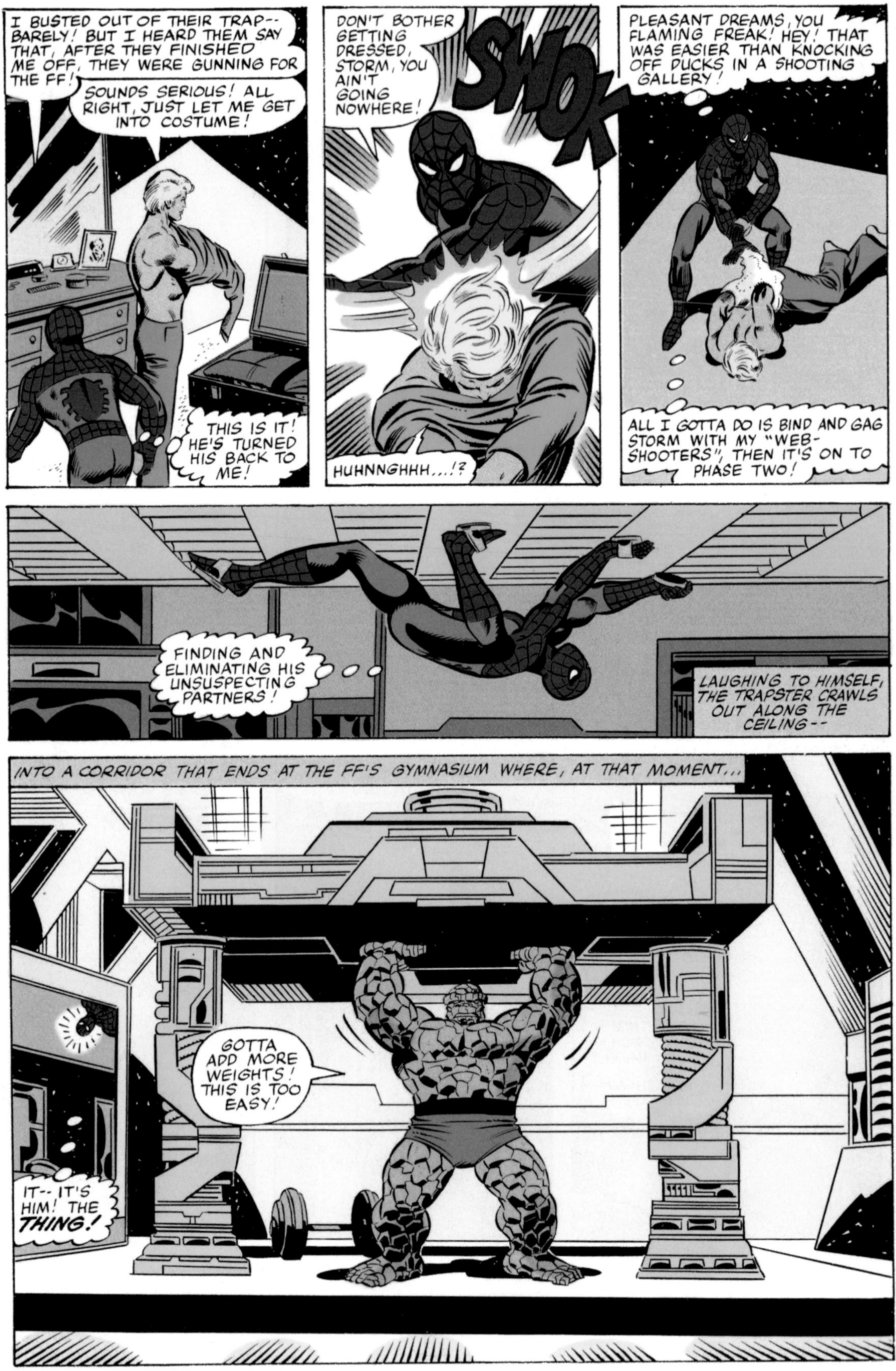
I BUSTED OUT OF THEIR TRAP-- BARELY! BUT I HEARD THEM SAY THAT, AFTER THEY FINISHED ME OFF, THEY WERE GUNNING FOR THE FF!
SOUNDS SERIOUS! ALL RIGHT, JUST LET ME GET INTO COSTUME!
THIS IS IT! HE'S TURNED HIS BACK TO ME!
DON'T BOTHER GETTING DRESSED, STORM, YOU AIN'T GOING NOWHERE!
SWOK
HUHNNGHHH...!?
PLEASANT DREAMS, YOU FLAMING FREAK! HEY! THAT WAS EASIER THAN KNOCKING OFF DUCKS IN A SHOOTING GALLERY!
ALL I GOTTA DO IS BIND AND GAG STORM WITH MY "WEB-SHOOTERS", THEN IT'S ON TO PHASE TWO!
FINDING AND ELIMINATING HIS UNSUSPECTING PARTNERS!
LAUGHING TO HIMSELF, THE TRAPSTER CRAWLS OUT ALONG THE CEILING--
INTO A CORRIDOR THAT ENDS AT THE FF'S GYMNASIUM WHERE, AT THAT MOMENT...
GOTTA ADD MORE WEIGHTS! THIS IS TOO EASY!
IT-- IT'S HIM! THE THING!

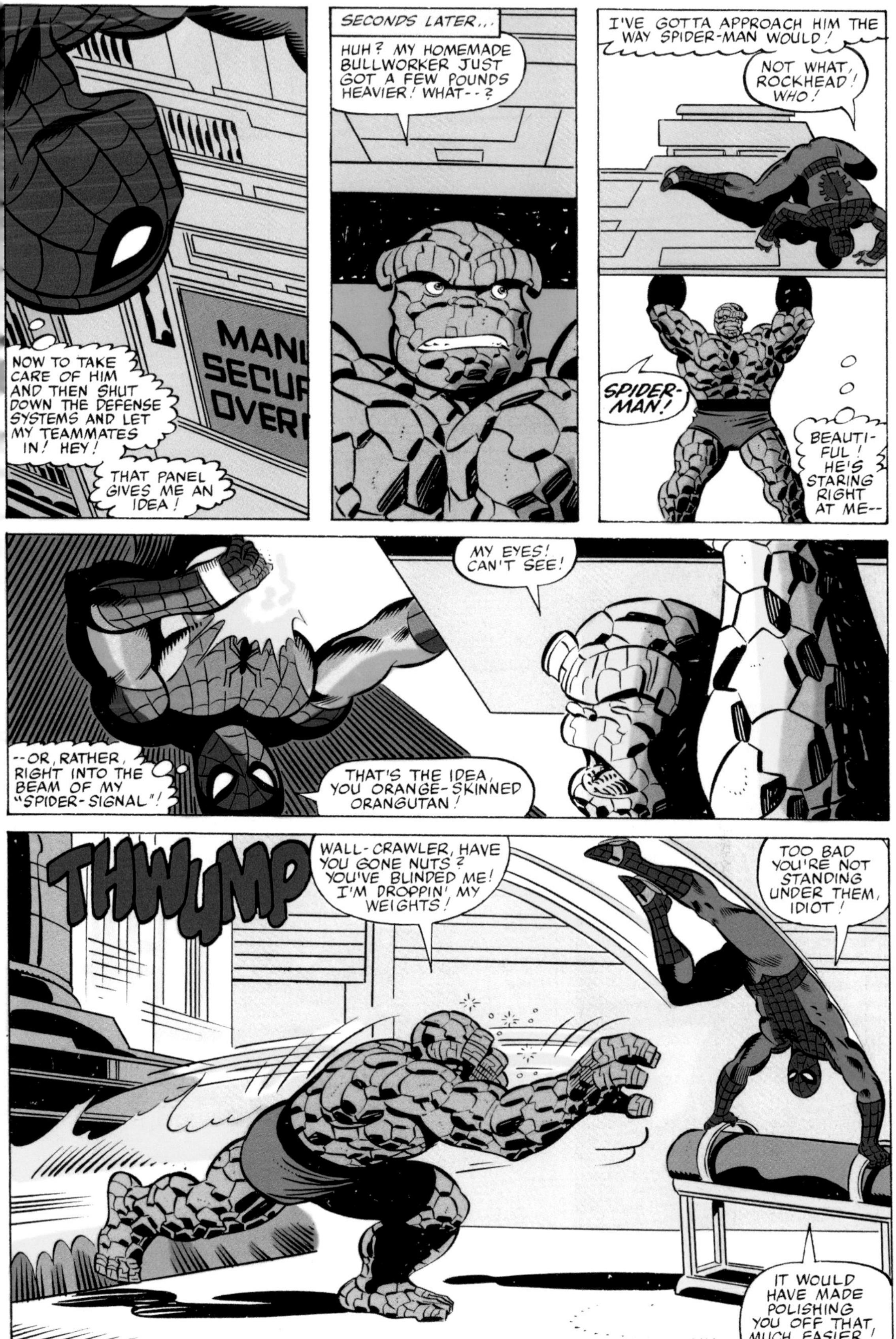
NOW TO TAKE CARE OF HIM AND THEN SHUT DOWN THE DEFENSE SYSTEMS AND LET MY TEAMMATES IN! HEY!
THAT PANEL GIVES ME AN IDEA!
SECONDS LATER...
HUH? MY HOMEMADE BULLWORKER JUST GOT A FEW POUNDS HEAVIER! WHAT--?
I'VE GOTTA APPROACH HIM THE WAY SPIDER-MAN WOULD!
NOT WHAT, ROCKHEAD! WHO!
SPIDER-MAN!
BEAUTIFUL! HE'S STARING RIGHT AT ME--
--OR, RATHER, RIGHT INTO THE BEAM OF MY "SPIDER-SIGNAL"!
MY EYES! CAN'T SEE!
THAT'S THE IDEA, YOU ORANGE-SKINNED ORANGUTAN!
THWUMP
WALL-CRAWLER, HAVE YOU GONE NUTS? YOU'VE BLINDED ME! I'M DROPPIN' MY WEIGHTS!
TOO BAD YOU'RE NOT STANDING UNDER THEM, IDIOT!
IT WOULD HAVE MADE POLISHING YOU OFF THAT MUCH EASIER!

NOT THAT IT'S GOING TO BE ALL THAT DIFFICULT OFFING A SIGHTLESS LUMMOX WHO CAN'T EVEN SEE WHAT HE'S FLAILING AT!

WHUMP!

WHY ARE YOU--? U-UNLESS, YOU AIN'T THE WALL-CRAWLER?!

I WOULDN'T HAVE CREDITED YOU WITH ENOUGH BRAINS TO FIGURE THAT OUT, GRIMM! NO, I'M NOT SPIDER-MAN!

SURELY YOU REMEMBER YOUR OLD FOE? THE TRAPSTER?!

MANUAL SECURITY OVERRIDE

HE'S COMING AT ME, LURED BY THE SOUND OF MY VOICE--

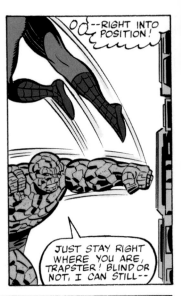

--RIGHT INTO POSITION!

JUST STAY RIGHT WHERE YOU ARE, TRAPSTER! BLIND OR NOT, I CAN STILL--

STRA- ZAM!

PERFECT! BY SMASHING THE CIRCUITRY BEHIND THAT PANEL, THE BIG GORILLA NOT ONLY KNOCKED OUT THE BAXTER BUILDING'S SECURITY SYSTEMS, BUT HIMSELF AS WELL!

NOW TO SIGNAL THE OTHERS!

SOON, ON THE ROOF OF FF HEADQUARTERS...

THE TRAPSTER'S DONE IT! THE FF'S DEFENSE SYSTEMS ARE SHUT DOWN!

I DIDN'T THINK HE'D BE ABLE TO PULL IT OFF!

AND I KNEW HE WOULD, PROVIDING HE FOLLOWED MY INSTRUCTIONS! ELECTRO, SHORT-CIRCUIT THE LOCKS ON THE ROOF DOORS, SO WE MAY GAIN ENTRY!

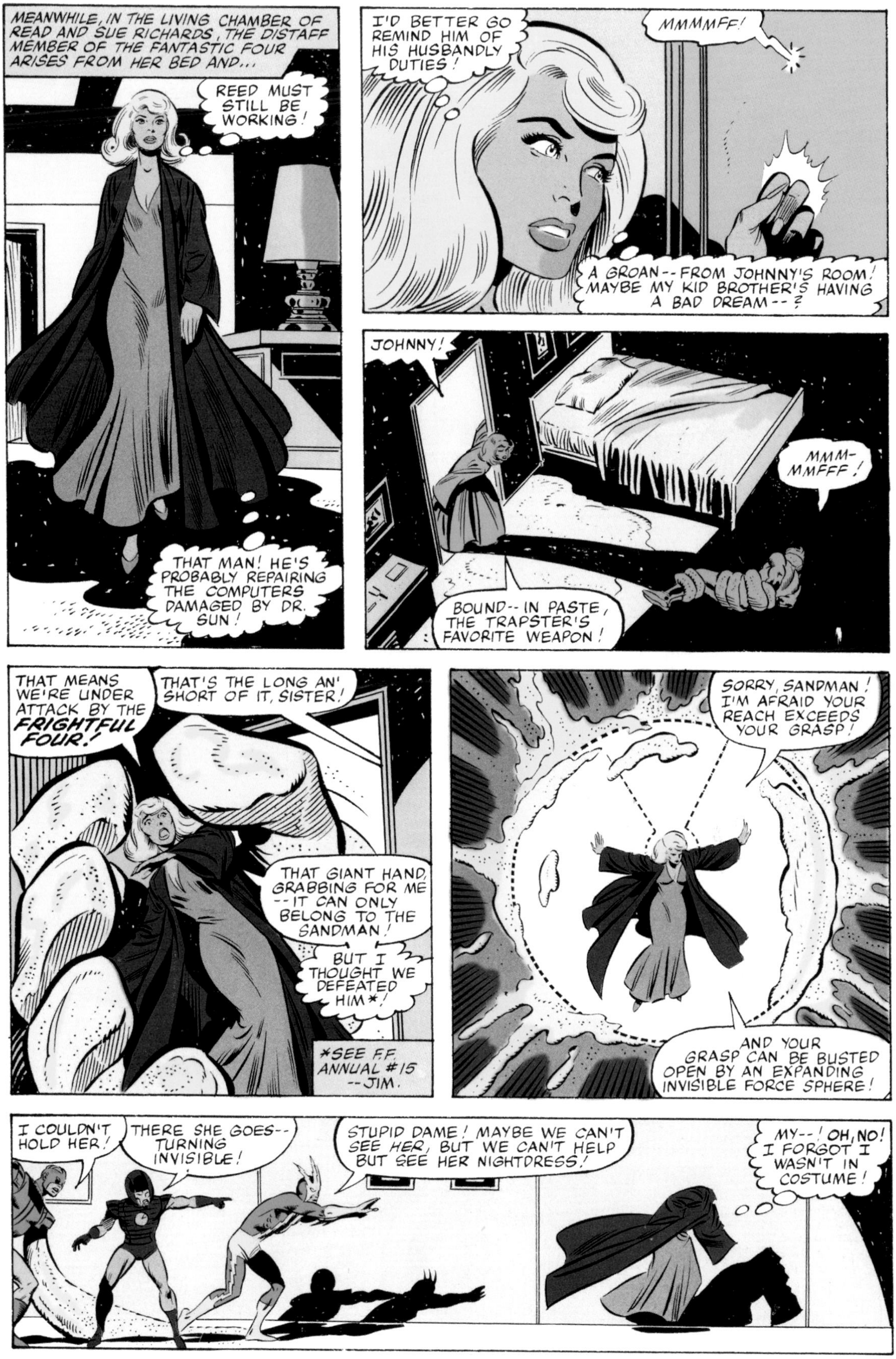

MEANWHILE, IN THE LIVING CHAMBER OF READ AND SUE RICHARDS, THE DISTAFF MEMBER OF THE FANTASTIC FOUR ARISES FROM HER BED AND...
REED MUST STILL BE WORKING!
THAT MAN! HE'S PROBABLY REPAIRING THE COMPUTERS DAMAGED BY DR. SUN!
I'D BETTER GO REMIND HIM OF HIS HUSBANDLY DUTIES!
MMMMFF!
A GROAN--FROM JOHNNY'S ROOM! MAYBE MY KID BROTHER'S HAVING A BAD DREAM--?
JOHNNY!
MMM-MMFFF!
BOUND--IN PASTE, THE TRAPSTER'S FAVORITE WEAPON!
THAT MEANS WE'RE UNDER ATTACK BY THE FRIGHTFUL FOUR!
THAT'S THE LONG AN' SHORT OF IT, SISTER!
THAT GIANT HAND, GRABBING FOR ME--IT CAN ONLY BELONG TO THE SANDMAN!
BUT I THOUGHT WE DEFEATED HIM*!
*SEE F.F. ANNUAL #15 --JIM.
SORRY, SANDMAN! I'M AFRAID YOUR REACH EXCEEDS YOUR GRASP!
AND YOUR GRASP CAN BE BUSTED OPEN BY AN EXPANDING INVISIBLE FORCE SPHERE!
I COULDN'T HOLD HER!
THERE SHE GOES--TURNING INVISIBLE!
STUPID DAME! MAYBE WE CAN'T SEE HER, BUT WE CAN'T HELP BUT SEE HER NIGHTDRESS!
MY--! OH, NO! I FORGOT I WASN'T IN COSTUME!

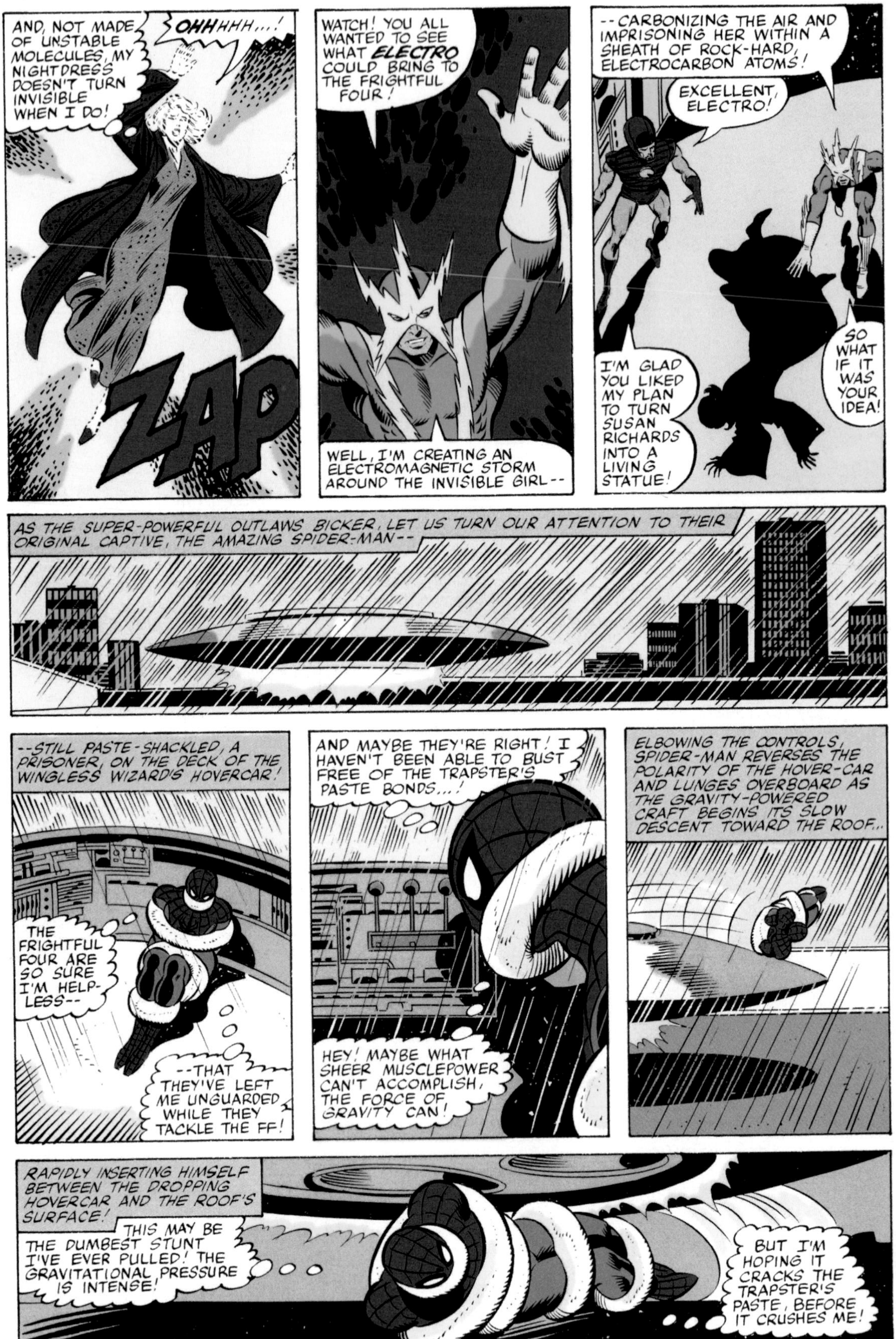
AND, NOT MADE OF UNSTABLE MOLECULES, MY NIGHTDRESS DOESN'T TURN INVISIBLE WHEN I DO!
OHHHHH...!
ZAP
WATCH! YOU ALL WANTED TO SEE WHAT ELECTRO COULD BRING TO THE FRIGHTFUL FOUR!
WELL, I'M CREATING AN ELECTROMAGNETIC STORM AROUND THE INVISIBLE GIRL--
--CARBONIZING THE AIR AND IMPRISONING HER WITHIN A SHEATH OF ROCK-HARD, ELECTROCARBON ATOMS!
EXCELLENT, ELECTRO!
I'M GLAD YOU LIKED MY PLAN TO TURN SUSAN RICHARDS INTO A LIVING STATUE!
SO WHAT IF IT WAS YOUR IDEA!
AS THE SUPER-POWERFUL OUTLAWS BICKER, LET US TURN OUR ATTENTION TO THEIR ORIGINAL CAPTIVE, THE AMAZING SPIDER-MAN--
--STILL PASTE-SHACKLED, A PRISONER, ON THE DECK OF THE WINGLESS WIZARD'S HOVERCAR!
THE FRIGHTFUL FOUR ARE SO SURE I'M HELP-LESS--
--THAT THEY'VE LEFT ME UNGUARDED WHILE THEY TACKLE THE FF!
AND MAYBE THEY'RE RIGHT! I HAVEN'T BEEN ABLE TO BUST FREE OF THE TRAPSTER'S PASTE BONDS...!
HEY! MAYBE WHAT SHEER MUSCLEPOWER CAN'T ACCOMPLISH, THE FORCE OF GRAVITY CAN!
ELBOWING THE CONTROLS, SPIDER-MAN REVERSES THE POLARITY OF THE HOVER-CAR AND LUNGES OVERBOARD AS THE GRAVITY-POWERED CRAFT BEGINS ITS SLOW DESCENT TOWARD THE ROOF...
RAPIDLY INSERTING HIMSELF BETWEEN THE DROPPING HOVERCAR AND THE ROOF'S SURFACE!
THIS MAY BE THE DUMBEST STUNT I'VE EVER PULLED! THE GRAVITATIONAL PRESSURE IS INTENSE!
BUT I'M HOPING IT CRACKS THE TRAPSTER'S PASTE, BEFORE IT CRUSHES ME!

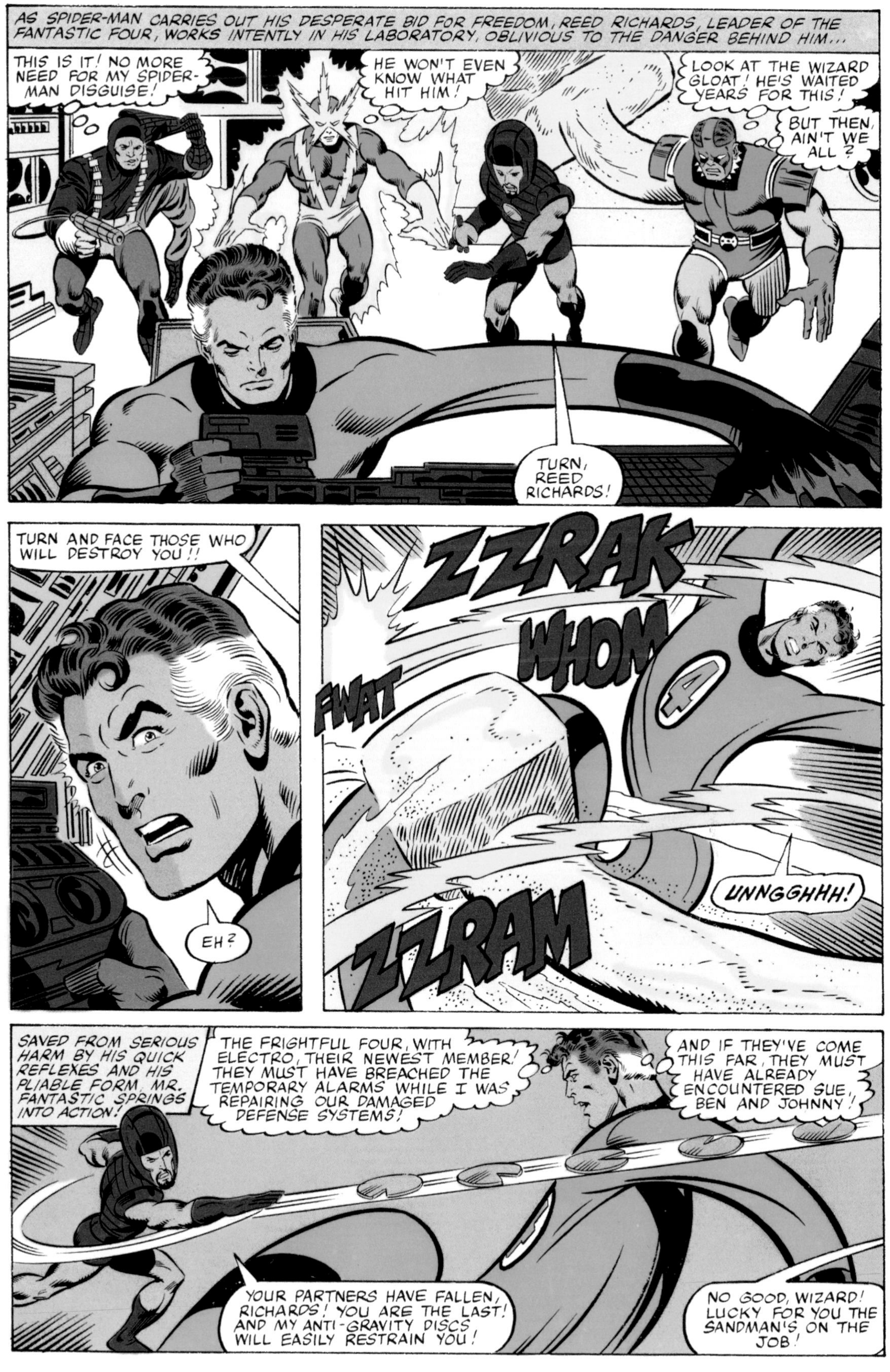
AS SPIDER-MAN CARRIES OUT HIS DESPERATE BID FOR FREEDOM, REED RICHARDS, LEADER OF THE FANTASTIC FOUR, WORKS INTENTLY IN HIS LABORATORY, OBLIVIOUS TO THE DANGER BEHIND HIM...
THIS IS IT! NO MORE NEED FOR MY SPIDER-MAN DISGUISE!
HE WON'T EVEN KNOW WHAT HIT HIM!
LOOK AT THE WIZARD GLOAT! HE'S WAITED YEARS FOR THIS!
BUT THEN, AIN'T WE ALL?
TURN, REED RICHARDS!
TURN AND FACE THOSE WHO WILL DESTROY YOU!!
EH?
ZZRAK
WHOM
FWAT
UNNGGHHH!
ZZRAM
SAVED FROM SERIOUS HARM BY HIS QUICK REFLEXES AND HIS PLIABLE FORM, MR. FANTASTIC SPRINGS INTO ACTION!
THE FRIGHTFUL FOUR, WITH ELECTRO, THEIR NEWEST MEMBER! THEY MUST HAVE BREACHED THE TEMPORARY ALARMS WHILE I WAS REPAIRING OUR DAMAGED DEFENSE SYSTEMS!
AND IF THEY'VE COME THIS FAR, THEY MUST HAVE ALREADY ENCOUNTERED SUE, BEN AND JOHNNY!
YOUR PARTNERS HAVE FALLEN, RICHARDS! YOU ARE THE LAST! AND MY ANTI-GRAVITY DISCS WILL EASILY RESTRAIN YOU!
NO GOOD, WIZARD! LUCKY FOR YOU THE SANDMAN'S ON THE JOB!

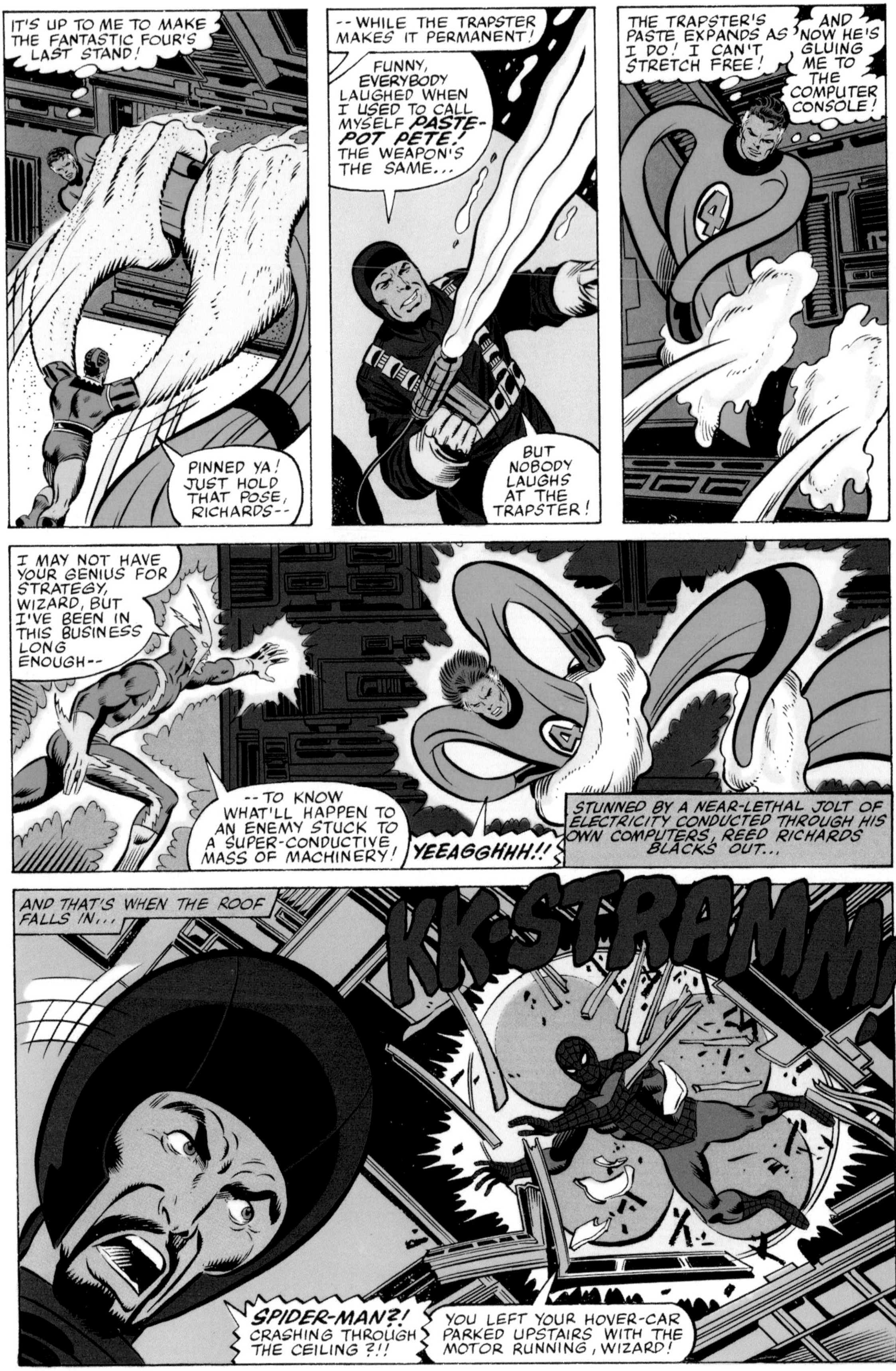
IT'S UP TO ME TO MAKE THE FANTASTIC FOUR'S LAST STAND!
PINNED YA! JUST HOLD THAT POSE, RICHARDS--
--WHILE THE TRAPSTER MAKES IT PERMANENT!
FUNNY, EVERYBODY LAUGHED WHEN I USED TO CALL MYSELF PASTE-POT PETE! THE WEAPON'S THE SAME...
BUT NOBODY LAUGHS AT THE TRAPSTER!
THE TRAPSTER'S PASTE EXPANDS AS I DO! I CAN'T STRETCH FREE!
AND NOW HE'S GLUING ME TO THE COMPUTER CONSOLE!
I MAY NOT HAVE YOUR GENIUS FOR STRATEGY, WIZARD, BUT I'VE BEEN IN THIS BUSINESS LONG ENOUGH--
--TO KNOW WHAT'LL HAPPEN TO AN ENEMY STUCK TO A SUPER-CONDUCTIVE MASS OF MACHINERY!
YEEAGGHHH!!
STUNNED BY A NEAR-LETHAL JOLT OF ELECTRICITY CONDUCTED THROUGH HIS OWN COMPUTERS, REED RICHARDS BLACKS OUT...
AND THAT'S WHEN THE ROOF FALLS IN...
KK-STRAMM
SPIDER-MAN?! CRASHING THROUGH THE CEILING?!!
YOU LEFT YOUR HOVER-CAR PARKED UPSTAIRS WITH THE MOTOR RUNNING, WIZARD!

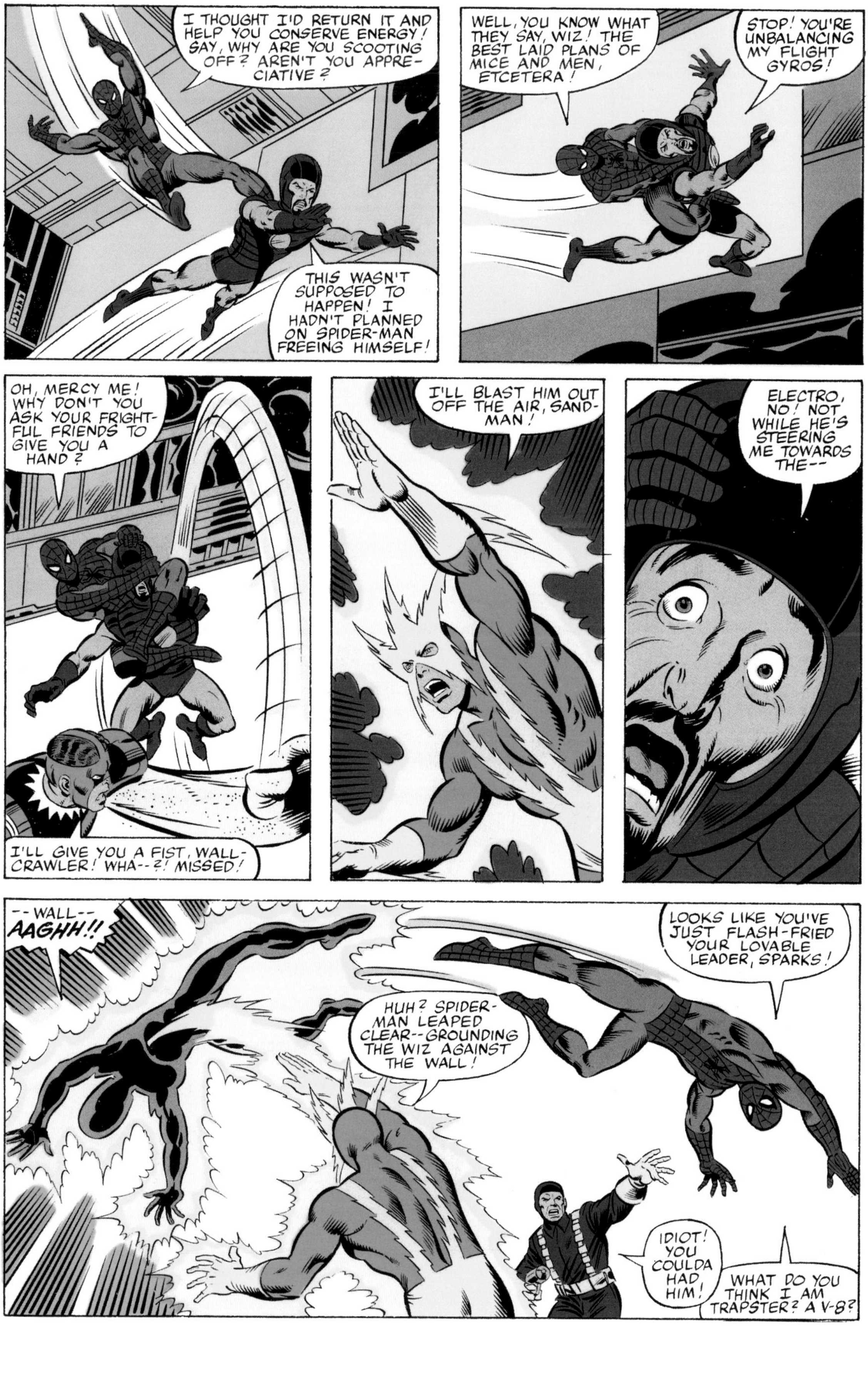
I THOUGHT I'D RETURN IT AND HELP YOU CONSERVE ENERGY! SAY, WHY ARE YOU SCOOTING OFF? AREN'T YOU APPRECIATIVE?
THIS WASN'T SUPPOSED TO HAPPEN! I HADN'T PLANNED ON SPIDER-MAN FREEING HIMSELF!
WELL, YOU KNOW WHAT THEY SAY, WIZ! THE BEST LAID PLANS OF MICE AND MEN, ETCETERA!
STOP! YOU'RE UNBALANCING MY FLIGHT GYROS!
OH, MERCY ME! WHY DON'T YOU ASK YOUR FRIGHTFUL FRIENDS TO GIVE YOU A HAND?
I'LL GIVE YOU A FIST, WALL-CRAWLER! WHA--?! MISSED!
I'LL BLAST HIM OUT OFF THE AIR, SANDMAN!
ELECTRO, NO! NOT WHILE HE'S STEERING ME TOWARDS THE--
--WALL--
AAGHH!!
HUH? SPIDER-MAN LEAPED CLEAR--GROUNDING THE WIZ AGAINST THE WALL!
LOOKS LIKE YOU'VE JUST FLASH-FRIED YOUR LOVABLE LEADER, SPARKS!
IDIOT! YOU COULDA HAD HIM!
WHAT DO YOU THINK I AM TRAPSTER? A V-8?

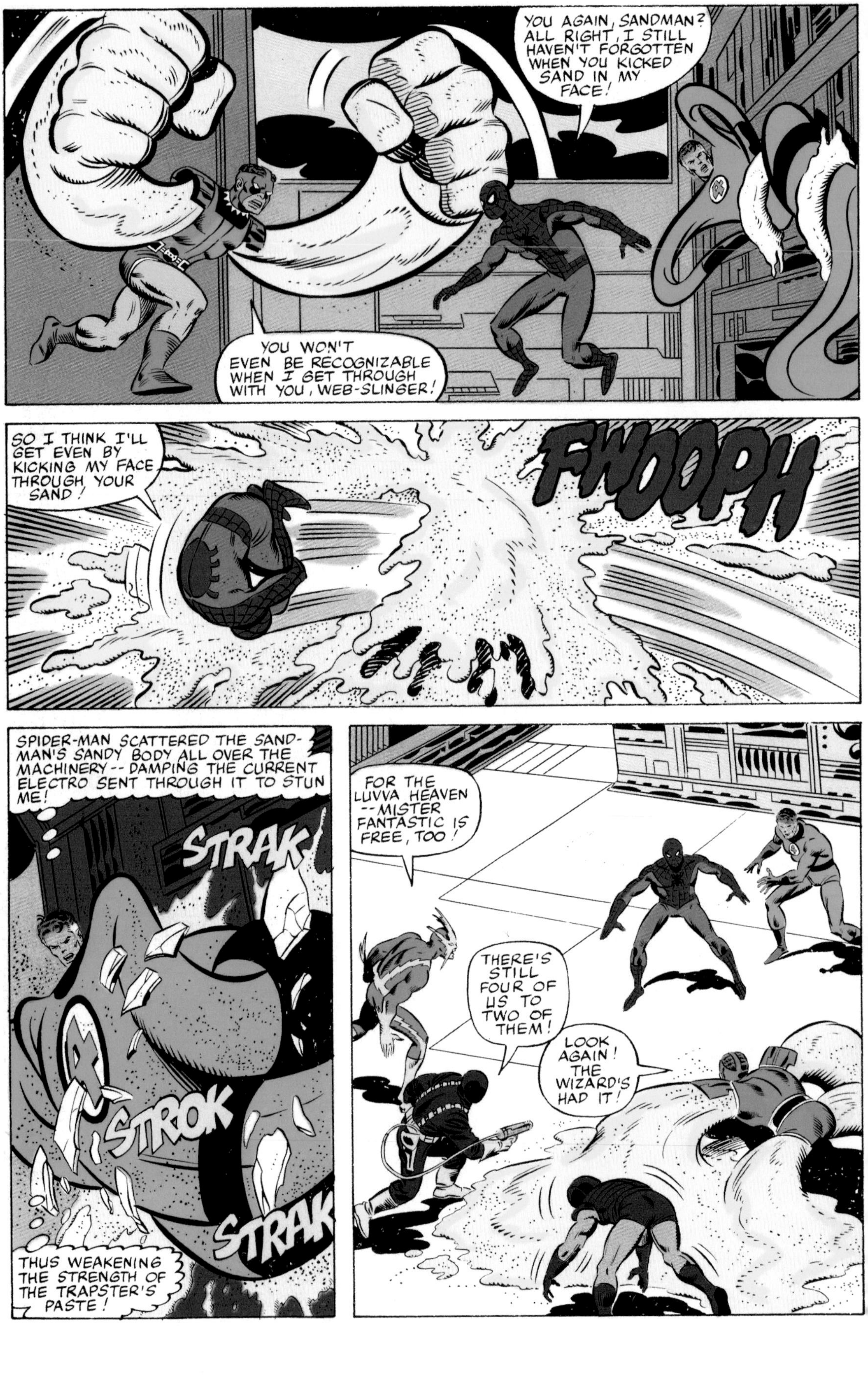
YOU AGAIN, SANDMAN? ALL RIGHT, I STILL HAVEN'T FORGOTTEN WHEN YOU KICKED SAND IN MY FACE!
YOU WON'T EVEN BE RECOGNIZABLE WHEN I GET THROUGH WITH YOU, WEB-SLINGER!
SO I THINK I'LL GET EVEN BY KICKING MY FACE THROUGH YOUR SAND!
FWOOPH
SPIDER-MAN SCATTERED THE SAND-MAN'S SANDY BODY ALL OVER THE MACHINERY -- DAMPING THE CURRENT ELECTRO SENT THROUGH IT TO STUN ME!
STRAK
STROK
STRAK
THUS WEAKENING THE STRENGTH OF THE TRAPSTER'S PASTE!
FOR THE LUVVA HEAVEN -- MISTER FANTASTIC IS FREE, TOO!
THERE'S STILL FOUR OF US TO TWO OF THEM!
LOOK AGAIN! THE WIZARD'S HAD IT!

WE DON'T NEED THE WIZARD! IT WAS HIS "GENIUS" THAT GOT US INTO THIS MESS!

WE'D BETTER START COUNTING ON OUR OWN SUPER-POWERS TO GET US OUT!

WHY NOT? THEY AIN'T NEVER LET ME DOWN!

AND, AS FAR AS I'M CONCERNED, OUR MISSION'S STILL ON! WE SMASH THE FF--

--AFTER SMOTHERIN' THE WEBHEAD UNDER A MOUNTAIN OF SAND!

AW, GOSH, AND I FORGOT MY BEACH BLANKET!

TO ENGULF SPIDER-MAN, THE SANDMAN'S HAD TO TRANSFORM HIS BODY IN ITS ENTIRETY TO A MASS OF FINE, SANDY PARTICLES...

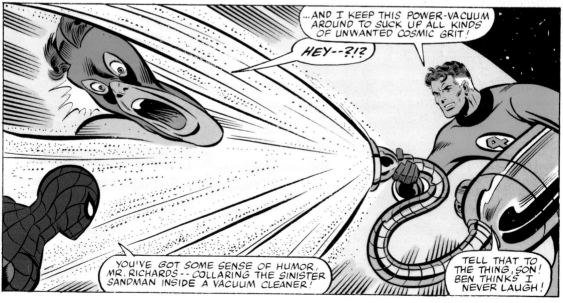

...AND I KEEP THIS POWER-VACUUM AROUND TO SUCK UP ALL KINDS OF UNWANTED COSMIC GRIT!

HEY--?!?

YOU'VE GOT SOME SENSE OF HUMOR, MR. RICHARDS -- COLLARING THE SINISTER SANDMAN INSIDE A VACUUM CLEANER!

TELL THAT TO THE THING, SON! BEN THINKS I NEVER LAUGH!

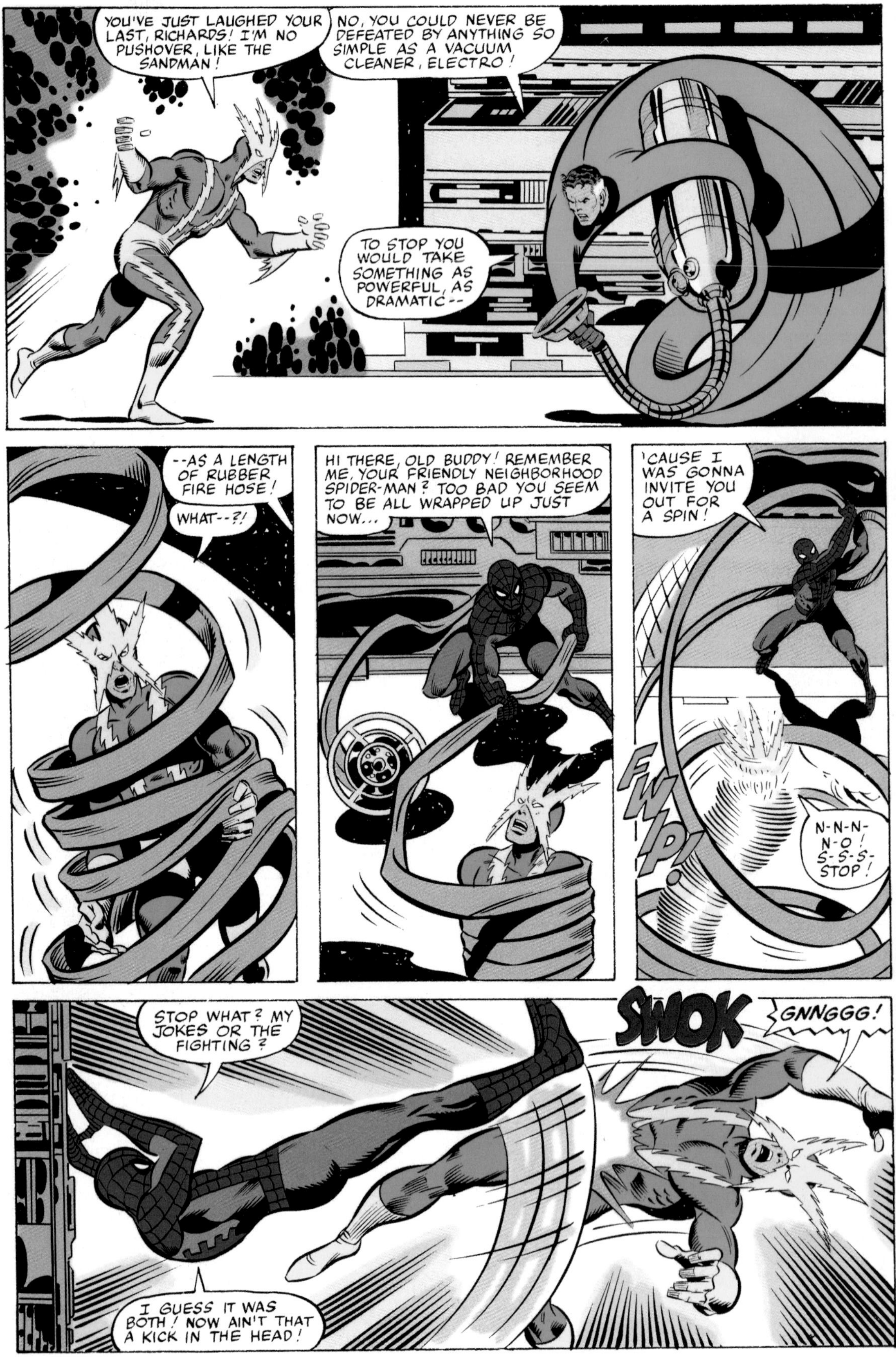
YOU'VE JUST LAUGHED YOUR LAST, RICHARDS! I'M NO PUSHOVER, LIKE THE SANDMAN!
NO, YOU COULD NEVER BE DEFEATED BY ANYTHING SO SIMPLE AS A VACUUM CLEANER, ELECTRO!
TO STOP YOU WOULD TAKE SOMETHING AS POWERFUL, AS DRAMATIC--
--AS A LENGTH OF RUBBER FIRE HOSE!
WHAT--?!
HI THERE, OLD BUDDY! REMEMBER ME, YOUR FRIENDLY NEIGHBORHOOD SPIDER-MAN? TOO BAD YOU SEEM TO BE ALL WRAPPED UP JUST NOW...
'CAUSE I WAS GONNA INVITE YOU OUT FOR A SPIN!
FWIP!
N-N-N-N-O! S-S-S-STOP!
STOP WHAT? MY JOKES OR THE FIGHTING?
SWOK
GNNGGG!
I GUESS IT WAS BOTH! NOW AIN'T THAT A KICK IN THE HEAD!

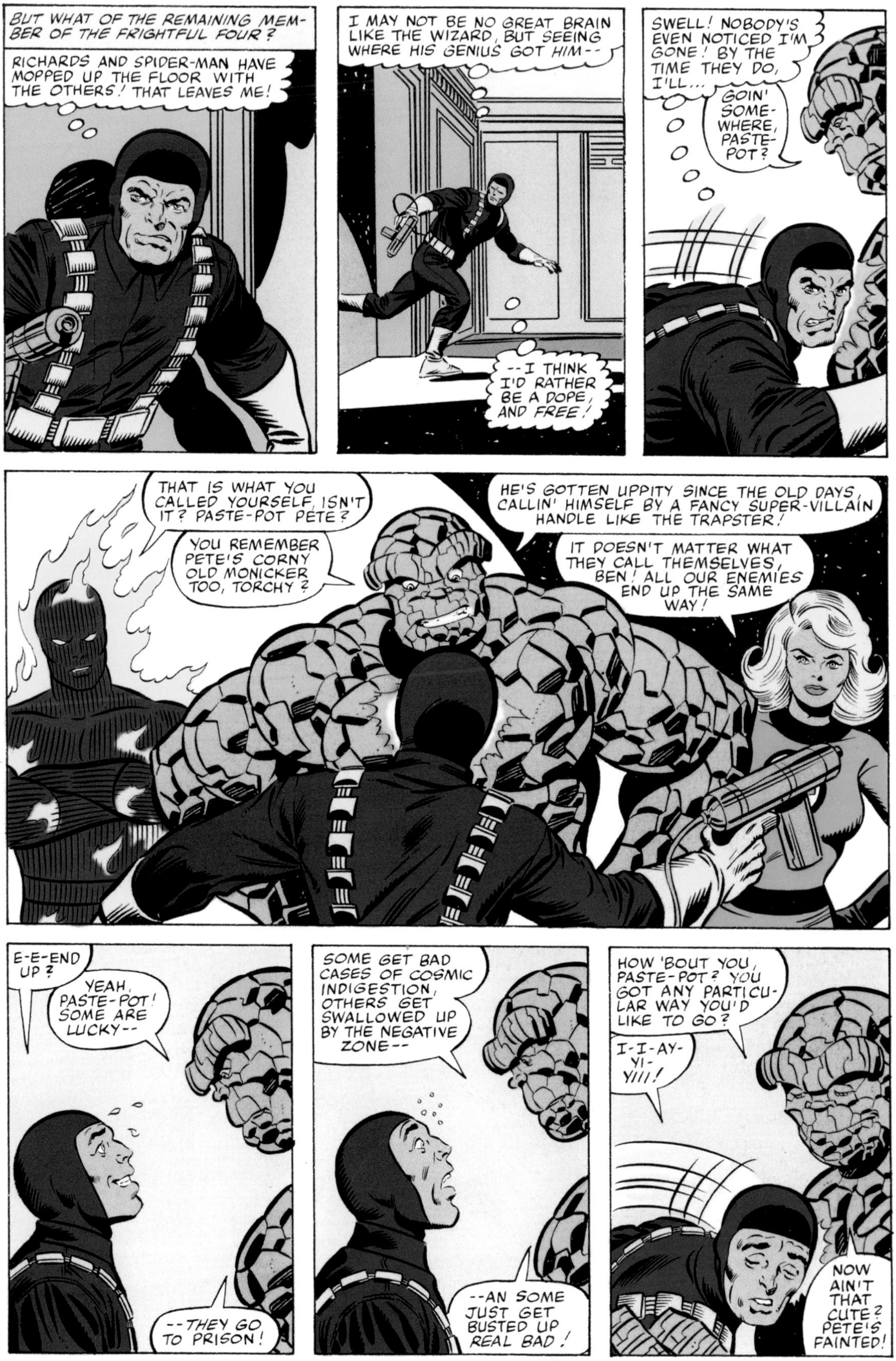
BUT WHAT OF THE REMAINING MEMBER OF THE FRIGHTFUL FOUR?
RICHARDS AND SPIDER-MAN HAVE MOPPED UP THE FLOOR WITH THE OTHERS! THAT LEAVES ME!
I MAY NOT BE NO GREAT BRAIN LIKE THE WIZARD, BUT SEEING WHERE HIS GENIUS GOT HIM--
--I THINK I'D RATHER BE A DOPE, AND FREE!
SWELL! NOBODY'S EVEN NOTICED I'M GONE! BY THE TIME THEY DO, I'LL...
GOIN' SOMEWHERE, PASTE-POT?
THAT IS WHAT YOU CALLED YOURSELF, ISN'T IT? PASTE-POT PETE?
YOU REMEMBER PETE'S CORNY OLD MONICKER TOO, TORCHY?
HE'S GOTTEN UPPITY SINCE THE OLD DAYS, CALLIN' HIMSELF BY A FANCY SUPER-VILLAIN HANDLE LIKE THE TRAPSTER!
IT DOESN'T MATTER WHAT THEY CALL THEMSELVES, BEN! ALL OUR ENEMIES END UP THE SAME WAY!
E-E-END UP?
YEAH, PASTE-POT! SOME ARE LUCKY--
--THEY GO TO PRISON!
SOME GET BAD CASES OF COSMIC INDIGESTION, OTHERS GET SWALLOWED UP BY THE NEGATIVE ZONE--
--AN SOME JUST GET BUSTED UP REAL BAD!
HOW 'BOUT YOU, PASTE-POT? YOU GOT ANY PARTICULAR WAY YOU'D LIKE TO GO?
I-I-AY-YI-YIII!
NOW AIN'T THAT CUTE? PETE'S FAINTED!

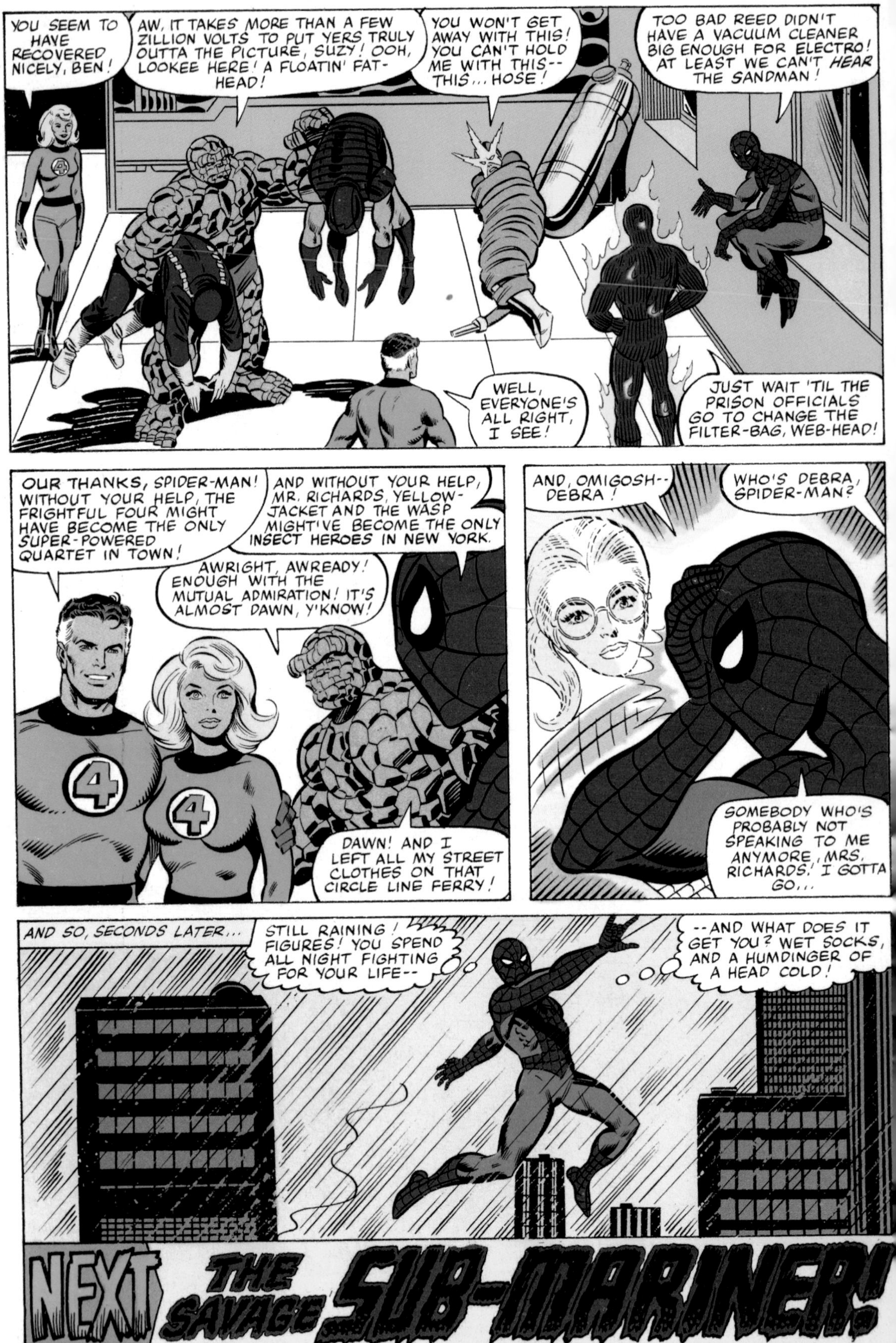
YOU SEEM TO HAVE RECOVERED NICELY, BEN!
AW, IT TAKES MORE THAN A FEW ZILLION VOLTS TO PUT YERS TRULY OUTTA THE PICTURE, SUZY! OOH, LOOKEE HERE! A FLOATIN' FAT-HEAD!
YOU WON'T GET AWAY WITH THIS! YOU CAN'T HOLD ME WITH THIS-- THIS... HOSE!
TOO BAD REED DIDN'T HAVE A VACUUM CLEANER BIG ENOUGH FOR ELECTRO! AT LEAST WE CAN'T HEAR THE SANDMAN!
WELL, EVERYONE'S ALL RIGHT, I SEE!
JUST WAIT 'TIL THE PRISON OFFICIALS GO TO CHANGE THE FILTER-BAG, WEB-HEAD!
OUR THANKS, SPIDER-MAN! WITHOUT YOUR HELP, THE FRIGHTFUL FOUR MIGHT HAVE BECOME THE ONLY SUPER-POWERED QUARTET IN TOWN!
AND WITHOUT YOUR HELP, MR. RICHARDS, YELLOW-JACKET AND THE WASP MIGHT'VE BECOME THE ONLY INSECT HEROES IN NEW YORK.
AWRIGHT, AWREADY! ENOUGH WITH THE MUTUAL ADMIRATION! IT'S ALMOST DAWN, Y'KNOW!
DAWN! AND I LEFT ALL MY STREET CLOTHES ON THAT CIRCLE LINE FERRY!
AND, OMIGOSH-- DEBRA!
WHO'S DEBRA, SPIDER-MAN?
SOMEBODY WHO'S PROBABLY NOT SPEAKING TO ME ANYMORE, MRS. RICHARDS! I GOTTA GO...
AND SO, SECONDS LATER...
STILL RAINING! FIGURES! YOU SPEND ALL NIGHT FIGHTING FOR YOUR LIFE--
--AND WHAT DOES IT GET YOU? WET SOCKS, AND A HUMDINGER OF A HEAD COLD!
NEXT THE SAVAGE SUB-MARINER!